Resistance, Imprisonment, & Forced Labor

Dear Mr. Hrvatin,
I shall always remember
with gratitude your interest
in my WW II experiences

Metod M. Milač

Syracuse, NY
12 January 2009

Studies in Modern European History

Frank J. Coppa
General Editor

Vol. 47

PETER LANG
New York • Washington, D.C./Baltimore • Bern
Frankfurt am Main • Berlin • Brussels • Vienna • Oxford

Metod M. Milač

Resistance, Imprisonment, & Forced Labor

A Slovene Student in World War II

PETER LANG
New York • Washington, D.C./Baltimore • Bern
Frankfurt am Main • Berlin • Brussels • Vienna • Oxford

Library of Congress Cataloging-in-Publication Data

Milač, Metod M.
Resistance, imprisonment, and forced labor:
a Slovene student in World War II / Metod M. Milač.
p. cm. — (Studies in modern European history; v. 47)
Includes bibliographical references and index.
1. Milač, Metod M. 2. World War, 1939-1945—Personal narratives,
Slovenian. 3. World War, 1939-1945—Prisoners and prisons, German.
4. World War, 1939-1945—Prisoners and prisons, Italian. 5. Prisoners
of war—Slovenia—Biography. I. Title. II. Series.
D811.M51518 A3   940.54'7243—dc21   2001050658
ISBN 0-8204-5781-7
ISSN 0893-6897

Die Deutsche Bibliothek-CIP-Einheitsaufnahme

Milač, Metod M.:
Resistance, imprisonment, and forced labor:
a Slovene student in World War II / Metod M. Milač.
–New York; Washington, D.C./Baltimore; Bern;
Frankfurt am Main; Berlin; Brussels; Vienna; Oxford: Lang.
(Studies in modern European history; Vol. 47)
ISBN 0-8204-5781-7

Cover design by Joni Holst

The paper in this book meets the guidelines for permanence and durability
of the Committee on Production Guidelines for Book Longevity
of the Council of Library Resources.

Printed in the United States of America

In Memory of My Parents
Ivan and Jerica

for their love, care, concern, guidance
and most of all
for their never-ending trust and faith
in us

Contents

Acknowledgments

During the entire period I was working on these memoirs, my friend and colleague, author and free-lance writer Paul Borštnik, was of great help to me, first by reading an early draft of the manuscript and later by suggesting corrections and changes. I am extremely grateful to him. I am also grateful to many individuals from whom I received specific information. However, so as not to be influenced in my recollections of the war, I did not solicit from others their perspectives of the events recounted here.

I wish to thank my two sons for urging me to write these memoirs and for their day-to-day help. Tom's thoughts regarding content and presentation were invaluable. Michael assisted me countless times with his knowledge of computer technology without which I could not have assembled this work.

I would also like to extend my thanks to several members of the Syracuse University faculty for encouraging me to persevere in my writing and to my colleagues at the University library who stood ready to assist me with their expertise. I am also indebted to Syracuse University for providing me an office where I was able to recall my war experiences in quiet seclusion.

For a person inexperienced with book publishing, the assistance of professionals is essential. I wish to express my most sincere appreciation to Ms. Phyllis Korper, Aquisitions Editor, to Ms. Bernadette Alfaro, Production Coordinator, to Ms. Lisa Dillon, Production Manager, and their staff for their expert help and always-ready advice throughout the process. I would also like to thank Dr. Frank Coppa, General Editor, for his constructive suggestions.

Finally, I would like to extend my heartfelt thanks to my wife of fifty years, Herta. Without her assistance in all things this work would not have been completed.

Introduction

❧

Quot homines tot sententiae:
suo' quoique mos.
There are as many opinions as there are
people: each has his own correct way.
—Terence c. 190–159 B.C.

My passage through the war was essentially no different from that of many others
who survived the cataclysmic years 1941–1945, but the variety of my predicaments,
my encounters with factions of all major ideologies in this struggle, and my ever-
present reminiscences of images, events, and consequences are some of the reasons
why I decided to record my personal history. Though over fifty-five years have
passed, in my memory these events remain as vivid as ever.[1]

I also have a deeply felt obligation to leave for posterity and history an account of my experiences. The obligation entails a binding loyalty to those who
never had an opportunity to express, to state, and/or to defend their associations,
actions, and their decisions. My gratitude is owed to those who, often at risks of
negative consequences to themselves, acted to help other human beings in crucial
situations. Throughout my long and difficult journey I was most fortunate to be
associated often with such unselfish companions. No matter how difficult the situation or how great the uncertainty or danger, being together with others helped
to soften the unexpected blows and circumstances.

Official histories of World War II, or any other calamity of that nature, re-
gardless how many details they include, cannot describe the totality of human suffering, especially by those not directly involved in the conduct of the war. The sufferings of the people thrown into and becoming part of the conflict, the agonizing

and terrifying experiences can never be sufficiently and adequately described. Only memory flashes, such as a few entries in these memoirs, might, I hope, raise in the reader's mind and heart the awareness of that side of the war's ugly face.

The deceptions during the war years were most depressing for me. Not the planned military deceptions, which are as much part of the strategy as anything else, but deceptions in interpersonal relationships. Total confidentiality and trust is expected of everybody in any group with common goals and objectives, especially during the war and in underground activities. What is the motivation of a traitor who, by his or her sinister actions often causes terrifying consequences for many?

It is quite possible that other people, who shared some of these experiences with me, looked at these happenings differently. I, however, have my memories deeply imbedded in my mind and in my heart. Therefore, I am convinced that my recollections truly represent the impressions and thoughts I experienced during those difficult and often tragic years.

A drawback in my memoirs is the sad fact that most of my closest friends during the key events are no longer around. I attempted as much as possible to render accurately what these friends would have said about this or that event or development. I feel comfortable that I have done my inner searching sufficiently and truthfully.

In the post-war period, while hearing, reading, and researching these events in retrospect, more factual and assumed information about the war came to light. Where my reminiscence and knowledge are different or where the recent documentation seem erroneous—according to my eyewitness recollections—I have made every possible attempt to lead the reader to the sources in question.

In describing events of great impact and far-reaching consequences, I have come in contact with many persons. Where known, the full names of persons who were helpful to me and of those who held any kind of official position, are included. Where I no longer remember the first name, I use letter "X," for family names, the letter "Y." For all others, where my associations may not have been either sufficiently positive or even negative, I use abbreviations only. It would have been impossible to locate these individuals to seek permission for inclusion of their names.

I am attempting to bring to the reader a slightly different look at the war, from the point of view of one young person who found himself in the turmoil of events, most often not by choice. To this author and to his generation—at the time they were still growing up, when they were inexperienced in practically all phases of life and human relations, and when they possessed only minimal understanding of the world's ideologies—the war brought the harshest realities of life much too fast and much too soon.

Of special interest in these memoirs may be the episodes of exposure to the authority and personalities of many ideologies involved in World War II and in different localities and under changing circumstances. Those in power came from various nationalities and so did the internees. People from all parts of Europe were present at the locations where I found myself during the war. Associations with such a variety of people was an experience of valuable and long-lasting benefit, though gained at the most inappropriate times and places. The reader should also be aware that at different times during the war, the status of internees often went through significant changes. Thus, toward the end of the war the chances for survival improved. It may also not be obvious that in general, internees had no rights or if any such rights existed, nobody observed or followed them. We were at the mercy of our captors.

The most tragic and catastrophic development, the forcible repatriations after the hostilities had already ceased in Europe on 8 May 1945, will never be sufficiently and satisfactorily explained. The question "Is the efficiency of military operations more important than thousands of human lives?" will be forever on our minds.

To those of us who survived the cataclysmic years of World War II and decided not to return to our native countries because of post-war developments, the generous international community came to the rescue. Not only the governments, but indirectly the people themselves, made it possible for us to start our lives all over again. Our gratitude is everlasting.

CHAPTER ONE

The Prewar Years

Even before the conclusion of World War I (Armistice signed 11 November 1918), two major events took place. The most consequential and long lasting was the Russian Revolution of 1917, eliminating forever a government and an administration practiced over centuries which allowed minor adjustments only when forced by the pressures of thought, necessity, or dangerous signs of strong opposition. The other important event had its roots in the tenth of the President Wilson's Fourteen Points (Address to Congress, 8 January 1918), which offered hope, gave impetus, and subsequently led to the realization of hopes and goals for many nations of the Austrian-Hungarian Empire. The independence movement initiated and formulated by the Spring of Nations in the year 1848, and the creation of new national states changed significantly the map of Europe during the years following the end of hostilities. The conclusion of World War I and the Peace Treaty of Versailles in June 1919, brought many negative after-effects as well; the war's ugly consequences were seen everywhere.

The depressing economic conditions and very low standards of living were very deeply felt by the entire population of Europe. After four years of sacrifices of all kinds and ten million victims of the war, the people were desperately looking for solutions, for ways to improve their daily life and cope with food shortages. The desperate conditions were opening the doors to new ideologies and to potential new leaders, especially those who kept promising fast and drastic solutions to the negative state of affairs.

The rise of Benito Mussolini in Italy (Prime Minister 1922, Dictator 1925), of Adolf Hitler in Germany (Chancellor 1933, Head of State 1934), and the consolidation of powers in the hands of Joseph Stalin (General Secretary of the Communist Party 1922, Dictator 1927) in the Soviet Union, brought some signs of improvements in some European countries in the 1920s and 1930s. These improvements, however, came with a price, a terrible price, hardly anticipated by anyone after the conclusion of the war of 1914–1918, the war that was supposed to end all wars.

The town of Prevalje, where I was born, is not known to attract distant visitors for reasons of enchantment. This is not to imply a lack of a beautiful natural environment or other features which generally contribute to the significance of a location. In this particular case, two historical churches and the Meža River are probably the key reasons for the existence of all towns and villages in this valley. Mežiška dolina (Meža Valley), as this region is called, extends from some distance west of Črna at one end, to Dravograd in the east at the other, where the Meža joins her much larger sister, the Drava River. My town, Prevalje, lies right in the middle.

Though the reader may have a difficult time finding Mežiška dolina on the map, this region at least for the last hundred fifty years, was a center for the coal and lead mining and the iron industry of Slovenia. These industries brought to the region either prosperity or depression, depending which decades of the last hundred fifty years we wish to examine.[1]

Mežiška dolina received special attention from international circles during the peace treaty negotiations after World War I, during the post-war border disputes between Austria and Yugoslavia, and at the time of the Carinthian Plebiscite in 1920. By decision of the Four Powers, this valley was excluded from the disputed territory and after the Plebiscite of 10 October 1920, it became the only part of the former Austrian-Hungarian Province of Carinthia assigned to the newly created State of Yugoslavia.[2] During and especially at the end of World War II, Mežiška dolina and its inhabitants suffered terribly. In the opinion of many, some crucial final battles in the European war were fought right in this area.

The plebiscite of 10 October 1920 decided the borders between Austria and Yugoslavia. Mežiška dolina was now separated from the rest of the Slovene Carinthian population by the new border. In his Introduction to the works of the Slovene Carinthian writer Franc Sušnik, Marjan Kolar remembers that Sušnik was never able to forget his homeland being cut in two,[3] and neither did thousands of others. In my own case, not only our homeland, but our families were now separated. As a consequence, my mother's family home belonged now to Austria, and one of my father's two brothers also had his farm on the northern side of the border.

My father and mother met during the Yugoslav Civil Administration of the disputed Carinthian plebiscite territory. My father, a lawyer, was assistant county administrator under the *okrajni glavar Kakl* (district head) in Völkermarkt/Velikovec. My mother, previously a teacher in Prekmurje, worked in the same county offices as one of the administrative secretaries. After the plebiscite, they had to leave Völkermarkt/Velikovec in a matter of hours, because the Yugoslav forces, who were controlling and protecting the territory, had to evacuate in a very short time and turn over the administration of the plebiscite area to the Austrian authorities. The Yugoslav Völkermarkt/Velikovec administration moved to Prevalje as did many other Yugoslav offices.[4]

My parents were married in a small mountain village, Koprivna, in 1921 on the Yugoslav side of the border. The village priest, Reverend Ivan Hojnik, before the plebiscite active as an educator and leader of the Slovene people in Carinthia, later a refugee from the territory, and an old friend of my father officiated. The old rule, that the marriage had to be performed in the bride's parish, did not apply since the Austrian authorities would not permit my father to enter their state.[5]

In 1922, my brother Ciril was born. On the second of October 1924, I raised my voice for the first time. I do not remember this, but so I was told.

On a little hill, just below higher mountains, a person traveling from Kranj toward Jezerski vrh/Seeberg Pass, a border point between Slovenia and Austria, will soon notice some distance away on the right a pleasant village with houses almost hidden by a multitude of trees of all kinds and with a prominent church steeple in the middle looking over the settlement. My father was born here on the last day of the year 1884. Officially it is known as Viševek, even though most people refer to it as Olševek. There is probably a good explanation for this variation, but I have never asked about it and so it has to remain a puzzle. As the oldest of five children, my father was destined, probably by his industrious mother and the village priest, to achieve the highest possible honor for a small village boy, a priesthood. To the big disappointment of his mother, who consequently withdrew her meager financial support, my father decided at the end of gymnasium/high school on the law. He took his degree under most difficult circumstances at the University of Vienna just before the outbreak of the World War I.

After crossing the border at Jezerski vrh/Seeberg Pass, a traveler will experience a road as steep on the Austrian side as during the climb from the south. The switchbacks are so sharp you get the impression you are stabbing yourself in the belly. There is no time to look at the magnificent mountains left and right; one just tries to get to a more comfortable terrain. The steepness levels off a little around the village of Bad Vellach/Bela. One of the last houses and homesteads on your left, once known as Skalarjev dom, is the birthplace of my mother. It is embedded under the Storžič mountain, which is usually given the prefix "koroški/Carinthian," to set it apart from another mountain of the same name, a little southeast of it, on the Gorenjska/Carniolan side of the mountain ridge. Here my mother was born in 1894 as the youngest of six children, three girls and three boys. Two of her brothers were victims of the war of 1914–1918.

I did spent time in my early years at both my father's and mother's birthplaces. Unfortunately, after the much-too-early death of Mother's last brother and owner of the property, the widow and her new husband mismanaged this property. Through an auction, it came into the hands of a German neighbor, who, in spite of an pre-auction agreement among neighbors, could not resist his greed, an action my mother would never forget.[6]

My earliest and strongest memories relate mostly to negative events. In one case, I must have been very young, because all I remember are two split seconds: in the first, my father entering our kitchen with blood running down his face; in the second, he is leaning over a pail of water, washing off his blood. Nothing else, no other persons, no sound, just blood. Many years later, I was told that it was an accident while he was splitting wood. The other event, which I not only remember but also often visualize, was a disastrous flood in our valley. The Meža River, normally only two to three feet deep except when the protective closures of the dam on the western side of the town were opened for water control, rose to unbelievable heights. I can still hear myself crying out of tremendous fear that our residence, completely surrounded by dangerous waters, will be swept away. The sound of the flowing waters in front of the house, during normal times so pleasant and comforting, now became loud, threatening, carrying with it possible destruction and an awareness of helplessness. This was no longer a river but a sea of threatening, dirty, brown, and fast-flowing waters, which for three days and nights brought disaster and destruction to our community as well as to all other villages and towns in the region. Our four-family house survived; several others in the vicinity suffered substantial damage. My memory, however, goes blank as soon as this great flood is over.

My mother told me how close I came to an early death at the age of two or three. In the fruit and vegetable garden behind the house, a water faucet was installed to facilitate the care of plants during the growing season. Under the faucet, set into the ground, was a sizable canister to prevent the often-spilled water from going to waste. My mother was talking to a neighbor on a bench with her back to this water source when she turned around to see two small feet moving back and forth in the air; the rest of me was submerged in the canister full of water. Maybe the flood and my head-down diving experience are reasons for my respect for rivers, lakes, and seas. But, in an unexplained contradiction, in my youthful years I always wanted to join the navy.

The years in Prevalje, however, were my happiest years. There were beautiful forests to explore, to pick blackberries, to search for mushrooms, to play hide and seek, and even to try some explorations deeper into the unknown. Ciril and I had plenty of friends, some older, some younger. A special enhancement came with the introduction of the scout movement into our town, for which I have to be grateful to Miha Rigl, who organized the first scout group in Mežiška dolina. This movement gave us a lot of outdoor experience and also a certain focus for our activities. Our summer tent camping was a great treat and well received by the local people. Landowners in fairly remote areas were always willing to let us camp on their properties with pre-agreed limitations. Most memorable was definitely the camping under Uršlja gora (Mt. Uršlja) at Bobrovo jezero (Beaver Lake). We lived under primitive conditions, and our home-made tents without extra covers often leaked. However, a sunny day usually took care of wet clothes and equipment. We were hungry most of the time, though the entry fee was very low to enable everybody to participate. Parents, if willing to help, were encouraged to bring extra supplies for the kitchen; any food for individuals was strictly forbidden. The scout movement had an added benefit for all of us. It brought together boys from all three social groups, that is, people from surrounding farms, from labor families, and those whose parents held government or business positions.[7] Even though social differences were relatively small, we learned a lot from each other.

Every night at campfire the most enjoyable part was group singing of scout, folk, and patriotic songs. Here and there some songs, introduced by our leaders, had political connotations, but we were not aware of that; for us it was only important that these songs were easy to sing. Why we had to stand guard at night, two hours each turn, was not very clear. Actually it was scary to stand guard, because the soft murmur of the adjacent forest brought to our minds all kinds of strange imaginings. It must have been an instructional device to prepare us for eventualities or to harden our self-confidence.

Our leader, Miha Rigl, checked with the property owners regularly to make sure that there were no misunderstandings. Most of the owners had served in the Austrian/Hungarian army during the World War I, and even though they were convinced that nothing of that kind would happen again, they felt that the experience we were exposed to could only be beneficial for us.

At one time during my elementary school years—I do not remember exactly at what grade—we were invited to join the Yugoslav organization *Sokol* (Falcon). While the scout organization was more or less independent, *Sokol* became, after King Alexander I's declaration of dictatorial powers and dissolution of the Parliament in 1929,[8] the only physical culture organization permitted in Yugoslavia. *Orel* (Eagle), a similar Catholic organization which had existed in the Slovene lands since the turn of the century, was dissolved, as were all other similar organizations throughout the country. *Sokol,* primarily an organization to develop physical fitness and sound minds, also promoted Yugoslavism over individual nationalistic tendencies. As such, it was instrumental in embedding in our minds the idea of one Yugoslav nation, but the programs of gymnastics and other sport activities were the important attractions. Never, at least at my level and as long as I was a member, were we subjected to any specific indoctrination. Most of the teaching and instruction were geared toward building a national awareness and love for the country of Yugoslavia.[9]

The most memorable events of my early years were family singing evenings under Mother's skillful leadership. She had a beautiful voice and a fine sense for four-part singing, a practice quite common in Slovene and Slavic lands. Mother often took out of a drawer a *citre* (zither) which was my mother's prize possession, carefully protected by soft cloth and always kept in a very special place. She assembled my younger sister Marija (soprano) and Ciril (alto), gave herself the lowest part, and assigned to me, because of my high register, the most important role to "sing over." Actually, this was the tenor part transposed to the highest register, to give this type of singing a very unique character. How I managed this art is not very clear to me; however, to my best recollections, I fully satisfied my teacher. Father was excluded from participation although he tried to join a few times. Mother claimed that he did not have a good ear. The real reason was most likely aesthetic; mother did not want a deep bass voice to interfere with our high registers of Alpine sonority and harmony. Many songs I have learned from my mother, a treasure I carry with me all my life. Not only Antonin Dvořak,[10] thousands of us have to thank our mothers for the songs in our hearts.

The decision that I should learn to play the piano came in an unusual way and without my participation. At my birth Mother decided to name me Marjan, but Father had other ideas. "Metod will be his name," he insisted. Knowing mother's great wish to have a piano, father negotiated. "If you agree to the name Metod, I will buy him a piano." When I was six or seven, a piano teacher moved into our four-family house, and Mother remembered and insisted. Thus started my long, pleasant, and rewarding association with music.

In 1930, an impressive show of national unity took place in Mežiška dolina, at Poljane near Prevalje; a monumental gathering was organized in the format of nineteenth-century *Tabori* (outdoor folk assemblies).[11] The people, many in national costumes, came to celebrate from all over and by all available means. Most admired were horseback riders dressed for medieval festivities, when elected princes still proclaimed their obligations to the people of Caranthania with a few Slovene phrases.[12] A replica of the Knežnji kamen (Prince's stone) was built especially for these festivities, heavily cemented into the ground to prevent possible sabotage.[13] The central event of this Tabor was the re-enactment of the solemn medieval proclamations.

The *Sokol* also organized national gatherings and sport activities on regular schedules. There was no lack of opportunity to develop a strong national consciousness.

On one summer day in the early 1930s, from the window in our apartment across town, we watched a large group of people walking slowly toward the railroad station, causing a lot of excitement on the way. Why so much interest in this group of people? The explanation was quite simple; a young woman was leaving for America. "How far is America and when is this woman coming back?" I asked my mother. I was not happy with the answer that America is so far away the young lady will never return.

The lost plebiscite in Carinthia in 1920 was always in the center of discussion in our family. Visitors, whoever they were, talked about those two years after the war, 1918–1920. Our relatives from across the border on their occasional visits reported about what was happening to the Slovene minority now under the new Austrian rule. A strong impression was made by my Uncle Lojze, Father's younger brother. His rough appearance was that of a hard-working farmer, and his strong voice convinced me that unusual things were happening, mostly detrimental, to our people on the other side of the border. I did not understand the details but sensed the hurt and suffering these people were going through. Known as active supporters of the Yugoslav cause during the plebiscite months, they were harassed on every occasion by their opponents either in their private lives or during the unavoidable business dealings with authorities.[14] For these reasons, occasional visits to the relatives across the border, although exciting in many ways, always left me unhappy.

My first awareness of the Nazis came in 1934 during the July *Putsch* in Austria.[15] Heavy fighting between the Nazis and various government troops took place near the Yugoslav border in Carinthia and in the vicinity where my relatives resided. After their defeat, many Nazis escaped to Yugoslavia, most of them to the territory under my father's jurisdiction.[16] Day and night, every hour, dispatches and telegrams with instructions kept coming, many directly from the central government in Belgrade. We lived at the time on the second floor of a four-family house, and such modern conveniences as telephones were not yet household items in those days; this equipment was present in government communication offices only. For those short night hours, when father came home for some rest, we put into place a primitive contrivance of a small wake-up bell on a string and several thin ropes with attachments to lift and lower dispatches and father's responses through a bedroom window. It seemed that the bell never stopped ringing. For us kids these were strange and frightening times. We did not fully comprehend what was going on and why. After we had heard so much about the Nazis and their actions during the uprising, when they were led away by Yugoslav soldiers to assembly points and to the railroad station they did not look any different to us than other regular folks.[17]

After they handed over their arms and ammunition to the Yugoslav forces, Nazi leaders were debriefed by my father, who as county head *(okrajni glavar)*, had political jurisdiction as well. During one of these debriefings, my father learned that one of my cousins on my mother's side, Hans Legat, had fallen victim to a Nazi bullet near Eisenkappel/Železna Kapla.[18]

A few months later, on the 9 October 1934, King Alexander I of Yugoslavia was murdered in Marseilles on the first day of his visit to France. Everything came to a complete standstill. Schools closed and several days of mourning were declared. Every house had candles in the windows at night. The king's pictures, decorated with black veils, were everywhere. During this month we rarely enjoyed father's presence, and when we did, we saw on his face his deep concern. A Requiem Mass in our local church on the day of the funeral in Belgrade—the king's body was brought back to Yugoslavia by the destroyer *Dubrovnik*—even though supported by the best music the town was able to offer, still left nothing but depressed feelings. Nature insisted on participation in kind as well; the days were cold, wet, dark, sinister.

Trips into surrounding hills and mountains were always of special attraction, whether they were organized by school, scouts, or family. My first major hike took place at a very early age with my parents and brother, on Peca Mountain with an overnight stay at the mountain hut. Both evening and morning hours were something new and wonderful. Over the top of Peca Mountain runs the border between Slovenia (formerly Yugoslavia) and Austria. Excellent views of both countries were well worth that extra climbing effort.

Among many hikes, the one on Uršlja gora/Mt. Uršlja meant something special to me—the first independent, unsupervised outing with some challenges. Franc Telcer was the leader; a friend, Ivan Kugovnik, Ciril and I made up the rest of the expedition. We carried one homemade tent and after ascending the peak, placed the tent not very strategically right on the top, too close to the almost vertical north wall. We recognized our mistake around 2:00 A.M. when strong winds threatened to blow us off the mountain. The next tent placement offered much more protection and allowed us some much-needed sleep as well. With pride we descended the next day, earning recognition as true members of the mountain club.

Elementary schools in the country were usually not considered equal to those in the cities. Whether this statement is correct or not would be difficult to prove. Certainly I don't intend to take anything away from my teachers, Ms. Alt and Mr. Stres, and the two principals, Mr. Doberšek and Mr. Lebič, but the fact is that we had to attend five grades before being considered fit to take entrance exams for admission to high school, while city kids usually attended only four years. Therefore, city children were slightly younger than country folks when they entered high school, but these age differences did not result in a maturity gap.

I took the entrance examination for gymnasium/high school in the city of Maribor in the spring of 1936. Soon after that our family moved to Dravograd. My father always felt that the county seat should have been in Dravograd not in Prevalje: the county's official name was "dravograjski." In addition, he felt that for people from Drava and Mislinja Valleys, who had to visit the county offices, it was inconvenient and time consuming to change trains in Dravograd in order to reach Prevalje. Dravograd's geographic location, connecting four valleys and being in the middle of the county, seemed to be the right choice. Leaving friends and such a suddenly dear place as Prevalje was a serious disruption in my life. Though the distance between the two towns was only twelve kilometers, we realized a major change had taken place.

That fall, 1936, it happened—a long trip to Ljubljana and to the outskirts, to Bishop's Gymnasium at Šentvid. Ciril was already a veteran at this high school, a school with emphasis on humanistic studies. For me it was a traumatic experience, the first time away from home, among strangers. Since we beginners were not permitted to see students in the higher grades, I rarely saw Ciril. To make the situation even more difficult, my speech or dialect was different from the others who came from regions of Gorenjska and Dolenjska. "Where are you from?" accompanied by laughs, was usually the reaction the moment I said something. On top of all this, when asked if I was ever a member of *Sokol*, not knowing any better I proudly declared my participation. I then suffered additional ridicule and almost isolation. I did not realize and I was never told that at this high school *Sokol* was derided. The scout movement had a slightly better reputation: the reaction to it was often indifference. There were no adverse feelings, however, ever expressed by those in authority. Were they even aware of our little internal differences? It took time, patience, and extra effort, but eventually I became friends with a few who did not consider my past actions a major sin. However, I soon realized that opinions and positions on variety of issues and topics were not uniform.

The Bishop's Gymnasium program was tough and most teachers were merciless. It was one of the few private schools tolerated by Yugoslav authorities. Bishop Jeglič struggled before receiving permission from the Austrian/Hungarian authorities before World War I to establish this private school and every year the school had to pass stringent review by educational inspectors from Belgrade.

In one sense, I lost my freedom of movement. Every hour from five in the morning to ten at night was scheduled, some for classes, some for studying, some for sports; we had no time on our own. For me, used to roaming around the countryside, this semi-prison was hard to adjust to. Study time was roughly five to six hours a day. Often I wished to have more time, but there were no exceptions to the schedule. For music and piano, I had two excellent teachers, Matija Tomc, a recognized composer, and Venčeslav Snoj, who was influential in my future musical development. However, practice time was highly restricted, and my appeals for additional practice time during play or sport periods received no favorable response. Still, the curriculum was excellent, and the efforts and expertise of our teachers first class. Gymnasium took eight years to finish. In the first year there were 120 students, in the eighth year, only about 20, signal of a tough process of elimination. Many transferred to other schools or trade schools or returned home after a few years to take over a farm or begin other employment. Many students left after the fourth year, because successful final examination at that point entitled the student to a lower-level certificate of accomplishment. The curriculum of the four higher levels was intended primarily for those planning to seek acceptance to universities or technical institutes.

My adjustment to living in Dravograd did not go smoothly either. Because

Ciril and I were now students at Bishop's Gymnasium, a private Catholic school, we were initially not well regarded by the fellows who were supposed to be our new friends. They had all belonged to *Sokol*, even though they were no longer active members of that organization. Our social status was different now. In Prevalje there existed a comfortable mixture of social groups; here the town's "high society" formed a separate group. The reason for our own social isolation was probably imbedded in the fact, that attending high school was still a privilege at the time and that fact gradually isolated us from others. For Ciril and I, as newcomers, knew no others in Dravograd, since we did not attend elementary school here.

The initial cool acceptance was definitely broken when Ciril and I introduced, with the help of Miha Rigl, the scout movement to Dravograd. Here again, this idea was so well received, that even those of German origin or those who considered themselves Germans joined. Our elders were delighted that for the first time the youth of the town worked together in a friendly and cooperative manner, something they were never able to accomplish before. Unfortunately, this friendship soon ended. The news must have come from above that scouts, although a non-political, non-religious organization, was nevertheless a British organization. Our new "German friends" of short duration departed as a group. The tensions grew deeper, not only in our town but in the surrounding areas as well.

This tension reached its peak in March 1938, when the German army entered Austria. The enthusiastic reception the Germans received throughout Austria in cities and towns completely obscured the fate of those who, to the very last, tried to prevent this from happening.[19] Everywhere, in every newspapers and on every radio report, we heard "Heil Hitler" and saw the raised right hands, the Nazi salute. It would be superfluous to mention how local Nazi supporters in our town welcomed this German action. From now on, these Nazi sympathizers became openly hostile toward anything Slovene or Yugoslav; more than that, some of them became involved in all kinds of (by Yugoslav laws) illegal activities.

After the annexation of Austria, the Anschluss, German students kept coming to Dravograd by train, unloaded their equipment, and set up their camp, always in the same place on the shore of the Drava River right across from our residence. After a day or two they broke camp and departed in their modern kayaks. Usually there were four or five kayaks with double occupancy in each expedition. It did not escape our attention, that the crew of each kayak consisted of a man and a woman, something we observed with interest also in their tent arrangements. The camp site was private and off limits, so a closer look at their activities was not possible. We were curious about an abundance of Leika cameras in their possession; each student was well equipped. The members of these expeditions, which started in our town and ended, after a long journey down the Drava River all the way to Donava/Danube by Belgrade, were skillfully disguised expert photographers and mapmakers assigned to bring back to Germany information about the Yugoslav defense installations. After several expeditions during the summer of 1938, these "student-tourists" stopped coming.

The friendship among the students in Dravograd grew stronger. We were attending high schools at different locations and thus enjoyed our association only during vacation times: two months in summer, two weeks for Christmas, and one week for Easter. In winter we skied with very primitive equipment; in summer we often went hiking. On one such hiking expedition in the region of Mt. Raduha, on a trip intended to take three days, we got lost on the first day on a poorly marked trail in the woods. It took us three days to get back to civilization. Fortunately, the high mountains served as general orientation points, and inhabitants of a few isolated huts pointed us in the right direction. We arrived back home at the exact day and time as planned, so our parents never knew about this misadventure.

Another misguided activity was our swim across the Drava River. Around Dravograd, the Drava was at that time a fast-running river, deep and with many whirlpools.[20] The idea to swim to the opposite shore and back was not an original one. An expert swimmer from a city athletic club visited relatives in our town. He demonstrated how to fight whirlpools. At the point where Drava crosses the border, there was a big bend in the river with a giant whirlpool permanently present and clearly visible. Local stories claimed that this whirlpool was so strong that at one time in the past it had swallowed a wagon and two horses which accidentally slipped down the steep embankment from the road above. This swimmer fearlessly swam toward this dangerous trap. With strong arm and leg motions he temporarily disturbed the center of the whirlpool and escaped the strong pull downward. None of us dared to follow. Instead, we followed his example of swimming across the river. As the youngest and weakest swimmer, I hesitated at first. My friends all made it across. The start was easy and smooth; the river just pulled me toward the middle. Here the struggle began. I fought with all my powers to get out of the dangerous center but was pulled back again and again. I saw and heard my friends waving and screaming on the other shore. One thing went through my mind "do not panic; do not panic." Almost half a kilometer further down from my starting point, a minuscule peninsula was intruding toward the center of the river and this saved me. Just as I was pulled past it, I was able with a few strong strokes to get out of the dangerous embrace, and I swam over a few minor whirlpools to the shore. Totally exhausted, I realized that this ordeal was not yet over. To get back, we had to swim again; under no circumstances would we dare to walk across the only bridge in swim shorts. This second time we knew better. We carefully selected our route and starting point and decided to swim in groups of three, close together. It worked much better. However, all of us learned a good lesson: "do not tempt the river unless there is a good reason to do so."

European political tensions touched us in many different ways: open hostilities of Hitler sympathizers, lenience of the central government in Belgrade toward activities of the fifth columnists, and construction of a defense line on the hills on the south bank of the Drava River were just a few. More and more Yugoslav troops came to the area, indicating a sense of urgency. On a few occasions we observed General Leon Rupnik, who was in charge of this defense work, and his entourage inspecting defense installations.

The chief engineer for the defense construction, a Serb, came directly from Belgrade. He let everybody know how unhappy he was to be assigned a job in this, to him, forgotten corner of the world. However, two special attractions came with him: two daughters. The younger one was a little reserved but very beautiful; the older was not as pretty but had a most pleasant personality and was a favorite of all of us. When she played the piano and sang current new popular tunes in her deep alto voice, we were completely enamored. Since there was a lack of young ladies of our age, these two Serbian students were a welcome addition to our otherwise almost entirely male society.

The news became more and more disturbing. My father regularly listened to Hitler's speeches. We did not understand what he was saying, but nobody missed the threatening sound of his voice.[21] Problems on the borders were constantly on the rise. The few border guards (*graničari*) were not able to cope with increased illegal traffic across the border, which involved smuggling of arms and ammunition as well as saccharin and cigarettes. The use of force was discouraged to avoid any possibility of an international incident.

The news about the life of the Slovene minority in the former southern Austria, now under Nazi rule, was equally depressing. All organizations and gatherings of Slovene ethnic groups were forbidden.[22] It became clear that the Nazi policy was the elimination of minorities by means of re-settlements or forced assimilation. The tragic death of the tortured Slovene priest Vinko Poljanec in the Gestapo prison in August 1938 clearly indicated in what direction the new rulers were heading.[23]

"Munich," "Chamberlain," "Peace in our time," "Sudetenland," became household words.[24] The conference in Munich provided some hope for resolution of conflicts, but misgivings and fears prevailed. We, with the typical reaction of youth, still did not realize the seriousness of the situation. Somewhere we got hold of a translation of Hitler's *Mein Kampf.*[25] We were reading, amid jokes and laughs, that Hilter intended to get his additional *Lebensraum* from the Slavs in the East. Future developments, however, eliminated all jokes and wiped the smiles off our faces.

September 1939 brought the start of a new war. We were always told that World War I was the war to end all wars. Now there was a new war. How big, how long, how destructive, how horrible, was the first question? When and where will it end? Will it end in another peace settlement in a few days? My history teacher in the gymnasium, professor Franc Trdan, told the class on one occasion, that no war ever ended the way expected by either side. What would that mean in this case? Successes of the German army against determined and courageous Poles left little hope for an early ceasefire or peace talks.

It was not easy to concentrate on studies at the start of the new semester after return to school in early September 1939. The war news we received was worse day by day. Our superiors and teachers tried to protect us by giving us as little news as possible. Nevertheless, we were sufficiently informed and regularly checked maps, hoping that the German advance in Poland would stop. The shock of the year came when the Soviet Union decided to enter the war against Poland, thus taking away from the Poles their last hope for survival.

At the end of November 1939, the Soviet Union decided to follow the German example of aggression and attacked Finland. Rumors circulated that, after the initial unsuccessful attempts to subjugate the Finns, it was Germany that advised the Soviets how to use their tanks more efficiently. Harsh winter conditions and determined resistance enabled the Finns to defend their land for four months before they had to surrender to a much superior force in March 1940.[26] The Finns' example of resistance gave everybody a little hope that courage and determination could still play a major role even in modern warfare.

This wishful thinking was soon dispelled by the German attack on Denmark and Norway in April 1940. While Denmark had no chance to offer much resistance because of the nature of its terrain, Germans encountered a few difficulties in Norway, especially in the northern parts around Narvik.[27] The German navy suffered substantial losses in operations along the Norway coast and inside the fjords. Our hopes that the advance would be stopped in this territory, however, did not come through.

A great shock came with the sudden German attack in the West in May 1940. The German divisions made rapid advances through Holland and Belgium in the direction of France, bypassing the Maginot defense line. Even though a sizable British expeditionary force was fighting side by side with the French army, they were not able to hold back the German motorized divisions. The situation on the front became desperate. Thousands of French people were trying to escape the German advance by fleeing south. The name Dunkirk, a place on the French coast where the British fairly successfully evacuated most of the expeditionary force and some French troops after the defeat on that front, was on the lips of everybody in those days.[28]

In June 1940, I was preparing for the lower-level final examination at the end of the fourth year of gymnasium studies. Since study hours were not sufficient for some of us, we took advantage of the only other opportunity for extra study hours, that is, sitting in the restrooms on the toilets after the lights went out in the bedrooms. Sitting there, of course, had its limitations, and one had to plan to get there just at the right time before every stall was occupied. How the director found out about our new study facilities, while our supervisors did not, remains a mystery. It was probably on one of his occasional night inspection tours of the buildings that he became suspicious. We had great respect for him, sometimes bordering on fear, because he never smiled. In a firm voice he called us out of our unusual study carrels. To our surprise, we were not reprimanded; instead, he said that sleep is more important before examinations than an hour or two of additional study. On the way toward our bedrooms, he gave us the disastrous news that Paris was already in the German hands. Few of us were able to close our eyes soon on that night.

In the summer of 1940 my parents decided to take the family on a one-week trip over the mountains of Pohorje. We started at the Maribor end and finished at Dravograd. These were well-established trails with convenient overnight accommodations, but the slow trail walking did not appeal to the two of us. For this reason we kept asking for permission to return home to our friends before the end of the trip, to which father reluctantly consented. My mother's words, before we departed, that this may be the last family trip, soon became prophetic. I will be forever sorry that Ciril and I did not realize the great uncertainty about the future that was in their hearts and minds; to this day I regret my insensitivity toward my wonderful parents. I should have known better.

In September, Ciril and I left for Ljubljana and our new student residence with the Čekal family in Kamniška ulica (street). Ciril started at the Teachers School; I entered the fifth year at the Classical Gymnasium/high school. I had made my decision to leave Bishop's Gymnasium at Šentvid primarily to study music. My piano instructor, professor Venčeslav Snoj, recognizing my strong desire for music, visited his former piano professor at the Academy of Music in Ljubljana and recommended me for acceptance as one of his students. Since I had not yet qualified for the entrance examination to the middle division of the Academy of Music as a piano major, I became a private student of Professor Anton Ravnik. This developed in time into much more then a student-teacher association. It was Professor Ravnik who introduced me to the beauty of the piano repertoire and to the rewards of music in the larger sense. He knew how to open the doors little by little and how to guide me to the right recitals and concerts. Our discussions about these concerts and artists are treasures I will always be grateful for. As a piano teacher he was strict and demanding. His condition for accepting me as his student was simple: start at the beginning and if you work hard, we will make fast progress. Lessons were twice a week for twenty minutes, time well spent.

The upper division of the classical gymnasium education consisted of four years, levels five to eight. The gymnasium in Ljubljana had much larger enrollment than my previous school. At the fifth year level there were three parallel classes of approximately forty students each. To my surprise and initial disappointment, I was assigned to unit A, the only unit which had female students. There were twenty-eight young ladies and only twelve young men in this unit: At first I felt uneasy. However, I soon realized that class spirit was even stronger in this mixed society than in all-male units. The one minor unhappiness were constant visits of the older students during the break periods. These visits pleased our female classmates but not the males.

The opportunities in Ljubljana for broadening music horizons were exceptionally good. Every Monday there was either a symphony or chamber music concert; solo recitals were on Fridays, opera on the weekend. In every concert hall and in the opera house there was standing room for students, so the cost of attending was minimal. Of course, standing for many hours through a Verdi or Wagner opera was not the most pleasant experience. Recordings, however, were very rare; equipment for listening even more scarce: The only way to learn was to go to live performances. My future looked bright and promising. The European war scene, however, presented an entirely different picture: defeat after defeat, tragedy after tragedy.

For the British, 1940 was probably the worst year. German U-boats were terrorizing shipments in the Atlantic; not a day passed without reports about torpedoed ships and often no rescue for the sailors. The Luftwaffe attacks, first on airfields in England and then on London, were on daily schedules. How long could a city like London survive such devastation? We admired the British pilots, who almost single-handedly defended their island day and night.

There were speculations that Germany was ready to attack England and that these air attacks were only a prelude to the invasion. My cousin on my mother's side, Franz Mubi, a police lieutenant in Graz before the annexation of Austria and who later served in the same capacity under the German rule in the city, was already assigned a post in England in the event of successful occupation. He and his colleagues with similar assignments were learning English and received instructions in preparation for their intended assignments.

The fall of 1940, however, brought unmistakable signs that Germany was not looking to England but east and south as the next area of interest. Even we young folks had to recognize the direction they were taking. In November, first Hungary joined the Tripartite Pact,[29] soon followed by Romania. Because the Italian Army suffered several defeats in Greece and was pushed back into Albania by the Greek forces in the fall of 1940,[30] the Germans also started pressuring Bulgaria to join the Tripartite Pact and to permit German troops a free passage through Bulgaria toward Greece. Bulgaria succumbed to these pressures in January of 1941.[31]

For Yugoslavia there were no more safe and friendly borders except toward Greece and the open waters of the Adriatic Sea.[32] The encirclement of Yugoslavia was almost complete.

The Christmas and New Year vacations of 1940–41 brought about the most depressing realizations. It became clear that Germany was putting all possible pressures on Yugoslavia. Nazi sympathizers were now out in the open; nobody could touch them. While walking to the traditional Midnight Mass across the town, all we heard was the German language—loud, boisterous, provocative. Many of these people came from the surrounding areas to re-enforce the town's German sympathizers. They enjoyed themselves in the local taverns, stood on the sidewalks, and let everybody know that, whatever they did, they could no longer be touched. I was walking next to my father and I sensed his anger at these provocations. His position as the chief county administrator became day by day more difficult. Yugoslav laws were broken daily by illegal acts against the state, by illegal border crossings, by smuggling of arms and propaganda items. These Nazi sympathizers, many active members of the Nazi party and of the well-organized Hitler's fifth column,[33] were dressed in paraphernalia closely resembling German costumes, the most obvious and, to us, the most provocative items of which were the white knee socks. Parents, leaders of youth organizations, and persons of influence were constantly reminding us that we should not succumb to Nazis provocations and by some incident or fight make this difficult situation even more difficult.

I did not listen to German radio news reports myself, but a few friends who spoke German told me that my father's name was often mentioned as one who, as chief representative of the Yugoslav government in this area, misused Yugoslav laws and unjustly sent to prison German nationals and sympathizers on trumped-up charges. Actually, the situation was entirely different. Yugoslav authorities were urging as much leniency as possible, and even the most obvious law-breakers were usually released from prison in a day or two under pressure from the German Embassy in Belgrade.

In our part of the world, Christmas was always observed and celebrated with beautiful festivities, church services, gifts, and family gatherings—the happiest part of the year. Not in 1940–1941. A nightmare was hanging over us; all attempts to show happy faces were in vain. The New Year festivities brought nothing more than another state of depression. All of us who were in schools away from home were rather relieved to leave home after the end of vacations. A feeling of guilt at leaving the rest of the families in such an unpleasant situation was also present and offset only slightly by parents' encouraging words that the future was not all that bleak.

Having completed the encirclement of Yugoslavia with ease and speed, Hitler did not wait very long to complete his southern political offensive. On 14 February 1941, Yugoslav Premier Cvetković was invited to Berchtesgaden to meet with Hitler. We did not know much about these discussions—only very brief and carefully worded diplomatic dispatches were released—but it was not difficult to guess what the discussions were all about. A surprise announcement came on 4 March 1941 about the Regent Prince Paul's visit to Berchtesgaden. Seeing Prince Paul of Yugoslavia in a newspaper photograph sitting next to Hitler in an open car, a depressed expression on his face, told us all. What burdens and responsibilities were on his shoulders? What was going on? These signs were not what we wanted to see or hear.[34]

On 25 March 1941, the bad news came: Yugoslavia agreed to join the Tripartite Pact. An agreement was signed in Vienna. The details about this agreement were only partially known, which opened the doors for all kind of rumors. Some claimed that Yugoslavia was privileged in reaching a positive agreement, joining the Axis Powers only as a formality, retaining neutrality and signing a kind of non-aggression pact.[35] Other rumors claimed that Germany would have the right to transport troops and material over Yugoslav territory to the front in Greece and to have some say in Yugoslav internal affairs, meaning removal of certain government officials considered openly hostile to the Nazi regime.[36] It is difficult to guess what the Slovene population actually thought about this agreement. No doubt there were opinions of all kinds. In school, among friends, we were all very disappointed over these developments, thinking it was a defeat of major proportions for Yugoslavia.

At least to our younger generation it came as no surprise when on 27 March 1941, a group of Yugoslav air force officers removed the government in a quick and well-organized *Putsch*. King Peter II was put on the throne; the three regents were removed, including Prince Paul, and the military took over.

The demonstrations in support of the officers and against the joining of the Tripartite Pact were widespread. When the news about the *Putsch* reached Ljubljana, I was in my high school class. At one of the breaks between classes at mid-morning, we noticed a large group of demonstrators on the street near our classroom, screaming and yelling all kinds of slogans. Our school director, Professor Marko Bajuk, made every effort to prevent us from joining those outside. One of the top students in my class read for us the king's proclamation and call for unity and support.[37] We were hanging out the windows on top of each other in this mixed class of boys and girls and yelling in support of demonstrators when Director Bajuk entered the room. He scolded us severely for our actions. The demonstrations lasted all day and into the night. Whether they were spontaneous or staged really did not cross our minds and probably would not have made any difference either.

The new government did not negate the Tripartite Pact. It tried to assure the German government of continuous cooperation in the matters of joint concern. However, partial mobilization was declared just in case. On the basis of the events in Europe of the preceding two years, one thing was clear: Hitler would not take this slap in the face without some response.[38]

CHAPTER TWO

Attack on Yugoslavia

6 April 1941

❦

There were only minor protests from European powers when German troops entered and re-occupied the demilitarized zone of the Rhineland on 7 March 1936, the first German military action after World War I. Neither was there much protest when Germany annexed Austria on 12 March 1938. The target for Hitler was the Sudetenland, a sizeable border area inside Czechoslovakia. Several strong diplomatic efforts by Britain and France to prevent this takeover were unsuccessful. At Munich, on 29 September 1938, Britain and France yielded to Hitler's pressure and signed the Munich Agreement which, according to British Prime Minister Chamberlain, the chief negotiator on the opposing side, was supposed to guarantee "peace in our time."

The peace reached at Munich lasted less than one year. In March 1939, Germany occupied the rest of Czechoslovakia. In April, following the German example, Italy invaded Albania. August 1939 brought one of the biggest surprises, the German-Soviet Non-Aggression Pact.

What everybody feared, happened in the early morning hours of 1 September 1939: Germany attacked Poland. Subject to previous agreements with Poland, Britain and France declared war on Germany. To make the situation even worse, the Soviet troops invaded Poland from the east a few days later, thus ending for the Poles any possibility of resistance.

In the spring of 1940 Germany demonstrated even further its true expansionist intentions. On 9 April 1940, it invaded Denmark and Norway, following only a month later, 10 May 1940, with an attack on the Netherlands, Belgium, and France. With unbelievable speed, the German Blitzkrieg overran these countries without much difficulty. To plunge Europe even deeper into the war, Italy, as an ally of Germany, declared war on Britain and France on 10 June 1940 and took minor military actions against France.

Germany then turned her aggression against England. The air attacks of the German Luftwaffe began on 15 August 1940 and continued until the end of October, but heroic

British Royal Air Force (RAF) pilots and the first-time use of radar allowed England to withstand the German attacks. These acts of terror from the sky are known in the history books as The Battle of Britain.

The Italian invasion of Greece on 28 October 1940 achieved only limited success. Nevertheless, with Germany moving by various means into Hungary, Romania, and Bulgaria, only Yugoslavia was still independent and non-aligned—but surrounded almost on all sides.

On Palm Sunday, 6 April 1941, I was on the way home from church in Ljubljana's suburb of Šiška where I usually attended service at eight in the morning for two reasons: to give me more time the rest of the day for study and to listen to the well-trained church choir and the soprano soloist, whose voice and interpretation of solo parts I admired. About half-way between the church and my rented room which I shared with my brother, Ciril, the unexpected sound of airplane engines suddenly disturbed a very quiet and peaceful Sunday morning, a sound soon followed by several explosions. My heart almost stopped, not willing to accept what was happening. As I spotted at some distance to the north a plane flying low and in circles above the Ljubljana radio station dropping bombs, I no longer had any doubt that Yugoslavia's turn had come and that diplomatic attempts by the new Yugoslav government to prevent an attack by the Axis powers and their satellites had not been successful.[1]

When I returned to my residence in Kamniška Street around 9 A.M., everybody was already assembled around the only radio in the house, in the kitchen of our host family, the Čekals. Listening to the news were Mr. and Mrs. Čekal, their two daughters, ages eleven and fifteen, my brother, and another student who also boarded there. Mrs. Čekal, a domineering figure, was in and out of hysterics not out of fear for herself but for her two girls and her husband. What would happen to them? Her husband, who used to tell us all kind of semi-heroic stories from his past, was pale and visually depressed. As a railroad official with some responsibilities, he knew that he would have to report almost immediately for an unknown assignment, most likely in a faraway region to help transport troops and military material. Radio news was not encouraging. Rumors, however, were coming from all corners. One person heard this; another knew that—in our naiveté and in desperate hope, we were still expecting some positive results or reports. However, in view of what we knew about the German forces and their quick successes during the first year and a half of the war, such optimism was difficult to sustain.

A state of shock enveloped the entire city and nation. Although the Ljubljana radio station was still functioning, the only news was the confirmation of the Axis powers attack on several fronts with almost no details, a description of the merciless German air attack on Belgrade, a few messages about resistance of the Yugoslav forces, repeated calls to military personnel to report to their stations, and calls for volunteers. Between the news and announcements, we heard broadcasts of military marches.

Ciril and I were very concerned about our parents, our sister Marija, and many friends and acquaintances in Dravograd, a town only two or three kilometers from the German border. Dravograd, because of its strategic location at the crossroads of four valleys, two of which were direct routes into Germany, was most exposed to a German advance. The accusations against my father in the past regarding alleged mistreatment of German nationals and sympathizers were very much on our minds.[2] But the uncertainty about our parents and Marija was our major concern.

A few days before the bombing, Ciril and I had received a message directing us not to come home for the forthcoming spring break. Why, I still do not fully understand. Our friends from the same town and vicinity received similar instructions. Dravograd and our residence there were both located in the north, on the left side of the Drava River, just a few hundred yards from the only bridge connecting this small area south of the German (Austrian) border with the rest of the Slovene lands.[3]

Not only the Yugoslav government, most of the population was convinced, after the *Putsch* of 27 March by the Air Force officers in Belgrade, that Hitler would take drastic measures: it was only a question of time. While the new government was making all kinds of diplomatic efforts to smooth things over and to find an alternative way out of the crisis, as a precaution it also initiated mobilization. To my father and other government officials in the border regions, intense activity by and assembling of large German forces on the German side was more than enough warning for preparatory measures. Thus, night and day, destruction of documents took place at the county headquarters under my father's direction. He seldom had time to come home even though our residence and his offices were in adjacent buildings.

The Yugoslav army had been building the first line of defense on the hills south of Drava for the last four years. This "petite Maginot Line" in Slovenia was, to the best of local information, completed a few months before the spring of 1941.

Because our residence was under constant surveillance for any unusual activity by the town's inhabitants and the government was trying by all means to prevent a panic, we were at great disadvantage. My father did not and could not allow removal of any personal items or possessions from our residence for the move south, which many people were doing, just in case. When permission for partial evacuation was finally given on 5 April, my mother left Dravograd in the very early morning hours of 6 April with some family possessions, unaware of the German attack, which started approximately at the same time or soon after.

It was fortunate for our family and others on the north side of Drava, that the main German assault in Slovenia was concentrated in the direction of Radgona and Maribor, with the clear intention of cutting Slovenia off from the rest of Yugoslavia, and not toward Dravograd.

According to some reports received later from friends, German forces did take control of the border-crossing station on the road leading from Lavamünd/Labot to Dravograd at approximately 5.30 A.M. but did not try to advance immediately toward our town only a few kilometers away. Expecting strong resistance, the Germans advanced cautiously in this mountainous terrain, overpowering first the widely spaced Yugoslav *graničari* (border guards), many of whom fell as the first victims of this surprise attack. I had often accompanied my father on his official visits and inspections of the *karaule* (border guard stations) and formed a very good opinion of these disciplined, professional, and dedicated men, who were mostly Serbs. Seeing later photographs of some of these *graničari* and other Yugoslav front-line soldiers' corpses in a pile, surrounded by German troops, was for me the first traumatic sight of the war—which is still strongly imbedded in my mind.

Because the German Army did not use *Blitzkrieg* strategy or because it lacked adequate mechanized equipment at the Dravograd sector, my father and his associates at the county headquarters gained sufficient time for successful transport of government offices across the river from the left to the right bank and were fast heading south toward the city of Celje as per plan. How far they actually came and how they disposed of the rest of the documents and government property or if they merged theirs with those at county seats in Slovenj Gradec and Celje, I never found out. As a reserve captain in the Yugoslav Army, my father's duty was to report for military service, and it is very likely that he was required to turn over his administrative responsibilities to others. I do remember, however, very distinctly when he suddenly appeared two or three days later at Ciril's and my student residence with only a briefcase and the Yugoslav flag from his county's headquarters in Dravograd under his arm.

That same day, 6 April 1941, Marija was, in effect, an orphan at the age of twelve. After my father's departure, knowing very well what kind of burdens and responsibilities he was facing, and in Mother's absence, Mrs. Kolenc and Mrs. Nendl became her custodians. With the help of Krista, our house-help, Marija packed two suitcases and walked over the bridge to the railroad station, arriving there at around 10 A.M.

Whatever was still in the house that was government property was left. By some consensus among those who decided to stay, most of our household items including furniture were allegedly removed from the premises to prevent confiscation by the occupation authorities with the intent of eventually returning it all to us.

When my mother arrived at her friend's residence in Laško, south of Celje, still relatively early in the morning of 6 April, she was stunned at the news of the

Germans' attack. Somehow she got back to Celje and was able to reach my father by telephone from the county office in that city. Father apprised her of the situation within the limits of security regulations and instructed her not to return but to proceed to the town of Mozirje, near Celje, to stay with Kolenc relatives, to wait for Marija and for further instructions.

Marija, her custodians, and many other refugees to-be, with their meager possessions, were "accommodated" on the freight cars of the last waiting train at the Dravograd railroad station. Their situation was that of a sitting duck; one plane or a piece of artillery would have blown that train off the tracks. From their most uncomfortable position, they were able to observe Yugoslav soldiers advancing toward the border. However, in the afternoon, the Yugoslavs were already pulling back from the border and taking more defensible positions on the south side of the river. When exactly the only bridge across Drava River went into the air, I do not know, but it happened well before the first German troops occupied Dravograd.[4] Velimir Terzić states in *Slom kraljevine Jugoslavije 1941* that German soldiers reached Sv. Duh, a mountain village north of Dravograd on the first day of this undeclared war.[5]

Dravograd, located on the north or left side of Drava, and its sister town Meža, on the south or the right side, hold a strategic position to four valleys: east to Maribor, northwest to Lavamünd/Labot, west to Prevalje and to Bleiburg/Pliberk, and south to Celje. It was imperative to hold positions here in order to gain time for others to regroup or at least to protect an orderly retreat.

One over-zealous Nazi sympathizer in Dravograd felt it was necessary to assist German troops in the battle with the Yugoslav Army and took his hunting rifle and started shooting from an attic window across the river at the Yugoslav positions. The smoke gave him away and he soon fell mortally wounded. I knew Mr. Lorber, a town merchant, as a pleasant and decent person. Why he took this action nobody in Dravograd understood. Promises of happiness and prosperity under the "New Order" probably misled him in his actions that day and cost him his life.

The train with those retreating from Dravograd, including twelve-year-old Marija, finally left the railroad station at 3 P.M. in the afternoon of 6 April in the only direction possible, south toward Slovenj Gradec and the city of Celje. This evacuation was successful because the Yugoslav troops were able to hold back the German advance first at the river crossing at Dravograd/Meža, and then on 7 April they prevented enemy advance into Mislinjska valley between Dravograd and Slovenj Gradec.[6] Thus, my father's group and those on the 3 P.M. train, although they both encountered many obstacles on the trip south, were not harassed by enemy planes and for the duration of the escape were out of reach of the German troops.

Ciril and I had at the time no communication with the family and knew nothing about their whereabouts or their fate. Naturally, we were most concerned about Father, knowing very well what would have happened to him if captured.

The fear of a German air attack on the city of Ljubljana on Palm Sunday and the following days was ever-present. Air shelters were few; there were none in our vicinity. To find out more about the situation, Ciril and I decided to walk toward the center of the city. On the way there, we saw the last army units leaving their barracks, orderly, fully equipped, but not mechanized. This single fact just increased our concerns not just for us but for the soldiers as well. The Yugoslav air force planes were nowhere in sight even though overflights on previous days had been fairly regular. Under severe pressure, one finds an explanation for everything; in this case, the planes had to provide ground support on the borders or disrupt enemy supply and communication lines. Surprisingly enough, many people were on the streets, asking each other what kind of future, danger, hunger, or persecution was on the horizon. Since Yugoslavia was surrounded on all sides by the Axis forces and their satellites, except in the narrow strip of border with Greece, even a non-soldier had to recognize the seriousness of the situation.

The news from Belgrade was devastating. The German air attack on a declared open city without defense was brutal, merciless, barbaric. Thousand of people were killed, many more thousands wounded; whole blocks were destroyed. Among those killed was the only Slovene minister in the Yugoslav government, Dr. Kulovec.[7]

Mr. Čekal received his orders the next day and soon departed with his co-workers—destination unknown. For him it was difficult to understand why my father, in addition to his own military duty, encouraged Ciril and I to volunteer as well and to proceed south to join the Yugoslav army. When we were on the way to register for the service, we met a few volunteers who claimed that they were stopped, mistreated, and forced back by armed Croatian groups. At the registration station we were told that registrations were suspended until further announcements because of the very confusing and unclear situation in the areas we were headed for and that we should wait for further instructions. When we returned to our student residence, Mr. Čekal was already back, visibly relieved that he would at least be able to share the uncertain future with his family.

That same afternoon I had been roaming around downtown, and when I got to the military barracks, which were located not far from our residence, I observed many civilians leaving this huge compound with various items, mostly food stuffs. The soldiers had already left, and this huge military establishment was completely abandoned. After a slight initial hesitation, with my conscience telling me that this had a smell of looting, I entered the compound and ran from one room to another looking for some food left by the Yugoslav army. People were encouraging each other to take as much as possible with the justification that otherwise everything would fall into the hands of the enemy. When I arrived, all

I was able to find was a small pile of dry white beans in a corner of one room. A woman who got there ahead of me had three empty sacks and after realizing that she would not be able to carry more than two, offered one of the empty sacks to me. I immediately went into action. Loaded with a heavy sack of beans, I willingly shared information about my acquisition with those who stopped me. Proud of my action, since this would be the only food my family had, but with some guilty feelings, I hurried home.[8]

To my great surprise and even greater happiness, I found my mother and my sister in the family room in the Čekals' house. My mother realized that she would not be able to stay for an extended period with people she never met before even though they had shown generosity every step of the way. She decided to try to reach Ljubljana and our house there. Not only did my mother look very tired, she appeared to be still in a state of shock and seemed distant. No wonder: She had left her home a few minutes before the attack to take a few of our possessions to a more secure place and never had a chance to return home. When she saw me with a sack of beans, which Mrs. Čekal immediately dragged into her kitchen, she embraced me and praised me for my resourcefulness and initiative, not really knowing how I had acquired it. As I was not known in the family as a practical person, she was rather surprised that I had risen to the occasion. I, in turn, had to admire Marija who, even though very young, took all hardships like a mature person; her attitude and disposition at the time was a small but important consolation to our parents.

During the first three days of the following week, the uncertainty continued. All local radio reports were brief, with sketchy information from the fronts. We heard about heavy fighting and strong Yugoslav resistance on the Bulgarian sector, where German troops were trying to break through in the direction of Greece. In addition, rumors of defections and treason by some Croatian military units northeast of Zagreb the Yugoslav-Hungarian front near the city of Bjelovar were most discouraging and depressing, especially since we realized what a sudden breakthrough would mean for Slovenia. Knowing the difficulties between the Croat nation and the central government in Belgrade, we realized that such a turn of events was not entirely out of the question.[9] We did not get much information about the day-to-day changes on the battlefields, not even in Slovenia, except when confirmations were announced about enemy forces reaching this or that town or a strategic point. From time to time, small groups of soldiers were seen moving south, hoping to reach the second defense line, a plan that was well known even before the attack.[10]

One of the first steps my father took after arriving in Ljubljana was to secure for us a permanent residence, since there was no hope of return to Dravograd in any foreseeable future. Two or three years before he had purchased a house in Ljubljana from one of his friends, Mr. Keržan, in anticipation of a forthcoming transfer to a new position in the capital city of Slovenia. Thus, he would assure for his three children an easier access to the university or any other professional school.

This small house in Dermotova Street was at the time of purchase rented to Mr. and Mrs. Hertle. Since Mr. Keržan described the Hertles as good tenants, their lease was renewed. Now that we were in a dire need for a home, father had a legal right to give them a two-month notice. When he came to the house, a sign indicated that there was one furnished room available for rent with kitchen privileges and he immediately decided to take it. The house servant, the only person at home, was delighted that she found a tenant. As far as I remember, the Hertles went to Germany a few days before the attack and were expected to return soon. Since we did not have any possessions worth mentioning, our move from the Čekal's house was accomplished immediately; the only piece of furniture that we possessed was my upright piano which had been transferred from Dravograd to Ljubljana at the beginning of the school year in support of my music studies. The Čekal family did not have a piano and welcomed this temporary addition.

During the day my father was rarely home: he was working with government officials on reports and documentation of the last days of his administration in Dravograd county. At the same time, he was trying to secure for himself a government position in Ljubljana. Here he encountered another unexpected disappointment. Even though the *Slovenska ljudska stranka* (Slovene People's Party) for which he worked diligently all his life, was in power the last decade before the attack and the *ban* (head) of *banovina* Slovenia was one of his colleagues, he did not even receive the courtesy of an appointment with *ban* Marko Natlačen, to whom he directly and regularly reported. A directive, announced a few days later, which stated: "Everybody back to your previous posts" was behind this cold reception. Even an intervention on his behalf by the Ljubljana bishop, Dr. Gregorij Rožman, who knew my father well from the Carinthian years of 1918–1920, did not help. Insistence on return to his previous Dravograd position would have been equal to travelling directly and voluntarily to a German concentration camp such as Dachau or Belsen. Fortunately, through some friends in the government, he found out that an official in the Agricultural Department was interested in his Dravograd position, and this "exchange" was then reluctantly approved by Dr. Natlačen.

Then the Hertles arrived back from Germany. Only my mother was home and she stepped out to meet them. Even though I did not understand the conversation (it was in German because Mr. Hertle refused to communicate in the Slovene language), I will never forget this "little Hitler" and his screaming voice, when he most rudely and in a tone of superiority asked my mother why we left Dravograd. All I understood was his frequent use of the words "die Lehrer und die

Pfaffen" (teachers and priests).[11] In short, as mother explained to me later, Hertle claimed that Germany was a legal state, not harming anybody unless serious crimes against the German people were committed, that he would investigate our situation in Dravograd, and that we had nothing to fear from the just authorities of the Third Reich. Germany was forced to attack because teachers and priests in Slovenia and Yugoslavia were involved in constant attacks against the people of German descent and were guilty of inflaming the population against everything German: We should thank the teachers and the priests for forcing Germany into this action. In addition, he had a lot to say about the traitorous Yugoslav government and the entire anti-German Serbian bourgeoisie. What remains so firmly in my mind is his dictatorial, screaming voice, which sounded to me as an amplified imitation of Hitler's loudest and most threatening speeches.

We never expected to find in our house a Nazi, particularly one of this caliber. Mother was devastated. She send me out to intercept my father so that he would know ahead of time what the situation was. When I found him, he just said that I did not need to worry. He never spoke to the Hertles; he never exchanged any greetings; he never stepped out of the room, except when leaving for work. To my additional surprise, one of the tenants in the house was my track and field coach, who spoke only limited Slovene and came to Ljubljana from Germany only a few years earlier. I made my own conclusions without any proof, however. Every day and every evening people were coming and going like on a railroad station and we had to listen to the constant "Heil Hitler, Heil Hitler." By that time we were expecting German troops to enter and occupy Ljubljana at any moment; thus, we felt trapped in our own house, or, to put it more realistically, in the house of a top Nazi or Gestapo agent in the city, with no way to escape.

One of the most crucial and decsive days was 10 April, Holy Thursday. Most of these past days we had felt as if we were in the dark. In this kind of situation, the outside world was probably better informed of our status through access to the official reports from both sides than we were who were being overrun. We had to depend mostly on the rumors, which were difficult to interpret between wishful thinking on the one side and panic on the other. However, two events on this Holy Thursday brought us back to reality.

Expecting an imminent occupation of Ljubljana, the capital of Slovenia, the *Narodni svet* (National Council), comprised of representatives of all political parties[12] under the leadership of the *ban,* Marko Natlačen, and organized as an interim authority in Slovenia, issued a *proglas* (Proclamation) to the people via radio, newspapers, and leaflets. The main points of this announcement were that, in expectation of an occupation, the population should remain calm and disciplined, refrain from any military action against enemy forces now that the Yugoslav Army had left the territory, remain at their posts, and obey Yugoslav laws that were still in effect.[13] The temporary government representatives wanted to prevent any unnecessary bloodshed in Slovenia when it became clear that this part of Yugoslavia could no longer be successfully defended. However, at the time of this announcement, many units of the Yugoslav Army were still in Slovenia. It was only on this day that the German troops advanced from Dravograd and Šoštanj toward Celje, which was occupied the next day, 11 April 1941. It should also be emphasized that the German troops advanced in this sector only after the Yugoslav Army started pulling back to the line south of the Sava and Kolpa rivers, due primarily to the events in neighboring Croatia. It was never clear to me, not even today, what were the correct steps for local civil administrations at the beginning and during the occupation. Life has to go on, but what constitutes collaboration and at what level? The morale of the Yugoslav troops was severely damaged by this proclamation: They felt that they were being stabbed in the back. Many soldiers of Slovene and Croatian ethnic groups, perhaps misunderstanding this directive, left their units and went home rather than continue their way south to Bosnia. The people of Slovenia gave all possible assistance to Serbian officers and soldiers who remained in the units, or tried to avoid capture by retreating south, either individually or in small groups, but the damage was done, as official support was no longer encouraged and provided.

To make the situation even worse, the news of the establishment of the *Nezavisna država Hrvatska* (Independent State of Croatia) came over the radio. After the uprising in Bjelovar and mass desertion of the Croatian soldiers from their units, Serbian officers and soldiers were killed or disarmed and turned over to the enemy: the whole Croatian territory was lost. The last step in this process was the establishment of the new Croatian state under the leadership of the pro-Italian and pro-German Ante Pavelič and his *Ustashi* movement. The rapid defeat of the Yugoslav army was caused not by enemy strength and force but by the internal problems in Yugoslavia. The *Ustashi* treason in Croatia eliminated both Slovenia and Croatia as viable defense territories and by massive desertion made the remaining units extremely weak and without access to support.

Slovene soldiers and volunteers in the Yugoslav Army, who were returning from Croatian territories and who were generally not mistreated by the *Ustashi* units, had horrifying stories to tell about the mistreatment of Serbs, military and civilian. Any long-standing grievances among Croats and Serbs in Yugoslavia did not justify any of these actions and atrocities. We listened with sadness to these reports, hoping that they were only exaggerated rumors.

Also unconfirmed were reports of very active fifth-column and Communist Party activities against defense efforts in the military units, encouraging soldiers to desert and return home. After all, the urgings explained, in the Third Reich there is no unemployment, the standard of living is high—why give your life for the bourgeoisie? The propagandist noted that the German-Soviet Pact assured future stability in Europe. Many returning soldiers talked about confusion in their units, not knowing what was the right course of action. Even some officers were unclear of their responsibilities and allegiances.

On the afternoon of Good Friday, 11 April, to our great surprise, the first units of the Italian Army slowly entered the city. When I saw three Italian soldiers walking down the city street, I just could not believe that an occupation could start in such a simple way. These three soldiers did not seem to be exceptionally concerned; their automatic weapons over their shoulders, they were curiously looking left and right. The population did not greet them or try to communicate in any way. We only stared at these strange people and their uniforms as they walked toward one of the many military installations in the city. What we really expected were German tanks entering in full force from the north and taking over the city in *Blitzkrieg* style.

Thus, on 11 April 1941, we had to accept the bitter truth that occupation of our land was an undisputed reality and that the future for us, starting on this fateful Good Friday, looked very dark—*tempora nondum cognita.*

CHAPTER THREE

First Year of Occupation

April 1941–June 1942

Following the defeat and dismemberment of Yugoslavia among the Axis Powers and their satellites, the Slovene lands of Yugoslavia were divided among Germany, Italy, and Hungary. By the occupation of Yugoslavia and by the defeat of the Greek and British forces in Greece and on the island of Crete, Germany secured the southeastern part of Europe. The attack on Crete on 10 May 1941 was carried out exclusively by German airborne troops.

On 22 June 1941, Operation Barbarossa, code name for the German invasion of the Soviet Union, began. This surprise attack inflicted on the Soviets great losses of territories and military manpower from the first. A few days after the attack, the Comintern in Moscow sent out urgent messages to the communist parties in Europe, calling for an all-out war against Germany. At the end of November and at the beginning of December 1941, German troops reached the outskirts of Moscow and Leningrad.

Though far away from the European view, Japan's unsuspected air attack on the U.S. naval base at Pearl Harbor in Hawaii on 7 December 1941 brought the war to an entirely new dimension—a conflict of world proportions.

Day by day, more and more Italian troops entered the city. In time it seemed that there was one soldier for each inhabitant, man, woman, or child. In one military installation near our home, where I did some "procurement" a few days before, there were at least twice as many soldiers stationed as when the Yugoslav Army occupied these quarters. We had no contact with the Italian military; the populace in general did not pay attention to them, except to display curiosity about their behavior and customs. These were the initial days.

Since we were now under Italian jurisdiction,[1] the Hertles soon left our house to our great relief. Before they left, they tried to remove everything possible from the house and from the garden. Father sent them a warning specifying the rules regulating tenants' departures, but they proceeded with their actions anyway.[2] Hertle was appointed mayor in one of the towns in Slovenia under the German occupation. How glad we were that they left our house and the city.

During the first few days of the war, we heard that one of our close friends from Dravograd, Bojan Nendl, who was attending high school in the city of Celje and probably volunteered to defend his country, had been captured as a Yugoslav soldier by the German forces and was taken away. His parents and his younger brother Dušan, also refugees, were offered temporary lodgings in our house. They had no place to go after they left Dravograd on 6 April 1941 after the German attack. Bojan was able to relay only one message to his parents through a person who recognized him among the captured soldiers. He reported that things changed overnight in Celje when German sympathizers started verbally abusing captured Yugoslav soldiers taken through the city streets. The German guards finally dispersed these people, telling them that these were Yugoslav soldiers, prisoners of war, and, as such, deserved proper treatment.

At home we were practically without the basic essentials. A few things, whatever mother had transported that fateful morning, were now stored in a village in German-occupied territory. Our parents had to act fast to get some of it to Ljubljana before the borders between Italian and German occupation zones were sealed. Fortunately, a distant relative in the German zone, Mr. Kuster, owned a truck and was willing to help. Thus at least a few essentials from our home in Dravograd reached us before the border closed.

When my father approached the firm of Čebin, suppliers of coal and wood for heating, and explained our plight, Mr. Čebin, in spite of shortages, assured my father immediate delivery of materials and kept his word.[3] My experience of how some people behaved in the time of shortages was less positive. Bread was in great demand at the time and its quality was very poor; the local bakery opened each day at 7:00 A.M. and only for a short time. To get a loaf of bread, one had to get in line at 5 A.M. and this was now my job. The first few days I took a lot of abuse from many people who claimed I was an intruder from another section of town trying to get a second portion. All my explanations were ignored. Standing there very unwelcome for two hours was extremely unpleasant, but I stood my ground. When my turn came on the first day and I offered money and reached up to get my loaf of bread, the lady at the window hesitated for a moment, then asked me a few questions about my residency. She told me to come back later in the day with one of my parents so that she would know who we were. Even though there were some protests from the back of the line that I was taking away the bread that belonged to their children, the lady handed me my share. I thanked her and took off as fast as possible. In the next few days objections were fewer and gradually ceased. However, I always felt very uncomfortable standing in that line;

I felt that I was begging. The food shortage brought another problem. Mother refused to eat under the pretense that, while cooking, she got enough nourishment. It took drastic action by the rest of us before she agreed to accept her meager share. Gradually we were able with the help of friends and acquaintances to get to additional supplies and food.

We were by no means the only refugees. The first wave moved south at the time of the attack, hoping for temporary protection behind the Yugoslav defense lines; partition of Slovenia into three occupation zones brought about another wave of refugees, this time from German-occupied territories. The German authorities had shown from the very beginning that they were determined to completely erase Slovene life from the regions under their administration. Daily, new refugees were moving into the Italian-occupied territory, primarily university and advanced high school students but also clergy and other people of higher education. How Ljubljana, its institutions and people, absorbed and helped the multitude of refugees remains a puzzle, but it did. I learned from one of these refugees the fate of one of my scout leaders who had come to Prevalje from Maribor three years before to teach and prepare us for scout skills examinations. He was last seen taken in chains into a Gestapo wagon: Nobody ever heard of him again.

How determined the Germans were to eliminate all that was Slovene from the territory they occupied was clearly demonstrated by their resettlement policy. For one week, trains from the region of Gorenjska, filled to capacity with Slovene intellectuals, political leaders, priests, and other influential individuals, including their families, traveled through Ljubljana to unknown destinations in Croatia, Bosnia/Herzegovina, and Serbia.[4] Word about passage and time of these transports reached the people of Ljubljana through railroad office connections. All major railroad crossings were barricaded and guarded by Italian soldiers. The people assembled at these crossings in large numbers to give our people from the north at least some expressions of moral support—this was possible because the trains had to reduce speed through the city. The screams and calls of encouragement were loud and continuous. Those inside the trains appreciated this attention, waved to us, told us who they were and from which towns or villages. The Italian soldiers guarding these crossings did not seem to mind these expressions of solidarity; one had the impression that they liked it. All this happened late in the evenings; we had to hurry home to get off the streets before curfew.[5]

For our family, the Italian policy of non-extradition of people from German-occupied territory of Slovenia meant at least a temporary feeling of relief. These feelings were, however, short-lived. Through friends and acquaintances we learned that Gestapo agents were inquiring about my father. It was clear from the questions asked that they did not know about our residence in Ljubljana—at least that was what our informants kept telling us. My father's duties as a reserve officer in the Yugoslav army were well known, so the assumption that he was away with the military forces was a logical one. It came as a great shock when we were informed that one of my father's colleagues from the Plebiscite years in Carinthia was kidnapped by Gestapo agents in the center of Ljubljana and secretly taken across the border into the German-occupied zone.[6] Gestapo agents successfully kidnapped another person in the city. From then on, someone always accompanied Father to and from work. It was assumed that in case of a kidnapping attempt, immediate assistance would come from other people in the vicinity. On one such occasion, when I was waiting for Father in the vicinity of his office to accompany him home, he stopped for a moment at the exit of his office building and exchanged a few words with a stocky robust man dressed in a large cloak and wide-trimmed hat. Father told me that the person was Prežihov Voranc, Slovene Carinthian writer and poet, whose works on the land and people of Mežiška dolina I enjoyed. To my wish to be introduced to this favorite writer of mine, Father simply responded that it would be too dangerous to attract attention on the street. I still remember my great disappointment during the walk home when after repeated questions about why it would be dangerous, I received no answers. Father was silent.

To my surprise there was no contact from the leader or members of my scout group during these first days of occupation. Because I'd become a member of the scout group in Ljubljana only a few months before, I didn't yet have personal contacts with other groups. But the Ljubljana scout group was entirely different from the one in my home territory, where emphasis was on outdoor life and skills. The indoor projects we were working on in Ljubljana did not attract my enthusiasm. A few days after the first Italian units came into the city, I tried to contact my scout group via facilities where our meetings were usually held. I found a note on the door, declaring that due to circumstances, this group had been disbanded. I was extremely disappointed, as these "circumstances" constituted the most important *raison d'etre* for this group to exist and work together. The content of the note made much more sense a few days later when I found out that my scout leader, H. H., left the city of Ljubljana, allegedly for an important assignment and/or training in the Third Reich. My belief that we were all united in these difficult times soon began to weaken.

The Italian military staged huge parades through the city on every possible occasion. Their military bands were first class. How the soldiers felt about these parades was another question, but those in command seemed to like these demonstrations of might and splendor. People in the city did not line the sidewalks in admiration; however, curiosity attracted us into the vicinity. On one such occasion, when walking on the sidewalk in the opposite direction next to the parade and ignoring passing Italian flags, a tall young man, well dressed, stepped in front of me and yelled in Slovene, "Don't you know how to salute the flag?" and at the same time tried to slap me across the face. I swiftly avoided his unfriendly greeting.

Then I became aware that there were three other men attempting to teach the populace in this unpleasant way how to pay respect to the flags of the occupation forces. What hurt was the fact that these four spoke perfect Slovene. Nevertheless, most of those assaulted preferred to take a few kicks rather than obey and salute the Italian flags.

In these early days of the occupation, it was still possible to travel outside the city to the Italian-controlled southern region of Slovenia. Mostly we traveled there by train to acquire food supplies. Ciril and I also took a few biking trips to this region (Dolenjska), an area not part of our travels in the pre-war years. On one such trip, on the way home, we heard some distance ahead of us the sound of an explosion. We did not pay much attention to it. However, a few minutes later, when we turned a corner on the road through the forest, we bicycled right into a group of Italian soldiers investigating sabotage-damaged railroad tracks. We were stopped, thoroughly searched, and kept under guard. Luckily for us, a couple who passed us a few minutes earlier in their shiny black car—the well-dressed man in the car spoke fluent Italian—explained to the Italians that they saw us riding our bicycles in this direction and that we could not have been involved in this sabotage action. We were then released and so were the two people in the car. We thanked them for the much-needed assistance in a difficult situation. During future bicycle excursions, we were much more attentive to our surroundings, not forgetting that these were war years. Eventually we had to stop bicycling outside the city because the Italian military truck drivers had great fun pushing bicyclists off the road by driving so close that we were forced off the road. Once Ciril and I ended in a ditch while a group of soldiers on the truck roared with laughter; we were not hurt, though, and no damage was done to the bicycles. These harassments were just too dangerous, however, and too much to take. It was no longer worth taking chances.

In June 1941, I ran into Dusan Pleničar[7] in the center of Ljubljana. I knew him from Bishop's Gymnasium at Šentvid and from the scout movement—he was a few years older than I. Because I trusted him, I agreed to help in the underground organization of the Yugoslav army resistance efforts in occupied Yugoslavia. I believed that out of the initial efforts, a strong organization would soon be formed to fight on the side of the Allies and help defeat the occupation forces. Some time in the future, according to Dušan, this participation would mean the launching of armed resistance in the mountains of Slovenia.[8] A week or two later a young man came to the house and asked Ciril and me to go with him for a little walk. He gave us only his underground name and told us that he would deliver some literature to be distributed in the neighborhood.[9] We took care of these distributions as early in the morning as curfew permitted to avoid being seen and identified. Our naiveté in the belief that all people were of the opinions expressed in this literature and in support of underground activities suggested there was short-lived. We were apparently "discovered" after the first few distributions in the neighborhood. Several neighbors secretly threw this literature over the fence back to our front door. A few but not all of these neighbors we eventually identified and discontinued deliveries to them. Nobody, however, reported us to the Italian authorities, something we became very concerned about.[10]

On only one occasion I met some of the other members of the underground group, and even this time only a select few, when we were assembled at a secret place for training in the use of small arms. A minor accident with a pistol at this session awakened us to reality, and even more, about the activities we were going to pursue. Fortunately, nobody got hurt on that occasion. However, it became clear that experts would have to be sought to prepare us adequately for any, even most basic, military action.

The Italian military took over not only all military installations in the city, but occupied several school buildings as well. For this reason we attended school only every other day; we were forced to share the remaining school buildings. Even though instructions were necessarily packed into the limited time span and there was a lot of homework to do, it worked well for me, because I now had additional time to pursue my music. I practiced the piano every possible minute. How my family and, to a point, our neighbors tolerated this, is hard to guess. I used every precaution not to disturb them too much, but still, twelve hours of piano practice on days off from school was a lot. I almost caught up with my colleagues who were ahead of me because of my late start.

In the fall of 1941, concerts, opera, and drama resumed. Many visiting artists, primarily from Italy but from other parts of Europe as well, were now enriching the cultural life in the city. Since opera libretti performed in Ljubljana were almost always translated into Slovene, on several occasions multi-language performances took place due to participation of foreign artists. What a special, unusual, and interesting conglomeration, hearing two soloists expressing their feeling to each other in two different languages and the opera chorus commenting in the third! I regularly attended symphony concerts Monday nights, chamber or solo performances Fridays, opera or drama on weekends. There were inexpensive standing room areas in concert halls, drama and opera houses to give students an opportunity to develop their cultural horizons and these were always packed to capacity. Standing through a Wagner opera was not, however, exactly a comfortable experience; if you were lucky, you could lean against the wall or on the dividing ramp, a special privilege requiring very early arrival.

Unlike the German occupation, where elimination of everything Slovene was on the immediate agenda, the Italian administration permitted continuation of Slovene cultural, scientific, and sport organizations, including school curricula. In the curricula they substituted the French language with Italian; the rest remained basically the same.

The prayer "Our Father" turned out to be for many of us, if not a very risky, certainly a very unpleasant and unexpected pivotal experience. It was the custom in our schools to say a prayer at the start of each day. Our Italian language teacher was a military chaplain and a Franciscan. On his first day in class, he told us that he came as a friend to help us continue our education. Most of us did not understand what he was saying, but we were able to deduce some of the meaning of his introductory speech because of similarities between Latin and Italian. He spoke very slowly and clearly. He selected "Our Father" for our first lesson in Italian, as a way of going from the known to the unknown. He made sure that each one of us was able to recite the text from the beginning to the end before he proceeded to other topics.

I do not remember how it happened that a month or two later the Italian class was scheduled at the beginning of the day; that had not been the case during previous weeks. Our professor entered the class, stood in front of the class, crossed himself, and started reciting "Our Father" in Italian. The class, however, followed in unison in Slovene. He stopped, told us to pray in Italian—the same result. Without any previous agreement among ourselves, we just repeated the prayer in Slovene. After the third warning, in visible anger, the chaplain took his things and walked out of the room while the class stood in complete silence.

Our feelings were mixed: some triumph, but some fear as well. We sat there, just waiting. About a half hour later, the director of the gymnasium, Marko Bajuk, stormed into the room. Angry and disappointed, he told us that the chaplain was extremely offended by our behavior and that he was demanding our immediate expulsion from the school. He threatened to close the school, if his demand was not met. Director Bajuk refused to take such drastic action and even begged for leniency and tried to calm him down; the chaplain, however, decided right then to refer the case to higher authorities. Through Bajuk's determined stand, we were allowed to stay in school pending further decision.

A thorough investigation followed. Professor Alfonz Gspan, our class supervisor and faculty representative, had to question each student individually about the happenings on that day. He had a list of questions, probably given to him, to prepare a report. Our answers went in several directions: (1) There were several weeks between the time we learned this text and the day we were told to pray in Italian; we no longer remembered the entire text; (2) Reciting in a foreign language did not give us the sensation of prayer; (3) Our understanding of the Italian language was not sufficient to understand fully what we had been asked to do by our instructor.

It took several months before the decision came. On that day, both the chaplain and Director Bajuk came to the class. From the day of this incident the chaplain never entered the school; Slovene teachers took over his responsibility. Director Bajuk spoke first in Italian, very diplomatically, addressing first the chaplain, thanking him for understanding and leniency on our behalf. After that he asked permission to address the class in Slovene. He did not spare us, telling us how much trouble we caused our professors, our school, and how we endangered the entire status of school curricula, which we still enjoyed, unlike other occupied regions of Slovenia where even speaking Slovene in public was forbidden. Then they both departed. The chaplain did not say a word but kept looking at us, person by person, with an angry expression. That was the last time we saw our Italian teacher and chaplain.

This was also the last time when we, as classmates, worked together and experienced a close relationship among ourselves. The situation was beginning to change: The German attack on the Soviet Union in June 1941, ending the Non-Aggression Pact[11] between the two powers, turned former allies against each other. The Soviet Union, with its ideological branches of activists throughout the world, the Communist parties, and the Comintern, now sent out an appeal for assistance. Immediately, the Slovene Anti-Imperialistic Front, which up to that time supported the partnership of Berlin and Moscow, renamed itself the Liberation Front. Though this Liberation Front was in reality led by the Communist Party of Slovenia, that fact was concealed by all possible means during the war years. People saw in this new conflict a new hope and a strong possibility of an early defeat of Nazi Germany. In 1940–1941, America was far away and Great Britain was struggling for survival. The Soviet Union had, however, since the defeat and division of Poland a common border with Germany, and here a final decision, à la Napoleon, was expected, even though the initial signs were not at all encouraging.

Questions kept entering our ill-prepared minds. What would happen if instead of one dictatorship, we got another? The Soviet Union at that time had certain advantages; first of all, it was far away. In addition, it possessed a strong Slavic base. We firmly believed that Germany would eventually be defeated. What the end would bring was much less clear.[12] It seemed reasonable to hope that the war would end eventually, in a year or two maybe. The post-war solution and type of government, if in the Soviet style, might last a hundred years, however. The reports from the Soviet Union before the war, of purges and officer trials, reports about the Soviet system and society as such, caused some uncomfortable fear in our minds. In our class, it soon became apparent that according to our backgrounds, associations, and families, we were drifting into different or opposite directions; polarization grew stronger, day by day. A post-war solution, our hopes for a pre-war status without a foreign influence and/or domination, seemed less and less realistic as time and the war progressed.

My father's health was visibly deteriorating during this time. He lost a lot of weight, looked depressed and ill. When we were expressing our optimistic thoughts about the war, he just listened and tried not to show his apprehension and concerns. Were there really any positive signs in 1940 and 1941? None, whatsoever!

In the spring of 1942 a few of us were playing table tennis in a small, all-purpose hall of a Catholic youth organization. This hall had large glass doors facing the inner court of a large circular building, at that time the United Insurance Building. I was standing with two friends outside this hall in the courtyard, waiting for our turn to compete.

All of a sudden we heard several rifle shots. A young man in a trench coat came running toward us from the corridor connecting the main street with the courtyard. He yelled at us, despair and great fear visible on his face, asking if there was an exit on our side of the courtyard. At the same time he turned around and started shooting with his handgun toward the corridor. We pointed to a door and he quickly disappeared behind it. A split second later, a few Italian soldiers appeared in the corridor shooting across the open court. Instinctively, we hit the ground trying to protect ourselves. Fortunately, the Italians immediately turned around and ran back toward the street; shooting and grenade explosions were heard from that direction. We immediately went inside the hall, closed the doors, and waited in fear. We were expecting an immediate and thorough search of the building and the surrounding area and were quite sure that this region of the city would soon be encircled by a large force of the Italian military.

What followed was a lot of commotion in the street, police and ambulance sirens, commands, and motorized movements. In such situations it was smarter not to get too close and take chances. We did not know what happened to the man in the trench coat. Did he escape, or was he still hiding in the vicinity? We assumed that he was alive since no further shooting took place in this area. Surprisingly, Italians did not enter the courtyard or search our side of the building.

When the sounds from the street indicated normal pedestrian and vehicular traffic about two hours later, I exited the encirclement, walking slowly with a book in hand right past the soldiers; they did not stop me. All my friends reached their homes without incident as well.

What had happened on that day, 26 May 1942?[13]

Two men entered the office of Ivan Peršuh, an officer of United Insurance, and mortally wounded him at his desk. After the attack they ran out on Miklošič street. A few employees of the firm, realizing what happened, ran after them, though they realized that the attackers were armed. After reaching the street, the two assassins separated; one ran through the corridor to the inner courtyard, the other down the street. The Italian military patrols, always abundant on the streets, hearing the shots and seeing the men running, went in pursuit. When the shooting on the street intensified, even the soldiers already in the corridor turned around to see and possibly assist those handling the situation on the street. The man we saw in the courtyard and in a split second, intentionally or unintentionally, helped to escape, probably survived because his partner, clearly visible running down the street and shooting at the pursuing soldiers, became the main target of the pursuers.

With no chance of escaping on an open street—the military patrols were closing in from all sides—this assassin jumped into a nearby store, hoping to find a rear exit. There was none. Italians who surrounded the store and the building offered him a chance to surrender, but the man refused. He, however, allowed employees and a few customers to leave the store. After a brief exchange of small arms fire, the man was killed by hand grenades.

These details and additional information came to us the same evening via media services, underground announcements, and through chain information from those who were present or in the vicinity. The two assassins were members of VOS, *Varnostno-obveščevalna služba* (Security and Intelligence Service), a special branch of the Communist Party of Slovenia and/or Liberation Front.[14]

I knew a few details about VOS long before that day in May 1942. My best friend in gymnasium, T. R., joined this group soon after it was formed in August 1941.[15] T. R. joined this organization for one simple reason: He wanted to fight the enemy at the first opportunity; he was not willing to wait for more opportune times. He was recommended to VOS by a classmate of ours, M. K., who apparently had the necessary connections. T. R. confided in me first about his intentions and then his decision to join, a serious violation of rules of any such secret organization. We had many discussions, pros and cons. So the sudden *fait accompli* came as a shock to me. Either T. R. did not have a clear idea what would be expected of him, about the intentions and goals of VOS, or he was not telling me everything he knew. A few months later, however, he realized, possibly when he received an order to execute a person, that the intended targets were our own people, not members of the occupation forces. When he resigned from this highly secret organization, he was immediately condemned to death by his former co-conspirators; apparently he knew too much. Though he now seemed relieved of a major burden, he became much more concerned about his future. T. R. told me only the very basic information about this organization and never revealed any names, except his immediate and initial contact.[16]

The execution of Ivan Peršuh on 26 May 1942, allegedly for the simple reason that he was instrumental in organizing a resistance group outside Liberation Front and not for collaboration with the enemy—as those who ordered his execution tried to convince the populace—was by no means the only one. Several individuals in the city and in the country were executed by VOS teams; actually, the list of names would be very long. The explanations provided by the Liberation Front were always the same: these individuals had to be eliminated because they were collaborating with the enemy. How, when, and where they collaborated was rarely stated and never documented. Those who were silenced had no way to defend themselves or to clear their names.

In addition to the burden of occupation, a nightmare of internal domestic terror was now hanging over the city and the land.

CHAPTER FOUR

With the Slovene Partisans

June 1942–August 1942

During the first half of 1942 attention was concentrated on the British/German struggle in North Africa. The desert war was different. The opposing forces pushed each other back and forth over extensive territories, capturing and re-capturing coastal cities. The names Tobruk and Benghazi became household words.

In the Pacific, the Japanese forces were unbelievably successful, overrunning Hong Kong on 25 December 1941 and Singapore on 15 February 1942. A bright moment came with the news of the U.S. naval victory at the Battle of Midway (June 1942), although only a few details became known to the general public in Europe.

The directive to extend air attacks on Germany to the general urban areas, in addition to the specific targets, was issued on 24 February 1942. Winter helped the Soviet forces to push the Germans away from Leningrad and Moscow and forced them on some sections of the front into partial organized retreat. The cities of Kiev and Kharkov and the Dnieper River were in the news in the first half of 1942.

Resistance movements in occupied Europe varied from one country to another. However, for any action against the German military, soldiers and officers, or other officials, reprisals were cruel and merciless, directed mostly against the innocent. The men, women, and children of the Lidice in Czechoslovakia (for the assassination of Reinhard Heydrich), Kragujevac in Serbia (for an attack on a German column and mutilation of dead German soldiers), and of the Slovene village of Rašica (for an attack on a German military unit in the vicinity of the village) were among the first unfortunate victims of the brutal vengeance, and there were many, many more.

Part I

28 June 1942, a Sunday, started as a brilliant day, one of those which offer tranquility and rest after strenuous weekly activities. I was working on a Latin translation in my parents' bedroom—they were early risers—so that I could concentrate in peace. We were dressed in our Sunday best, ready to go to church.

We had discovered at dawn that morning that the Italian military forces were strategically placed on all streets and corners as far as we could see from our windows.[1] Our guess was that they were searching for something specific and would soon depart from the neighborhood. With so many soldiers on the streets, it was not advisable to step out; why ask for trouble?

At around 9 A.M., strong knocking on the door indicated the arrival of unwelcome visitors. When my parents opened the door, a lieutenant and three soldiers entered the vestibule. My father spoke some Italian, which he learned before and during the First World War in Gorica/Gorizia and as an officer in the Austrian army on the Italian front. He was told that all male members of the household between sixteen and fifty-five were to be taken to the military barracks for census purposes by order of the Military Command. In every house the names of male residents had to be posted with dates of birth. In our house, Ciril and I belonged to that group. Thus, without even a chance to close my books, out I went to join the others already assembled on the Italian military trucks. Before departure, the young, polite lieutenant assured my parents that the whole procedure would take only a few hours, and we would soon be home again.

When we arrived at the military barracks—the former Yugoslav Army center in the city, known as Belgijska kasarna—we noticed in the middle of the huge courtyard a section enclosed by barbed wire. There we joined people of all ages (but most of them young) who had arrived before us. This collecting procedure took three to four hours. Gradually, the place became crowded; there was not enough space to sit down, and we were hot and thirsty.

Early in the afternoon we were led out of the enclosure in a single file, guarded by numerous soldiers, toward a tall Italian officer. We were able to observe from a distance that something of importance was taking place at the moment each individual came face to face with this officer. Some men were directed to go to the right and others to the left. Those going to the left were accompanied by several soldiers; not a promising sign. Coming closer, we noticed that almost everybody refused to raise his arm in the Fascist salute, so a ritual developed—an immediate, rather unfriendly rough up and a few kicks with rifle butts. After this encounter, two soldiers lifted the victim's right arm to satisfy the greeting procedure. Our neighbor, a lawyer in his early fifties, was in front of us. We could not hear what was said because we were held some distance away; we did see, however, that he went to the right. Then came Ciril's turn. He survived the beating ritual with flying colors but was waved to the left almost immediately. When you are prepared in advance for some rough treatment it really is not so bad, as I soon found out. It must have been strenuous even for the Italian soldiers who had to repeat this required exercise over and over. After one of the soldiers pulled my ID from my hand and gave it to the officer, he asked for my name and my profession. In such circumstances, the profession of "student" is second only to "demolition expert." Before I realized that this was not just a nightmare, I was grabbed and unceremoniously dragged to the left into a building, down a long corridor, and with a few kicks pushed through a door. All those assembled there greeted me with loud cries of welcome, and that immediately lifted my spirits.[2] Ciril was waiting for me right inside the entrance to the prison, correctly anticipating my fate.

Our neighbor reported upon his return home that we had been detained. The section of Ljubljana subjected to the Italian *razzia* on the 28th of June 1942 was Bežigrad. People who were anticipating additional *razzia*s in other parts of the city (which took place over the next few days) were able to seek cover or move to parts of the city previously searched, thus avoiding deportation. Unfortunately, we had been the first targets.

I do not recall if we were given anything to eat or to drink that day. I do recall my hunger and thirst very well.[3]

No new arrivals came after the middle of the afternoon. Our initial defiance and courage gradually deflated because of the uncertainty of the future. After a while, natural needs had to be attended to; a long line soon formed waiting for permission for a short walk toward the restrooms, one person at a time. These restrooms had no escape possibilities. On the way there and back we were heavily guarded. The soldiers did their duty but were not hostile.

When darkness set in and the curfew was already in effect, we were led in long columns, three abreast, Italian-style, from the barracks to the Ljubljana railroad station. Ciril, who always carried a miniature pencil and small pieces of paper, wrote a note to our parents and dropped it in the darkness, just before he was pushed into the freight car. Two or three of us behind him successfully disguised this drop. A railroad man found the note and brought it to our home the next morning.

After the train pulled away from the station, we tried to establish the direction of travel. Freight cars have only a few small air vents high under the roof. A few men formed a pyramid and served as observers. We soon found out that we were traveling south, most likely toward Italy and one of the concentration camps.

Ciril and I were fortunate in securing a place next to the wall. Conditions were very crowded. It took a little patience and adjustment for everybody to settle down in anticipation of a long journey.

I started feeling sorry for myself sitting there leaning against the wall. This sudden denial of freedom negated everything I was working so hard to achieve. Regular school work can be done later in life. My ambition, however, to be a pianist immediately suffered a serious blow. The important techniques have to be mastered at a very early age. My serious piano studies had started very late due to various unfavorable circumstances, and now, just as I was catching up with my more fortunate contemporaries, this sudden and uncertain interruption.

I was distracted from my morbid thoughts as the train slowed down in preparation for crossing the great viaduct at Borovnica. After we crossed the bridge a few minutes after midnight, the train resumed speed and we were relieved that no mishap had happened at such a height above the valley. Our observers reported seeing occasional flashes of light in the hills ahead of us to the east and left of the tracks.

About ten minutes after midnight, just as I started tormenting myself again about my miserable situation, we heard the train whistle, brakes were applied, and a salvo of rifle shots hit the train. By instinct, we hit the floor and screamed as loudly as possible, "stop shooting, we are prisoners." Because the train came to a halt, someone heard our desperate cries, and the shooting soon stopped. It was probably less than a minute before a partisan reached our freight car and yelled to us to get away from the door. With one shot he eliminated the lock, opened the door, and ordered us to exit, declaring that he would blow up the car with a hand grenade. I was among the last who jumped into the darkness.

It is hard to believe how a person's athletic abilities improve when bullets fly! The Italian guards apparently recuperated from the initial shock and started pounding up the hill with everything they had. The slight low curve in the terrain probably protected me from being hit. I did not see the others but heard the movements of people left and right and ahead of me trying to get away from the train and over the first ridge. I stopped, when, in spite of darkness, I saw the first partisan.[4] A women, dressed in khaki pants, a jacket, a red star on her headgear, with a rifle in her hands, stood calmly with a raised fist, and greeted me with "Death to Fascism." I did not know the right answer; I saluted in the old way.

The shooting stopped when we were a safe distance from the train. Our pace uphill slowed down. Without knowing the direction or destination, the only thought in our minds was to get away from the train and from the Italian forces as far and as fast as possible.[5] I last saw Ciril when he jumped from the freight car; we found each other an hour later.

While advancing up the hill, a schoolmate of mine, M. K., caught up with me and started explaining the goals of the partisan movement. He was thoroughly convinced that the ideas and goals of the movement were right, just, and achievable.

The partisans started taking control of us as soon as there was sufficient daylight. They led us further into the hills. At around seven in the morning, we assembled at an open area near some abandoned buildings.[6] It took a little time before other partisans arrived and set up a control station. It also became obvious—little by little—that we were under guard, no longer free to depart from the area, although nobody said anything of the kind. The partisan guards were clearly visible and strategically placed. We were wondering why this was necessary, since until then there had been ample opportunities to walk away.

We were assembled in mid-morning and addressed by a higher official or a military officer; the uniform did not reveal his official position or rank. The officer's explanations and instructions were simple and direct. For the partisans we were an unexpected but welcome addition.[7] Because of severe lack of arms and ammunition for such a large number of new arrivals, we would not be at this time incorporated into any regular units. The commander, therefore, decided to give us three choices:

(1) To join partisan fighting units immediately, even though it would take some time before military training and equipment would be available;

(2) The command would organize us into a labor battalion, there being a need for all kind of work in preparation for winter. Therefore, such a labor force would be crucial for success and survival;

(3) If anyone wished, for any reason, to be released, the partisans would provide a safe passage out of their territory. (He stressed that this promise was made on partisan honor.)

We were instructed to sign in at the tables set up for this purpose. After these instructions, the most welcome news was that we would get something to eat toward the evening.

Strange things started happening. First, more and more armed partisans started circling around the camp and keeping watch. Second, when Ciril and I sought consultation from a few we knew, everybody was tight-lipped. As refugees from Dravograd, we felt isolated. All of a sudden one had the feeling that this was no longer an open society, even though nobody exercised any kind of pressure. We were undecided until the last moment as to how to declare ourselves. Then, in our naiveté, not thinking that the alternative would be an Italian prison and not a "status quo ante," we opted to go with those who asked to be released. The most convincing reason for this decision was the promise given on partisan honor.

The announced count was approximately 30–40 for armed units and 50–60 for release. The rest, a majority, decided to join the newly formed labor battalion.

Our serious mistake became apparent almost immediately. The 50–60 who wanted to be released had to assemble in a separate area for further instructions. Three machine gun crews were set up, pointing their barrels dangerously into our direction. From time to time, partisans came into the enclosure, asking for our clothes and shoes, often saying, "You will not need this anymore." Since we did have a chance, as instructed, to change our minds, Ciril and I decided to get out of this dangerous encirclement. Another schoolmate of mine, E. L., who made a good impression on those in command by loud and convincing analyses of the current political situation and by praising the importance of the partisan movement, came to assist, just before we were to be liberated of our shoes and jackets. At the registration table they seemed to be pleased with our change of heart. There were no questions asked; we became members of the labor battalion.

The number of people in the encirclement dwindled during the day. Only ten or twelve remained at the end. They were led away toward the evening under heavy guard and, as far as I know, were never seen again.[8]

At around midday on the 29th, after we had been questioned by our new authorities, my brother was approached by one of the partisans, who took him to one side. The conversation was not encouraging. The person, a tradesman from our home-town in Carinthia, Dravograd, was very direct, stating that people like my father—referring allegedly to his Slovene People's Party (SLS) affiliation—are summarily executed here. In this difficult situation, my brother uttered something like, "It is not necessary that sons should always be of the same persuasion as their parents." Ciril was later depressed about his effort to improve our situation by being disloyal to his father.

The tradesman, who was commanding a small unit of ten or twelve partisans, including two women, approached us in the afternoon again. He suggested that we join his unit which was already designated to depart for Carinthia and Styria with the base in Pohorje, as he put it, "To put some fear into the Nazis in our home territory." He added again that the situation here was not safe for the two of us. Under such circumstances, we saw no other alternative and consented. The question of approval by his superiors was still, however, to be resolved.

Late in the afternoon a cow was dragged into our camp. It was such a welcome sign. We were, of course, not concerned with who had to give up this unfortunate animal; our stomachs were empty. For us inexperienced city folks, the dinner seemed to take a long time to prepare. Our admiration went to those who skillfully converted an innocent cow into a very delightful dinner in such a short time. In the soup, reinforced with a lot of cornmeal, were big pieces of meat. What a dinner! A guerilla of any type, large or small, has to eat in order to function: a partisan half jokingly said to me that the first piece of equipment needed for life in the woods is a spoon, a large spoon. "Obtain one as soon as possible," he added.

Toward evening the Italians attacked. Slowly but surely they were coming closer and closer to our location. Before our new acquaintance departed with his unit to help hold back the advancing Italians, he told us that he could not take us along this time but that he would try to incorporate us after this immediate danger is over; he assured us that he would help wherever or whenever possible. Our paths never crossed again.[9]

When darkness approached, the Italians were still coming closer. The command came to break camp. We were organized in a single file, forming a very long column, and instructed to hold on to something on the back of the man in front to prevent disorientation during the night retreat. It was pitch dark. From time to time, instructions were passed from the front about special obstacles such as a narrow pass, roots, rocks, fallen trees, or dangerous drops too close for comfort. The progress was slow; the column had to stop several times because of falls or similar accidents. Here and there we heard some swearing, when, due to inexperience with such night marches, someone's face hit something unpleasantly hard on the back of the man in front. Bloody mouths often resulted from such encounters. The sounds of enemy advance were gradually ending. The Italian forces probably took positions to protect the railroad line at the location where we were liberated the night before.

Around midnight, we entered a small village. A few houses had to provide accommodations for a select group. The majority, however, found comfort in covered haystacks. A call came for volunteers to stand guard; there were not many takers. Ciril and I volunteered, trying to establish ourselves with our new masters and because we had previous camping experience as scouts. We were assigned first and second guard, midnight to 2:00 and 2:00 to 4:00 A.M. Nobody questioned our qualifications or even reliability. Instructions were quite simple. Italian lines were only a little more than a few hundred yards away. There was no fear that they would move during the night. However, noise, talking, movements of people, or any unusual activity should be avoided so that the Italians would not suspect that a large and unusual number of people were bivouacking in their vicinity. "Call the alarm only if a column is detected approaching the village." We were given a password and that was it. We were not armed; only the partisans were carrying rifles and grenades, and there were two machine guns in the column at the time we left our provisional camp. The night passed without incident. Before the early light, we carefully and silently left this village and continued our journey into the unknown.

We were on the move for a while, sometimes in small units, but all heading toward the same destination. The territories of our movements were not familiar to me; this was not the land of my prewar hikes. This unfamiliarity with the terrain was also one of the reasons Ciril and I were so ready to depart for Pohorje, where we knew our way around and would be more at home with the population as well.

For a short period our location was an open area surrounded by protective forests, with good views toward an unknown valley. Single Italian air force planes occasionally disturbed the quietness of the place. The sounds from the engines and propellers always alerted us to the need to take cover. We were also very impressed with the extent of the territory, in which we felt fairly safe from the occupation forces.

There were no recognizable limitations to movement; we considered the armed partisans as our protection. However, we were aware that a departure from this group would be considered desertion. There were no escapes; everybody was determined to do his part.

This was most likely the time when plans were in the works for our assignments. While waiting, we were provided in the evenings with a cultural program of some sort. Poet Matej Bor usually recited some of his latest witty rhyming jokes, mostly attacks on either political opponents, real or imagined, or descriptions of alleged sexual encounters between Italian soldiers and fictitious native women. The person who seemed to play a leading role among this cultural group and among the command was identified as a professor from a gymnasium in Bežigrad, a northern part of Ljubljana. Even though I probably heard the name Edvard Kocbek at the time, it did not mean anything of significance to me.[10]

The cultural officer in charge was E. C., who was trying hard to improve the level of cultural activities. He questioned the new arrivals in order to identify people with some skills in art, theater, music, and literature. Always dressed in an oversized dark cloak, he stood out among the partisan community. When he learned that I had studied to be a pianist, he tried to recruit me for his nonexistent band. Realizing that a piano would be tough to carry around and was also out of place in a band, he suggested that I join as a drummer. When I replied that I intended to do more for the liberation than just play drums, he kindly explained that even seemingly insignificant roles would play an important part toward the expulsion of occupation forces from our land.

More unpleasant and intimidating were private visits and interrogations by the political commissar Fric Novak. Many knew him from Ljubljana University. He was dressed to perfection in an officer's uniform (rank unknown), as if he were prepared to participate in a military parade in a liberated city. He did not look like a political commissar as they became known to us in subsequent days. His interrogating technique was unusual to say the least. He would corner individuals and ask questions such as, "Are you regularly attending church services?" "Are you a member of the Catholic Youth Organization?" and similar questions which were usually ill-received and did not seem relevant to the goals of the liberation efforts. Ciril and I answered those questions in the affirmative; instead of a reaction or a comment, we were subjected to a cynical sneer.[11] We had the feeling we would be entirely at his mercy from then on.

Midmorning a few days later, we were assembled in a forest clearing in the vicinity of Otave. Top partisan brass conversed and exchanged papers. After a few introductory remarks, welcomes, and excuses for not being prepared for so many newcomers, we were assured that there would be a responsible role for each of us. The thirty-plus volunteers for the partisan army were called and departed after a short ceremony. Among this group was my classmate, M. K., who in the preceding days had told me a few basics about the Liberation Front and its goals.[12]

The next selection came as a shock. Twelve names were called; the two of us were numbers three and four. We were immediately surrounded by armed partisans and separated from the rest. To make the situation even worse, one person selected, a university student, became hysterical and started screaming about how could he, as a member of a communist troika cell in Ljubljana, possibly be selected for this group of White Guards *(belogardisti)*. He named the other two troika members.[13] His desperate appeal was directed especially toward Polak-Stjenka, his colleague from the university, who, on his famous horse, was among the command group.[14] Nobody responded or reacted, the hysterical fellow was just pushed back into the group. The fear and shock in the eyes of those who were not called yet told me very clearly what was on their minds. We were led away immediately. A solo partisan was in the lead, with five others, all armed, in a V-formation behind us. We walked almost an hour down a narrow country path; not a word was spoken. We were completely numb. All we could hear were heavy footsteps, ours and theirs. When we were approaching a forest, a son of a Ljubljana industrialist—his name was called first—walking in front of me, spoke what was on all our minds, "They will execute us in that forest." A few minutes later, a partisan on a galloping horse caught up with our detachment. A brief discussion between the newcomer and our guards followed. Result: the guards seemed visibly relieved; some even had smiles on their faces. The leader then informed us of our new orders to join a partisan group in the Polhograjski Dolomiti, some distance away. The armed escort was then sent back to the camp, and only our leader remained.[15]

Relaxed, we continued our march for another hour, talking and smiling. We wanted to know something about the situation in the Polhograjski Dolomiti. All our leader could tell us was that he would turn us over to a new guide, who had excellent orientation experience of the terrain where we would be crossing several roads and railroad tracks. We stopped when we reached a little valley with a sizeable stream of clear, rushing water, where another group of partisans was already resting.

It was a sunny day. A few men from the other group were standing naked in the middle of the stream, taking advantage of this washing opportunity. Our leader organized a stove and started preparing soup. The hills on both sides of the stream were thickly covered with bushes and small trees; they were steep, with the elevation to the top approximately two to three hundred feet. It was so pleasant to lie in the sun, to dream about the future, while waiting for the soup to boil.

And then suddenly rifle bullets were hitting all around us. The Italians apparently reached the top of the hill on the opposite side from our group in complete silence—the noise from the rushing waters prevented detection—and they now had a clear view of the valley. Apparently, those who arrived there before us were not concerned about safety and had placed no guard at a strategic point. In panic we started running toward the hill, desperately trying to reach the bushes, the top, and to escape to the other side. Our leader was screaming, "Someone help me carry the stove and the soup." While running toward the hill, I spotted Ciril coming to the leader's help. I yelled at him, "Leave that damn soup and save yourself," and off I went up the hill, practically on all fours, scratched by the bushes and branches along the way while bullets hitting around me sounded like heavy summer hail.

I rolled over at the top and stopped, trying to calm my pounding heart and over-worked lungs. Shooting continued for a while and then stopped. There was no partisan response. One learns to distinguish between the sounds of friendly and enemy fire very fast. I started looking around for others and for Ciril. Gradually a few of us found each other, probably fifteen in all, but we were without a guide or a leader. For about twenty minutes we continued walking away from the stream and then sat down in a forest to wait for others. Then, out of the blue, a single bullet landed right in the midst of us, three feet from me. In great panic, we were up in a split second and running as fast as we could, thinking that the Italians spotted our resting place. There were no additional bullets. Ashamed, we stopped. Inexperience, having no means for defense, and unknown territory contributed to this unpleasant sequence of events. I kept inquiring if anyone saw our leader or Ciril.

It was getting dark and with darkness came the need for a comfortable place to survive the night in the middle of the forest. Two hours or more passed and still no trace of anyone else. We were very concerned about the others, especially those washing themselves in the stream. Were they hit, killed, or hurt, or did they have sufficient time to escape? Then, a most happy sight. Our leader, still holding his rifle, and Ciril came through the woods, bringing with them the stove and the soup. I was so happy to see Ciril alive. Neither Ciril or the leader made any comments about our behavior or accused us of cowardice. On that day the two of them were in our eyes real heroes. The soup tasted very good, but we ate it with some guilt. The two soup-saviors did not receive or take bigger portions. We spent the night in the woods, and, after learning a good lesson, we took turns standing guard and listening for possible dangers and the chance that others would find our location. We never heard further details of what happened at that stream after our fast retreat.

What next? Our leader was not quite sure where we were, but the fast-approaching night gave us little time for proper orientation. We walked uphill and eventually settled in tall grass out in the open at the highest point possible. Exhausted, we soon fell into deep sleep. In the very early morning the grass was wet from morning dew, and when I tried to get up, I felt strong pains in my hips and knees. The same happened to a few others. I could hardly take a step. It took a little time to realize that some form of arthritis resulted from sleeping in the wet grass. After several minutes of walking, these pains diminished a little but never completely disappeared. Every step was associated with pain.

The leader kept observing landmarks in several directions and then decided on a new course. No doubt, we were a burden for him. He did not know where to turn or how to look for connection to the higher authorities. We, on the other hand, depended on him. It was not his Mauser rifle, which was always in his hand or at his side, that meant something to us: It was his skill as a provider of essentials that was most crucial. Every time we passed near a house or a small village, he would tell us to stay hidden in the nearby woods and then he carefully approached a few houses trying to get something to eat. Being from the region himself, he was usually successful. Small pieces of old bread, sometimes even a little milk, were all these folks were able to share with us. After one such trip, I became a beneficiary, not a rightful owner, of a much-needed spoon. Eventually, all of our new group came in possession of spoons; handy cups or bowls were not far away.

The same day or the next, we arrived in the vicinity of a picturesque village; Sveti Vid (Žilce). Its church steeple was visible from far away. There were at least twenty to thirty houses or more, nicely located on the hilly surroundings of the church. We were stationed in the woods not far from the village and instructed not to take individual trips to the nearby houses but to stay put. Some tacit agreements were negotiated with the local populace to give us permission to bivouac during the night in the covered haystacks, certainly more convenient than sleeping in the woods. These precautions were necessary to prevent discovery of our presence in the area. All this time we were under control or guidance of one single person, one meagerly armed partisan. He gave us from time to time special assignments, such as picking up prearranged provisions at certain houses. To avoid attracting attention, only one person walked into the village each time and only to a few select houses. On my assignment, I visited two houses; one which served the village and wider neighborhood as a diner or restaurant, the other, a shoemaker's shop. At both places they were generous and gave me a little extra to eat. However, I was told to eat it there and not to mention to the others. The promised provisions I carried back to the camp. It was not much, but sufficient for the group for a day or two.

One day the leader took me to a spot with a clear view south toward the valley and pointed to a house a considerable distance away. He told me to go there and tell the man or woman in the house that a certain person was waiting. That was all. I hesitated for a while, thinking of a trap. Seeing my reluctance, he told me that all this territory is safe and that I should not encounter any problems on the way but to keep my eyes open nevertheless. He also said that he could not leave the group himself for the several hours which this trip would require.

It took me more than two hours to reach the designated house. Only one woman was home; she looked at me with distrust. I gave her the message and received no response. She reluctantly gave me permission to drink from the fountain next to the house, and I left that unfriendly place in a hurry.

Hiking up the hill, weak from hunger, was a struggle. I came to the point of complete exhaustion. The hill was steep and the terrain rough. I was lifting my legs by pulling on my trousers about the knees since my legs just refused to cooperate.

In desperation, I disobeyed one important instruction: not to stop at any but the designated house. When I came into the vicinity of an isolated small house, I approached the woman working outside the house and begged for the first time in my life for food. The woman looked me over. I was still in my Sunday best, even though my suit was showing the effects of living in the woods. Without saying a word, she went into the house. I sat down and waited with my heart pounding. I could not avoid fear. It seemed an eternity, but the woman finally came out of the house with a small glass half filled with milk. I drank it to the last drop, wishing for more. However, I realized that that small amount of milk was probably the most she was able to spare. With energy miraculously restored for the time being, I was back in the camp in a little more than five hours total. I reported leaving the message; there were no questions asked about whom I saw or anything else.

One day, during these initial stages with the partisans, Ciril came to me and told me that among us was also the poet Miran Jarc, a name we both knew from the book *Odmevi rdeče zemlje*.[16] Ciril introduced me to him, a tall, skinny person, always sitting by himself and involved in his own thoughts. He was pleasant and enjoyed questions and conversations; however, he never initiated any such exchanges. We noticed that he had extremely weak nerves. At the sound of an airplane he started shaking and was the first in the woods to hide behind a tree. No assurances of any kind, that the enemy was far away and that they would not discover us, were of any help. He simply could not control his nerves. I don't recall when he was taken out of our group; however, I will always remember this gentle, kind, and interesting individual.[17]

Part II

We knew our inactivity could not last forever. The command finally came for us to move again. It was probably handed to our leader outside the camp, in the village of Sveti Vid (Žilce), because we never noticed any couriers. How many were in our group? Fewer than twenty. Destination? Not the Polhograjski Dolomiti as originally intended but a reunion with the labor battalion. The location of the labor battalion, however, was not revealed to us.

We set out, still without any equipment and with one armed partisan in the lead. He was young, enthusiastic about his assignment, and seemingly knew his territory well. As a proud owner of a good pair of new hiking boots, he had the appearance of an experienced scout leader rather than that of a partisan. His walking pace was much faster than ours, and many had difficulties keeping up. Once in a while he would stop and encourage our efforts. His job was to bring us to a certain point before the evening, and he was determined to accomplish that. Even though he was a pleasant companion, we were happy when he turned us over to a partisan, who in appearance and behavior was more what we had become accustomed to. As we soon found out, the new guide also had a talent as a provider. After all, to get supplies on the march was crucial. Our new guide knew his business.

On the second day of the march we faced a new and difficult task; we had to cross the well-protected railroad tracks. Our leader told us that we would cross toward the evening, while it was still daylight. There were fewer Italian patrols on the railroad tracks in the early evening, if any, and we needed daylight for a successful crossing. We waited all afternoon hidden in the nearby woods. This was an especially good day for provisions. Our guide provided us with a large quantity of dark, heavy bread and sufficient amount of milk. A problem with this kind of food was loud burping when complete silence was essential.

Toward the evening we were ready to go. The leader was at the head of the column. He instructed us that as soon as he jumped over the tracks, he would take a protective position facing Italian bunkers, which were only about two hundred yards to our left and clearly visible. If the Italian soldiers started shooting, those already across the tracks were to continue up the hill; the others were to retreat and wait for him at the bivouac we had just left.

I was right behind the leader. With a few big jumps, I was across the railroad tracks, running past the leader, who was behind a bush aiming at the Italian bunkers. In a few seconds I was away from the tracks and climbing as fast as possible up the hill. The railroad crossing was an example of a smooth and efficient operation, without a mishap. We wondered if the Italian soldiers saw us and just ignored us. Anyone in those bunkers should have noticed people crossing the tracks such a short distance away. Furthermore, that trail was so well worn that there was no question about its purpose. However, we felt safe again. Our leader was very proud, and so were we.

The first town we entered after crossing was Kompolje. From there we went to Žvirče and then to Hinje. Everywhere the local population thought we were strange characters, as we seemed to be under guard but we often sang. We enjoyed singing as a group, but the song, "Avanti popolo, alla riscossa," was not popular with us. Why sing in Italian? We did not pay much attention to the text and did not fully understand the thoughts expressed in the song, but the language at the time was offensive. We wondered what kind of message this song delivered to the folks in villages and towns. I remember well a group of people in one village standing with a priest in front of the church, when we were marching by and singing "Avanti popolo . . ."; the expressions on their faces were those of disbelief.[18]

At Hinje both Ciril and I had a chance to speak to a brother and sister who were residents of that town. He was my schoolmate at gymnasium, and she was in the same class as Ciril at the teachers' school. They promised to inform our parents of our well-being. All the inhabitants at Hinje were generous with extra food.

It was afternoon when we passed through Smuka. We arrived late at night in Stari log, our final destination.

From the time when the twelve of us were separated from the rest of the labor battalion near Otave on that unfortunate day until we reached Stari log to rejoin the labor battalion, we stopped at several partisan encampments. Some of these were of a permanent, some of a temporary nature. Two made quite opposite impressions on us.

At one camp, a small group of partisans was sitting around a campfire. We, as a group, were not invited to join but were resting and waiting to spend the night a few yards away. We were, to a point, included in the conversation. Some narrations were probably intended for us, mostly about their experiences in the Spanish Civil War. These partisans were older and very sure of themselves. They were neither hostile nor friendly but indifferent toward us newcomers. One among them, a younger man, approached our group and recognized the son of the Ljubljana industrialist who was with us. This person told us that he was for a while employed in the factory owned by our companion's family. He then added a few negative remarks about his work experience there while he was circling around us. This man did not show any hostility toward the owner's son, but we nevertheless sensed a sharpness in his words. More than that, he wasted no time in telling us how he executed his first victim. In complete silence we listened to details. He told his victim to walk ahead of him and to say a few prayers; while this unfortunate person was praying, he put a bullet in the back of his head. The grin on this fellow's face when he was telling us about his first kill drove chills throughout my body and a fear in my heart. I am sure all my companions felt the same. The other partisans did not pay much attention, even though they heard at least part of what he was telling us. That terrible impression on that evening was only slightly softened by the unexpected arrival of an Australian man, allegedly an escaped prisoner of war. He had a beautiful horse, was comparatively well-equipped, and moved around independently; he was not part of any partisan unit. The Australian brought some news from recent radio reports, news from the fronts, translated for us by the only English-speaking partisan, a former navy man. The news from the fronts was positive. Of course, nobody would dare spread negative information.

The second camp, where we rested for an hour or two, had the word "proletarian" as part of its official title. These people knew what they were doing; everyone had a well-defined assignment, the camp was clean, and their defense installations were built at strategic locations. We were spotted long before we came near the camp; our leader presented his papers. We were given a warm meal. These partisans did not say much nor mingle with us or ask questions. After we left, we were in agreement that members of this unit had definite goals and excellent discipline in their routines.

We were accommodated in Stari log in a large storage building, where most of the labor battalion members already had their quarters. Stari log was the largest settlement in this area. Most of the houses in town were empty. The original inhabitants, known as *Kočevarji* (in Slovene) and *Gottschee Deutsche* (in German) were, after the defeat of Yugoslavia in April 1941 and by an agreement between the German and Italian governments, relocated to German-occupied sections of Slovenia—from where Slovene families were expelled to Croatia or Serbia—not to Germany proper as they were led to believe.[19] When we were stationed in this town, only a few houses had occupants—Slovene, not German families. Partisans used some houses for their needs; many houses, however, were left empty.

One of the first things I heard the next day was that one of the labor battalion members, J. H., took off on the first day after the labor battalion arrived in Stari log, right after renewed interrogations were underway. I knew little about him but was aware that he was higher up in our own underground organization. For Ciril and me, the situation and participation with the partisans did not seem encouraging when we assessed all negative signs of the past weeks and added J. H.'s escape to it. We, who arrived in Stari log several days after the others, were again interrogated about our backgrounds. These interrogations went fairly smoothly since interrogators only recorded our answers. Naive as we were, we did not think anything wrong about providing details. I was, fortunately, never asked whether I belonged to any underground organization. The interrogator did ask, however, whether I received an invitation in gymnasium to join the Liberation Front. My answer was negative. I also believe that Ciril and I had some backing or even support from one of the political commissars, who told us that he was originally from Mežica, a town only a few kilometers from Prevalje and Dravograd, our pre-war homes. He never mentioned my father, although he must have known at least his name and his position in Dravograd County.

We were doing a variety of work in and around Stari log: work in the fields, repairs in the town, preparing food and making preparations for the winter. For a short while, I was assigned to a butcher who was kind enough to look in my direction when extras became available. Most of these extras were in the form of cracklings, which, because of our half-starved state, caused unwelcome frequent bowel movements. This was dangerous in itself because on our starvation diet, we were supposed to suffer from constipation. Extras for anybody were strictly forbidden, although reality, especially at the command posts, was frequently a different matter.

Emergency alarms sounded often. On such occasions we took our meager possessions and went into the nearby hills and woods. Most of the time nothing happened. On one such occasion, the alarm was called a few minutes before the noon meal; after we returned to the village two hours later, our meal was gone. This almost caused a rebellion, because we concluded that the alarm sounded for the sole purpose of depriving us of our meal. We were offered no explanation about the disappearing nourishment; we just did not get a meal on that day. From then on, alarms were looked at with suspicion, especially when called mid-morning.

The commander of the labor battalion was a short, husky man in a dark uniform and heavy black boots. This kind of uniform seemed to prevail among people in command. One day the famous partisan, Daki (Stane Semič), visited the village with his group; in appearance he looked similar to our commander. We often heard about his many encounters with the enemy, always with victorious results. However, when we were standing around him to hear about some of these battles, we heard only how the alleged domestic enemies of the Liberation Front were eliminated or, to be exact, murdered. These executions were narrated in gruesome detail, and the expressions on his and his companions' faces indicated that such acts provided a special pleasure. Such talks frightened us and generated in our hearts and minds a determined refusal to conduct the war in such an irresponsible manner. We did not dare to express disapproval or even leave the group when this was going on. We felt that Daki and his companions were behaving like this on purpose, to enjoy seeing fear on our faces.

The battalion received orders to built defenses on the road leading to Stari log from Kočevje, the nearest Italian stronghold. We were to cut down all trees on both sides of the road for a distance of about two to three miles between Stari log and Kleč(e), the last village still in the so-called liberated territory. We had no experience in forestry work, and the only instruction we received is how to cut a tree so that it falls in the desired direction. It is very surprising that no accidents happened. These were very tall old trees, mostly spruce. The constant sounds of falling trees filled the air every day, and teams competed with each other to see which one could cut down more trees. It must be in human nature that acts of destruction provide more pleasure than acts of construction. Only one person asked who owned the trees and expressed some reservations about the legality of our destructive action, which gave our group a little pause. The work had to be done; these were our orders.

We were almost finished with tree-cutting, when a call came for eight volunteers to carry barrels of soup from Stari log to the partisans at advance positions in Kleč(e). The road was now impassable for any kind of vehicular traffic or transportation. Ciril and I volunteered right away; the offer sounded attractive. In Stari log, the eight of us were accommodated in a small cottage on the village outskirts. Once a day, on a variable schedule, we carried a large barrel full of thick soup to Kleč(e) over and around the trees we had just cut down a few days before. We carried the barrel on a heavy wooden stick, one man in front, looking for the best path, the rear man holding the barrel to prevent it from swinging. The barrel was very heavy; we had to pad our shoulders. Ciril and I were a team. He was the lead man; I took the back position. It took roughly one hour and a half to two hours to get to the destination when conditions were favorable, a little less on return since the barrel was empty.

On the second day Ciril and I got lost. After we crossed the tough part of fallen trees, we took the wrong turn. The land did not look right and we were concerned. We were out in the open, marching down a well-worn path. Two partisans on patrol spotted us. When we explained that we were taking soup to the forward positions, they asked us, half jokingly, if we had Italian or partisan positions in mind. We were perplexed by such questions. It turned out that we were already very near Italian positions. Would they enjoy our soup? Probably not. Fortunately, the two men on patrol did not accuse us of a desertion attempt, but led us back to the right trail.

The weather is usually at its best at the end of July and beginning of August. Not so on one afternoon when it was Ciril's and my turn to carry the barrel. The person in charge in the house where the soup was prepared told us that in such a terrible storm with thunder and lightning, we did not have to go. However, thinking of those on the other end who would not get anything to eat until late next morning, we decided to try anyway. We covered the open barrel of soup with canvas and started down the road despite the storm. We had to depart then in order to arrive before darkness. It went well for a while. However, the fallen trees were now wet and slippery, and the ground was muddy. The established technique of crossing did not work, and we had to spend extra time to pass the barrel over individual logs. At one point, in desperation, we tried to bypass the road and walk through the woods, but this did not work either. We were almost in a state of panic, because darkness was fast approaching and we were still among the fallen trees. When we finally exited the fallen-tree area, it was completely dark. Once on the road, however, we had no difficulty proceeding in the right direction even in complete darkness. We were able to differentiate the feel the rough road under our shoes. That touch provided a correct and secure guide.

We arrived two hours late. Those on duty had given up on us long ago. The partisans were taking cover from the heavy rain in a storage building. Our posts were, after all, only forward observation points for early detection of any unusual movements of the Italian armed forces; no bunkers or defenses existed there.

We were praised left and right for our efforts. Normally, we would have gone back with our empty barrel immediately, but that day a return trip was out of question. We were shivering in our soaked clothes, and the commander suggested that we spend the night in a haystack. Once there, we realized that the only way to stay warm was to remove all our clothes, but hay, even though it offers warmth, is not exactly comfortable to a naked body. In case of a sudden Italian attack, unlikely during the night or in such inclement weather, we kept our clothes within reach. In first daylight, we put our "Sunday best" back on our bodies, went to the storage building, picked up our empty barrel and departed, after receiving a few more thanks from those on the morning watch.

The trip back presented no difficulties after our bodies warmed the wet clothes to a comfortable level. When back in Stari log, we dried our clothes, first in the house where soup was prepared and then in the afternoon in front of our cottage.

The assignment of carrying soup to forward positions, which we enjoyed, lasted unfortunately only one week. One day, when Ciril and I were resting in front of the cottage after the early morning delivery, the battalion commander came by on his horse. To his not-too-friendly question about what we were doing, we told him that we were delivering soup to the forward positions. He was very surprised and his reaction was quick: "You two are delivering food to the forward positions? March immediately back to the battalion!" We were very disappointed; we thought that the commander knew about our assignment.

Soon after we were unceremoniously removed from our important and responsible job; the battalion was on the move again. The new home for the labor battalion became the picturesque village of Pugled, high up in the mountainous terrain southeast of Stari log. When we arrived, the battalion command was already there, well situated in the middle of the village in an attractive house. In addition to the battalion commander, there were three other unarmed partisans housed there who were responsible to assign and supervise our work. Two armed older partisans, and two young girls, who had household and cooking duties for command personnel only, also shared command quarters. This command post enjoyed separate and better provisions and better meals. We were "privileged" to enjoy from time to time the pleasant smells escaping from the kitchen windows, reminding us of the good old pre-war days. These special arrangements were not in tune with the spirit of partisanship and were local in nature. We felt very offended by these dual standards, because the constant preaching of complete equality was here thrown right into our faces or, to be more precise, into our noses. It did not take us long to discover why the two armed partisans were constantly on patrol. They were in reality successful providers for the command post, but no crumbs ever found their way into our direction.

Our own quarters were at least under a roof. However, I do not remember seeing any kitchen facilities or stoves, so we were probably quartered in storage buildings or something similar. We slept not in beds but on hay-covered floors. My blanket was still just my coat.

The village itself had good views in several directions. We were the only people stationed there; the previous inhabitants were gone. Here we worked almost exclusively in the fields. Those who were skilled in the use of the scythe rose very early in the morning while the grass was still wet to get the best cut. For us unskilled laborers the shift started later, when it was time to turn the grass over several times before it was completely dry and ready to be picked up or put in piles. These fields were not on level ground but had various degrees of gradient. After all, these were mountain villages, where all the work had to be done by hand in the traditional way. Our supervisors, who were used to field work, were not satisfied with our performance, and we were often criticized for slowness. Empty stomachs do not foster speed.

It was strictly forbidden, punishable by death they said, to pick up an apple or anything else to supplement our meager daily diet. Some of us discovered here and there a few horseradishes left in the ground. These caused pains in the stomachs, but they were something to chew on. Someone, more knowledgeable about internal affairs then we were, eventually persuaded us to discontinue eating horseradishes, and we thus prevented permanent damage to our interiors.

A special signal came into being as we were working in the fields. One of the partisan songs contained a line, "O kmet, spametuj se, spreglej" (Oh, peasant, come to your senses, open your eyes [take notice])! It became a favorite greeting among us. Our supervisors did not like hearing this verse, but this was our only way to express our occasional displeasure or complain in an indirect fashion.

The labor battalion consisted almost exclusively of gymnasium and university students. Only a few people were older and established in their profession. One who I remember well was Dr. Avgust Plajh, a lawyer. He did not hide his deep ideological disagreement with the way partisans were conducting their activities. The rumors circulated that Dr. Plajh had been invited to meet with the partisan high command while serving in the labor battalion, although he never mentioned that. Dr. Plajh had a positive outlook. He would often say, if he noticed signs of depression in a person or detected inner suspicious thoughts, "Men, we have to do the job assigned to us even though we may not be in agreement with tactics and goals our superiors stand for." He also stressed repeatedly that trying to escape would not be the right thing to do and that it would endanger the rest of the battalion members. He performed his work in the fields without complaints and with exemplary patience.[20]

At Pugled we had among us three Italian prisoners, two of them older men. They clearly suffered in our midst. We did not associate with them; they were isolated even though they had similar assignments. These two soldiers worked very diligently, rarely talked to each other, but stayed together whenever possible. We heard them sometimes praying in the evening. The partisans did not abuse them. I often thought how hard it must be for them to think of their families or the fact that their families knew nothing of their fate. Their faces showed that they were very much afraid for their lives.

The third Italian prisoner had a higher rank; some claimed that he was a sergeant. I recall that he was addressed by many as *tenente* (lieutenant). His name was Mario. It was easy to understand why he had earned a special status. Mario possessed a beautiful tenor voice and used it to his advantage. Evenings he would sit on a bench in front of the command post with the two young girls and sing everything from popular tunes to operatic arias. It was a pleasure to listen to him; his singing brought back so many nice memories. Mario was a tiny person, always cheerful and pleasant. He did not associate much with the two other Italian soldiers or show compassion or concern for them.

On a pleasant early evening, when the sun was just beginning to hide behind the distant hills but still sending great red rays over the fields, we collected our work tools and started marching home to get our evening meal. Something, however, was not quite right. We noticed one of the field-work supervisors running around, greatly upset. During the evening meal we were informed that tenente Mario and a university student were missing; presumably they were trying to escape. The supervisor found their work tools in the bushes near the fields where we were working that day. The two armed partisans from the command posts were immediately dispatched after them, and a large area was searched in pursuit of the two alleged deserters. We were told that the two would be caught, brought back, and executed in front of the entire labor battalion. We feared the worst for them and for us.

Our status immediately changed to semi-imprisonment, and new interrogations took place the next day. This time interrogations were rough. They wanted to know, among many other things, who attended Dr. Lambert Ehrlich's funeral and why.[21] We were questioned in what appeared to be a cowshed. The room contained a small table and two chairs, one for the interrogator and one for the person being interrogated; the rest of the dark room was empty, the floor covered with hay. I had already been questioned and was sitting on the hay in the back of the room with two others when Ciril was brought in. Without any hesitation, he told his interrogator everything he knew about Dr. Ehrlich and his many contributions to the formation of Yugoslavia as a member of the Yugoslav delegation at the Paris Peace Conference after World War I, and about his work in support of the Carinthian Slovenes. The interrogator did not expect such an answer. After he collected himself, he told Ciril that his information was only half of the story about Dr. Ehrlich and that Ciril apparently did not know about Dr. Ehrlich's more recent and traitorous activities. The questioning ended there.

For some the questioning resulted in further detention. These few were allegedly officers of Catholic organizations at gymnasiums and at the university and thus suspected of being in opposition to the Liberation Front. One of them, X. R., was one morning taken under guard into the woods and we feared the worst. He was composed and calm. Fortunately, half an hour later he was brought back; it was a scare tactic. Rumors were circulating that law students and lawyers among the partisans were proposing development of a legal system to achieve some judicial independence. Apparently this call for legality, even though at an embryonic stage, had some positive consequences for our status as well.

While in detention, we were not spared verbal attacks from a few fanatics, but most of the partisans did not show any hostility toward us. The most painful situation involved a young boy with gangrene in his left arm, who used all possible insulting words against us and was praised for his insults by one of the adults. We felt sorry for this boy and his empty ranting. Even to a non-specialist, it was clear that his gangrene was past any possible surgical help which certainly could have been an explanation for his abusive state of mind.

After two days of uncertainty, it became obvious that the two escapees must have reached Italian lines. For precautionary reasons, we left our comfortable lodgings at Pugled and moved into the nearby woods, expecting an Italian air attack. Surprisingly, there were no overflights and no attacks on our positions. The command then decided to return to Pugled that same evening even though it was assumed that the Italians must have received many details about our numbers, activities, armament or lack of it, provisions, and extent of operations.

Our semi-imprisonment, which was already considerably relaxed, suddenly took an unexpected turn. At the morning battalion assembly, approximately fifteen names were called, mostly those of us who were in disfavor after the escape. The battalion commander announced that the High Command had decided to form a new unit, a mobile pioneer detachment (*pionirski vod*), and that we had been selected for this unit. A political commissar was assigned to join us, and one armed partisan was officially put in charge of the detachment. We all praised the battalion commander for appointing X. Novak, who went through a lot during the interrogations, as the superintendent of this new pioneer detachment. We were apparently fully rehabilitated.

We departed immediately, destination unknown. The political commissar was *de facto* in charge of this detachment. He tried to learn something about each of us by casual conversations during the trip. He said that he would encourage open discussion and that he respected different opinions. We learned that he had joined the Communist Party at an early age.

It was mid-afternoon when we reached the village of Topla reber.[22] The village looked most attractive on that nice afternoon though there were no people there; all the houses were empty. The largest structure was a school, where we established our new quarters. First things first, so under Novak's directions, we set up the kitchen, stored provisions, and helped to prepare the evening meal. After the meal, the political commissar informed us that our assignment was to prepare storage facilities for the winter at various locations in the region of Kočevski rog, Topla reber being the first one. He added half-jokingly that he hoped there would be no escapes from this unit since he accepted personal responsibility for this first mobile pioneer squad, its members, and its operations.

The political commissar apparently had prepared storage facilities before. He examined potential areas for storage even before our detachment was formed. At Pugled he examined wells by climbing down into them and assessing the possibilities. In addition to storage facilities in villages, additional facilities were scheduled for construction in the nearby woods, he said. On the first day, when he was working with two university students cleaning a well, an interesting debate took place among the three of them regarding possibilities for post-war transformation of the social structure in Slovenia. Even though some of us were not intellectually able to participate in these discussions, we, nevertheless, formed a good opinion of our commissar. He was entirely different from political commissars we had met; he was intelligent and well spoken.[23] We did wonder why we were all of a sudden completely free after the unpleasant times of only a few days before. However, we were pleased with the current status, the new assignment, new location, our company, and our independence. We now had better provisions; meals were adequate, and everyone received the same quality and quantities.

In August one does not usually think about winter. However, when it is necessary to find overnight shelter in the woods, especially on a rainy night, the winter immediately comes to mind; it presents new and more serious challenges. Preparing storage facilities, knowing their locations, and what kind of resources would be available became important goals, so we were anxious to work diligently on these new tasks. What kind of storage facilities these would be or what would be stored there, the commissar did not know as yet. He told us that the nature of facilities and their location would determine where supplies and materials for daily life or for military needs would be stored. The future looked much brighter.

In the morning of 13th of August, only three days after we arrived in Topla reber, a major shock hit us suddenly and unexpectedly. The tranquility of our peaceful village was broken. Only a direct lightning strike would have matched what we experienced that morning. Loud, terrifying, thundering sounds of motorized machinery came from all directions. These sounds were everywhere. Worst of all, these disturbances sounded so close, much too close. We were completely taken by surprise. We had no warning, not a single indication that something big was in the plans against us. We had no idea of what to do or where to run.

The only person who knew the terrain well, our commissar, had gone to Pugled the evening before, so we were on our own. Our leader was as scared as we were even though he tried to keep his composure. How far away were the attackers? Would their vehicles, or whatever advance equipment they had, move up into the hills? Was this a major attack or just a daily skirmish into our territories? The commander decided that we should leave the village, take a few supplies with us, and go into hiding until the danger was over. Nothing very useful was ready to be taken; our meals needed to be cooked. There was no time for that, however.

We proceeded up the hills and into the woods. The leader told us to stay put while he searched around, trying to establish links with others. No luck. One of our members lost his senses, advanced down a hillside and started yelling, "aiuto, aiuto" (help, help)! Two men went after him, silenced him, and brought him back.

He was embarrassed. For punishment we gave him a new name, Aiuto; the name stuck. The uproar, rumbling, and thunder continued all day and into the night, sometimes some distance away, sometimes too close for comfort. How close they came we did not know; it was difficult to judge, maybe one to two kilometers. Our hopes were that the Italian attack was limited to the valleys. We did not see any foot soldiers. From the vehicular noise, frequent explosions, machine gun and rifle fire, we easily deduced that large forces were engaged and that they were definitely in our vicinity.

The second day was not much different. We were completely isolated; we had seen no other partisans all day. We tried unsuccessfully to get closer to Pugled to join the others—if they were still there. We walked through the woods and that slowed our progress. The threatening sounds were even stronger from the direction of Pugled. We were very hungry, thirsty, and tired. Toward the evening we went back to the woods near Topla reber and spent an uncomfortable and scary night there.

The next morning all seemed back to normal. We relaxed a little but were still cautious and undecided. There was no rumbling of motorized equipment, no unusual sounds; tranquility was here again. We guessed that the Italian forces retreated to their initial positions, as had happened a few times in the past. Silently we proceeded to the edge of the woods above Topla reber and carefully observed the village. Nothing was changed; the village was empty. The commander, therefore, decided that it was time to get something to eat. He ordered us to go to the village and prepare a meal. In addition, he told Ciril and me to go through the houses and search for blankets and canvas, just in case we had to stay in the woods for a while longer

Slowly and fearlessly we walked into the village. Nothing was disturbed at our quarters in the school building; the kitchen facilities were intact. We felt secure. After preparations for the first meal in two days were well underway, Ciril and I went to a large house some distance away to search for blankets.

The doors were not locked. Everything left by the departing owners was undisturbed, giving us the impression that we were the first intruders. Ciril immediately started searching. I spotted a nice bookshelf holding richly bound large volumes and could not resist my curiosity. When I pulled one from the shelf and opened it, to my great surprise, I had the full score of a Wagner opera in my hands. With great enthusiasm, I tried to hear what was on the pages. I did not get far.

Two rifle shots, Italian rifle shots, brought me out of my musical dream. Ciril was already running toward the door. I pulled a thick reddish tablecloth from the nearby table and followed Ciril, who was empty-handed. We ran as fast as possible toward the school. Stepping into the kitchen, we discovered to our horror that the potatoes were still cooking; however, our companions were no longer there.

In panic, afraid to be left alone, we ran through the center of the village, between the houses, trying to get to the woods the shortest way. All of a sudden, in front of us from both sides of the street a few dozen black shirts appeared from behind the houses and pointed their rifles and automatic weapons at us. Instinctively, we turned around. There was no way out in this direction either. The black shirts were everywhere, slowly and calmly coming toward us. . . . Without being told, we raised our arms in surrender.

It was 15 August 1942, 9:00 A.M.

CHAPTER FIVE

In Captivity by the Italian Armed Forces

August 1942

━━━━━

By mid-summer 1942 Axis Power reached its peak. On the Russian front German forces reached the Don River on 4 July 1942 and crossed it on 31 July.

In Africa, after recapturing Tobruk, Field Marshal Rommel was again advancing toward Egypt. On 30 June 1942, Rommel's Afrika Korps reached their farthest point east, El Alamein in Egypt, before being driven back by the British a few months later (October 1942).

Only the German U-boats, from the start of the war the terror of the Atlantic, were in 1942 encountering more difficulties, and their successes were on the decline. Because of heavy losses, they abandoned attacks on shipping along the North American coast and concentrated on the convoys. Their "wolf packs" brought them some success; however, their losses were tremendous.

The first deportations of Jews from the Warsaw Ghetto to the concentration camps were underway in the middle of 1942.

The approach by the black shirts was terrifyingly slow; it lasted forever. That is, it took a few seconds, but they were the longest seconds I have ever experienced. The two of us stood there, numb, scared, frozen in place. In a split second my mind went back to the freedom of the last two months, and suddenly, very clearly, this freedom emerged in an entirely new, most positive and colorful light, despite some unpleasant experiences.

When we lifted our arms in surrender, Ciril dropped his sack of small unripe pears, which he had picked up in the kitchen prior to our desperate attempt to escape into the woods. I let go of my newly acquired tablecloth and my small metal cup, a helpful item for scooping and drinking water, picking berries, or accepting occasional donations of food.

Four soldiers started searching us; the others stood leisurely around just watching. One soldier emptied Ciril's sack, nothing incriminating there. After searching me, another removed my wristwatch and put it in his pocket. At the same moment I noticed an approaching lieutenant and, pointing to my wrist, called to him *"l'orologio!"* On the lieutenant's order, the soldier immediately returned my wristwatch.[1]

The soldiers who captured us belonged to a Fascist military group identified with insignia "M."[2] Rumors had circulated during our partisan days that the members of "M" battalions were the cruelest among Italian military units. We also heard that often every tenth prisoner would be executed. So the fear of what would happen to us next was deep and strong.

The soldiers then led us around the corner to the back of a house and, to our great surprise, ten other members of our group were standing there under heavy guard. They were happy to see the two of us safe and sound. We noticed right away that our commander and two or three others, including Aiuto, were not among those captured; they apparently remained in the woods when we were given orders to prepare a meal and escaped in time. A university student in our group of twelve spoke fluent Italian. He explained to our captors that we were from the train of prisoners attacked by the partisans at Verd on 29 June 1942. This interpreter concluded his report by saying that *carabinieri* who were supposed to guard us ran away at the start of the attack instead of protecting the train. Surprisingly, Italians liked this part of the attack story the best.

We also learned through our interpreter that the soldiers of battalion "M" had been in the woods on the opposite side of the village early in the morning. With binoculars they had watched our leisurely walk into the village and into the school. It was obvious that we were not armed. They saw Ciril and me walking to a house a little distance away. Our companions, who were preparing a meal, were devastated when Italians entered the kitchen. After they were led away, the two rifle shots were fired to make Ciril and me run back to the school so they wouldn't need to chase us. Ciril and I were not questioned by the Italians; if the others were, I do not recall hearing about it.

After an hour or two, while the Italians were searching the village and the surrounding areas, we left Topla reber. The last thing I remember was seeing Italian soldiers cutting apple and other fruit trees. That unfortunate sack of pears that Ciril carried was probably the reason for this action, but they did not burn the village, at least not on that day. We would have noticed that even kilometers away.[3]

We were not physically mistreated, but we did not receive water or food. We walked in the middle of the main column, at first surrounded by soldiers, later between two tanks. These tanks occasionally accelerated, and we were forced to run. The empty space between the two tanks was often reduced to a minimum, which further frightened us. The driver in the tank behind us probably enjoyed his game with the captured enemy. On both sides of the main column, nearer the edge and in the forest, we were able to observe heavily armed Italian patrols searching the area and protecting the main column.

Toward the evening, Italians established a camp and started their evening meal. We were not included—no meal for us, but we were allowed access to drinking water. After their evening meal, one soldier brought to our Italian-speaking interpreter a piece of bread, probably from his own ration. The interpreter immediately turned over this piece of bread to our member in charge of provisions. He cut the bread into twelve equal pieces, only a very small piece for each one of us. Seeing that, many soldiers of lower ranks brought food, some already divided into twelve pieces. One soldier even baked twelve apples and delivered them in a ceremonial fashion. The Italians thought that our sharing was based on the communist doctrine of equality. We had to explain to them that we were doing this for the simple reason that we cared for each other. The commanding officer observed these gestures of help by his subordinates and did not object. But neither did he change his policy of no food for prisoners.

Around 9:00 P.M. that evening we heard a few rifle shots not too far away. An hour later we were called, one by one, to the commanding officer. He held in his hands an identification paper with a photograph of a man approximately forty years old. The person appeared to be dressed in outdoor clothes. The photograph was not very clear, and none of us knew the person. We, of course concluded, that this person had been killed when we heard the shots an hour before.[4]

The second day was not much different. For nourishment we still depended on the good hearts of a few Italian soldiers. We circled around in the general direction of southeast from Topla reber. From time to time we stopped, the officers held consultations, and messengers came and went. We did not hear a single shot all day, not Italian, not partisan. In 1942, the partisans were poorly equipped with what was salvaged from the Yugoslav army. Much of the armament was in poor condition; ammunition was scarce. In one camp, during our trip to Stari log when I was standing guard at night, I was handed a Mauser rifle without ammunition. There was really no need for bullets since the rifle was already damaged beyond repair. The best equipment, such as machine guns, was assigned to units with more important tasks than accompanying Labor battalions. During the August 1942 offensive, the Italians engaged thousands of well-equipped soldiers, with mechanized units, tanks, and air support. The only chance for the partisans to avoid defeat or capture by this superior force was to break out of the encirclement or to seek hiding places in the caves in Kočcvski rog. To facilitate their escape from an encirclement, units were split into smaller groups and left to their own skills and initiative.

On the third day we arrived at an important Italian assembly center. This was either at the villages of Rdeči kamen or Podstenice. Here we were turned over to another branch of the Italian military. We were still dirty and unshaven. A photography session followed. Tall, heavily armed soldiers with rifles pointing at us were an essential part of this activity. Still no food.

About three hours later, Italian army trucks were ready for us and for other civilians arrested in their homes, mostly the young and a few older men. The twelve of us were on the first truck, six on each side, facing each other. There were at least five or six additional trucks, two of them reserved for the Italian military escort crew. We were ready to depart.

At that moment another Italian transport column arrived from our intended destination with several wounded Italian soldiers. A few minutes before we had heard sounds of machine gun fire some distance away. The Italians were very upset and very angry; everybody was running back and forth; the wounded were carried into the houses. Two enraged soldiers from the arriving transport ran over to our truck, climbed on, and started beating us, screaming, "Banditi, banditi!" An officer, seeing what was happening, ordered them to desist and saw to it that they left.

After an hour, the officer in charge of the transport received orders to proceed. The commanding officer, a lieutenant, first ordered his soldiers off the trucks and placed them in a single file on the right side, the protected side of the trucks. He himself jumped on the step next to the driver of the first truck where we were sitting. That was the exposed side, toward the steep wooded hills, a great place for an ambush.

Our progress was very slow, at a walking pace. I had my back to the hill; right under me, a little in front, the lieutenant talked encouragingly to the driver. Scared as I was, I was aware that across from me were the terrified faces and eyes of my co-prisoners and the same expression of fear on the faces of two Italian soldiers seeking protection on the right side of our truck. On that side of the road the land dropped off considerably and was therefore fairly safe from attack. The fear of a repeated partisan ambush at this location, suitable for just such an attack, hung over us for almost one hour. We all admired the commanding officer, who, instead of taking his place next to the driver on the safer side, decided to protect his lead driver with his own body by standing fully exposed on the step next to him.

After approximately one hour, we reached a much better and more level road. There, the lieutenant stopped the transport and ordered soldiers to climb on the trucks. He then went around and took his seat next to the driver in the lead truck. We sped away as fast as the road allowed, out of danger, out of partisan territory.

To make matters worse, our new captors lined us up at the next stop in front of a white wall facing the sun. We were forced to stand at attention with guards watching us and yelling if we moved even a little. Hunger, lack of water, and the hot sun brought us to exhaustion; nobody fainted, however. Here our stubbornness played a role. After an hour and a half, an officer came over and asked our interpreter a few questions. When he found out that we were from the train at-tacked at Verd, we were permitted to stand in a more relaxed posture, but we were still forced to stand. Other officers and soldiers then started coming over, asking who was studying in this or that field; they themselves were high school or univer-sity students. With the help of the interpreter, I exchanged a few words with a music student, a pianist, from Milan. These conversations did not last long. The new commanding officer, seeing what was going on, angrily forbade any further association. Those who talked to us were visibly disappointed and almost apolo-getic when they walked away.

The rest of the journey was uneventful but long. Our destination was the prison in the city of Novo mesto. The accommodations were poor, all twelve of us in one completely empty room without any furniture in the rather cold and damp basement. There were plenty of graffiti on the walls, some informative, others of questionable value. The doors to our room were left open so that air could circu-late since there were no windows. This was toward the end of August, the best sea-son for such accommodations.

There were some benefits associated with this prison. After a long time we were able to shower and shave. What a nice feeling, all of a sudden you are a *homo novus*. I suffered a lot from a bloody wound on the right heel caused by my dress shoes. In the mountains I used thick leaves trying to avoid further damage and pain while walking. Nothing really helped; the wound just got bigger and bigger. Here in prison, the Italian military doctor took good care of my problem; the wound started healing fast.

In the afternoon of the second day, Ciril and I were standing with two others at the door, when, to our great surprise, three Italian soldiers brought down our neighbor from Dravograd, Dr. Erat. When he walked by we made eye contact, nothing else. In such situations it is better not to indicate to your captors that you know the person. In those split seconds the three of us followed that unwritten rule. Dr. Erat was taken further down the corridor and locked in a single cell.

Dr. Erat, whom we last saw at Christmas 1940 back in Dravograd, in addition to his medical profession was a key leader of the *Sokol* movement as well as the leader of many other liberal political and cultural organizations. No patriotic cel-ebration of any kind took place without his active leadership. On this day he was well dressed with a light raincoat hanging over his arm and he carried a sizeable utility bag. He did not give the appearance of being captured in partisan territory; most likely, he was arrested at home. Ciril and I were very puzzled, because we knew that he had remained in Dravograd after the German attack and occupa-tion. We also knew that he had been imprisoned by the Gestapo. Now we saw him in the Italian zone, almost at the other end of Slovenia.

We saw Dr. Erat only once more when he was taken to his interrogation. Un-fortunately, this time our door was closed, and we only caught a glimpse through the keyhole. Nevertheless, the sight of a neighbor from our Dravograd during the few days we were kept in the prison in Novo mesto was a coincidence of an almost unbelievable dimension and shrouded in mystery.[5]

Another very surprising event happened in Novo mesto prison. In a secret manner, which I am not willing to disclose even after so many years, one of the twelve of us received a strange message. Anyone willing to sign up for a period of one year to protect our villages—protect them from whom was not explained— would be released from prison. Nobody in our group was willing to take such chances. We decided to stick it out.[6]

We stayed in Novo mesto only three days. The next step was a walk to the railroad station. Before we boarded the cattlecars, we saw a few others from the Labor battalion already on the train but were unable to talk to them. The train took us back to Ljubljana and back to the Belgijska kasarna. This time, however, we were taken to the first floor, to a completely empty room. We discovered that it is much tougher to sleep on a concrete floor than on wood; no matter how you turn, it hurts. A great advantage was windows, facing one of the main streets of the city. We were now looking out into freedom only a few yards away.

Our hopes for release from captivity grew with every hour. On what grounds this would happen did not really cross our minds. When we heard a few names called for release, all our hopes immediately went up. Then one of the two brothers in our group of twelve was also called. In his great hurry to leave, he even forgot to say goodbye to his brother. We concluded that one by one we would be released. In this facility we received regular, although very small, amounts of food. The day after, more people were released, all, except for a few, under eighteen years of age. Our guess or wishful thinking was that the Italians were releasing people by age groups. These hopes were gone early the next morning. We were taken to the courtyard again, organized into a column, and marched toward the railroad station in Ljubljana. It all became clear, very clear. We were finally going to the concentration camp from which we had been diverted by the partisan attack at Verd on 29 of June. On the way to the railroad station, very early in the morning, there were almost no people on the streets. A former professor of mine at the classical gymnasium, Vlasta Pacheiner, spotted me in the group of prisoners. She was standing at the side of the road to check whether her husband was on the transport to Italy. Professor Pacheiner was kind enough to inform our family that we were taken to the railroad station. She noticed as well that I was carrying something. She was right. I still had with me my metal cup and the tablecloth from the house at Topla reber.

Now all hopes for release were gone. This time, the Italians would make sure that we reached our destination. On the train we lost track of where we were going, since we could not reach up to the openings in our cattlecars. To our great surprise, the train stopped near a large harbor. Before we even saw the first signs, a sailor among us identified this port city as Rijeka (Fiume) in the Adriatic Sea. From the train we were taken directly to the harbor facilities and were turned over to the Italian navy.

There was not much chance to look around after we boarded a small ship. In the belly of the ship there was a place for us, again in a completely empty storage room. We guessed the trip would not be long because of the complete lack of accommodations. It was impossible to get a glimpse of the outside world from this dark, not very clean, dungeon, which resembled, in our opinion, the slave ships of not so many decades ago. Where were they taking us? To an Italian port on the other side of the Adriatic?

Fortunately, we did not have to wait more than five or six hours for an answer, though these were very long and exhausting hours. It was hot, humid, and hard to breathe down below. After the ship docked, we were ordered out of the stinky hole. The Italian army took control of us at 7:00 P.M. It took the Italians a long time to get us into a properly organized column, Italian style per tre. They counted and recounted us again and again before they were finally satisfied.

While the formalities were going on, we enjoyed the beautiful view of a very picturesque town with nice surroundings and a neat harbor. The air was something extraordinary as well, especially after long hours in the dungeon.

The name of this town was Rab (Arbe in Italian), on the island of the same name.[7] The sun was just going down. The reflections around the houses and hills were blending and changing every minute. For many of us this was the first look at the Adriatic and its so-often-mentioned beauty.

It took almost two hours before we were ready for departure. What we were going to do here on this island was much on our minds. The clock on the town's steeple showed exactly 9:00 P.M. when the column received orders to march.

CHAPTER SIX

Concentration Camp Rab in the Adriatic

September 1942–January 1943

Germany and Italy declared war on the United States of America on 10 December 1941. It took only until 17 August 1942 for the first American bombing raid on Germany to leave from the bases in England.

On 19 August 1942, the raid on the French coastal city of Dieppe took place. Participating in this attack were 5,000 Canadian and 1,000 British soldiers. The raid was a catastrophe: The attacking forces suffered tremendous losses. It was, as judged later, a premature experiment of techniques to be used for the eventual invasion of Europe.

On the same day, 19 August 1942, the German Sixth Army moved toward Stalingrad on the Volga River, where the opposing forces engaged in fierce fighting at the beginning of September. The Red Army in the last moments prevented German takeover of the city.

On the southern section of the Eastern Front, German troops reached the Caucasus region, threatening to occupy the rich oil fields so crucial to both sides.

Part 1

The clock on the town's steeple sounded nine times, and these sounds provided us with a little music for the start of the march; the music was much too short but nevertheless sweet. We felt that this must be a nice place; nothing bad would happen here. Even the first steps of the men on the march were livelier than is usually the case with forced marches of prisoners. The darkness was setting in fast. In front of me an Italian-speaking prisoner engaged an Italian soldier in conversation, trying to find out something about our destination, accommodations there, and what kind of work we would be doing. Those of us who heard this exchange did not believe everything the soldier said; nevertheless our hopes were elevated. The soldier talked about comfortable accommodations, easy work assignments, and adequate food. He claimed that we would be pleased or at least satisfied with everything at the new location. Our hopes were high.

We walked approximately one hour and there was still nothing to see. It was now completely dark, but the full moon provided sufficient light for us to realize that we were walking inland, away from the coast.

After another twenty minutes, a sudden hush of disbelief came over the column. The first lights and the first tents of a distant camp came into view. There were no doubts anymore; this must be the concentration camp, our destination. The sights even at a considerable distance were unbelievable, almost impressive, and at the same time very intimidating. More than a thousand tents, surrounded by barbed wire and high watch towers, were spread out in military precision on a slight incline below a modest hill. All those positive hopes of a few minutes ago were now gone; fear set in. This was our destination—Concentration Camp Rab.[1]

We arrived at the reception area late at night at the end of August 1942. Nothing much happened that first night. In the quarantine area, attached to the camp, we fell asleep almost immediately, even though the facilities there were very primitive and uncomfortable.

In the morning we had to give away everything we brought with us except our clothes. There was a blanket on the ground, and we fell to our knees and emptied our pockets. My little water cup and my tablecloth from Topla reber fell victims to this action. When Ciril pulled out of his pocket his tie pin and threw it with too strong a motion on the blanket, the soldier in charge hit him across the face. That slap hurt all of us. We stopped and just stood there for a few split seconds. The soldier himself seemed surprised at our firm but silent reaction and from then on showed a changed attitude and almost a civilized and friendly face. After this incident we lost our hair, on the top only. These introductory routines did not consume much time.

After these procedures we marched as a group through the main entrance into the camp to a section where several empty tents were waiting for us. There they turned us over to an Italian officer and a Slovene capo, his assistant.[2] Six men were assigned to each tent. An Italian military tent became our new home. Bales of straw were delivered, two for each tent, supposedly for comfort. But they were full of lice and other unpleasant creatures.

Before we even settled in our tent, we had visitors; a few women with small babies begging for food. Most of them were from the region of Čabar.[3] It was heartbreaking seeing these poor women in rags holding their starving babies. We had nothing to give.

Who were the prisoners on Rab? A great majority were Slovenes from the Italian-occupation zone of Slovenia. Only a small percentage were from Čabar, maybe 10 to 15 percent. Generally, the Slovenes belonged to two categories: (1) those captured during the Italian offensives against the partisans, as we were, and (2) men of all ages and some women and children from the villages not under Italian control and protection. Because of their geographic location, these villages were capable of providing support for the partisans, their goals and their efforts. When we arrived, men and women were in the same camp, living under identical Italian military tents and under identical conditions.[4]

Overlooking the camp was a large building, probably a former school—the headquarters of the Italian command. On the first evening we received instructions to get out of our tents at the sound of the trumpet and stand at attention while the Italian flag was lowered. Standing at attention and facing in the direction of the flag were all that was required. There was no demand for the Fascist salute.[5]

The very first night made us realize what would face us throughout our stay in this camp. The little creatures in the straw started biting almost as on command. We couldn't guess what kind of pests these were, but they did a good job on us. In addition, the tents, too narrow for three men to sleep comfortably on each side, immediately presented a serious and long-lasting problem. During the night, the three men on each side were forced to turn from one side to another in unison. Every time a man wanted to turn, the other two had to do the same. That first night we experienced some difficulties, but in time this simultaneous turning became a serious problem. Ciril and I shared one side with another man of fairly agreeable disposition, but problems came up, nevertheless. The opposite side of our tent was less fortunate. Although we were friends trying to help each other, these interruptions of sleep during the night did not reinforce our friendships.

The first muster took place the next morning. The officer in charge went from tent to tent and called each prisoner by name. On that first morning one man from our group asked for permission to make some changes in tent assignments so that we would all be in two adjacent tents, a request the officer flatly refused, and in confirmation of his absolute authority he quickly added, "Qui commando Io." At the same time, our capo standing behind him was signaling to us not to ask any questions.

At the end of August, during September, and part of October the island was hot during the day and cold at night. The only comfortable time was one hour in the morning and one in the evening. There was no shaded area to be found anywhere during the hot and sunny days. The only cover from the strong sun was the hot interior of the tent. We also very much desired at least a glimpse of the Adriatic Sea or any part of the coast. Being denied that view was an additional punishment. Since we marched to this place at night, we did not even know from which direction we came. Alongside the camp was a dirt road wide enough to accommodate large trucks. After some observation of the road traffic, we eventually guessed the direction of our arrival.

The dining utensils, distributed during the registration process, were a mess can and a spoon. Daily meals consisted of fig coffee in the morning and soup twice a day. The thin, watery soup contained some vegetable leaves and either five to fifteen grains of rice or an equally small amount of piccolo noodles. The only solid food was a small apple or onion, and a miniature piece of bread in the middle of the afternoon. As a result we were extremely hungry for the first two or three weeks; after that starvation set in: the hunger remained and, in addition, severe weakness of the entire body became part of daily life.

At one end of the camp, near our tents, there were six large barracks equipped with bathrooms, showers, and toilets. A very nice set-up, but no water was available. These barracks were locked so we could not even shelter from the sun inside of them. The only water in this hot climate came from a very large barrel that the Italian soldiers brought into the camp mid-morning each day. In desperation, the prisoners attacked that water barrel with their mess cans, fighting each other to get at least a few drops. More than half of the water was spilled during these water fights. The Italians did not make any attempt to organize water distribution, and the thirsty prisoners acted under the rule of "every man for himself." The soldiers enjoyed from some distance the spectacle of these daily ordeals. Most of us, after one or two bad experiences, did not even try to get a drop of this water.

How Italians handled deaths was a puzzle at first. The very sick were taken out of the camp to another facility. Soon, however, we realized that to be taken out of camp to a quasi-hospital nearby meant certain death. If a person died in camp, he or she was immediately removed. What happened after that was not clear. The first coffins we noticed on trucks outside the camp were small. The babies started dying first. If there were ever any "official" funerals, we never found out.

A few days after our arrival at the end of August, the women and children were relocated to a new facility a short distance away. We did not have a view of this camp. Once a day the children were taken for a walk; most often they walked on the road next to our camp. Thus, the fathers whose families were in the women's camp had a chance at least to glimpse their offspring. Fathers and husbands were permitted to visit their wives and/or children for a short time on Sundays.

Our *Campo Concentramento* was encircled with high barbed wire and guard towers. The cooks often threw their useless stuff, including vegetable remnants, on the piles next to the barbed wire. More daring prisoners tried occasionally to retrieve some of this junk to supplement their diets. They were never successful. The guards were very alert, day or night. If a person came to the vicinity of the barbed wire, the guards immediately yelled and pointed their rifles in his direction.

Because of the non-existence of the toilet facilities, we were forced to use the most primitive of latrines—a big hole in the ground near the tents, covered with wooden boards—a real nightmare. There we had to squat in the company of many; each prisoner involuntarily exhibited his unique intestinal problem. The wooden boards were in time covered with excrement, causing additional problems for the feet; the boards were slippery and the particles of excrement stuck to footwear. After a visit to the latrines, one had to walk around for a while, day or night, to remove from one's shoes that terrible stench. The most common intestinal problem during the first three weeks in the camp was constipation. I was not the only one suffering from it. Many would think that fourteen days of complete constipation was impossible, but that was exactly what happened to me. I do not wish to describe "the techniques"—and there were several—we used to deal with it.

In the evenings, after dark, we could hear prayers from many tents, most often the rosary. Older prisoners from those unfortunate villages in the so-called "liberated" territories did most of the praying. Those of us who were captured as partisans didn't associate with other prisoners. Often, when we tried to do so, these men were curt and not willing to disclose any information or even to talk. We thought they blamed us for their misfortunes. The question was often raised as to who would bear the ultimate responsibility for everything happening here? The Italians exclusively for their conduct and for the conditions in this camp? Or would it be shared by those back home in charge of development, politics, and strategies who indirectly caused this relocation of so many innocent people to this terrible place?

Anything positive in Concentration Camp Rab was a rarity. However, strongly imbedded in my mind is one positive memory in connection with the distribution of soup twice a day. An insignificant activity it might seem, but it was of vital importance to all of us standing in line for the watery but warm nourishment. The soup was prepared in several primitive kitchens, then brought in huge barrels to the distribution points. The person distributing the soup had a difficult job. Because the solid ingredients in the soup were such a rarity, it mattered a great deal to us that these miniature solid pieces of nourishment were divided among prisoners as equally as possible. It took a special skill, almost an art, to keep stirring the soup in the barrel with a continuous circular motion while at the same time pouring into each mess can an equal amount of liquid and an appropriate amount of those rare nutritional pieces. In our sector, the man who had this job, a prisoner himself, was a perfectionist in the art of soup distribution. Never, never, were there any complaints against him for not doing his work right or for favoring people from his own village. Not all areas were that fortunate; sometimes we heard loud screaming and accusations, here and there leading to minor fist fights. On such occasions, the capos had a hard time keeping things under control. Fortunately, it was never necessary to call the Italian guards for help.

After the first month in the camp—many people arrived days or even weeks before we did—the general situation started to deteriorate very rapidly. Lack of water, lack of washing opportunities, and the dirt we lived in caused depression, despair, and loss of hope. Our nerves were deteriorating almost faster than our bodies. Every little action or word resulted in unnecessary disputes and accusations. Our life became unbearable. Many prisoners were having difficulties getting up for either physical or mental reasons. The morning and evening musters became a torture for many. There was no way to avoid standing in line next to the tents. Some prisoners had to be supported by their tent partners to comply with the rules. A special slogan soon became known throughout the camp in reference to these rules. Everybody soon learned the real meaning of the command, "tutti fuori, anche morti" (all out, including the dead ones).

At that time we also came to the conclusion that a fight against the lice was a must. We could no longer take the merciless attacks by these creatures. We have been killing them only on the upper parts of the body, now it became necessary to take action against these pests at the bottom of the belly as well. Once a day, the six of us would sit in the tent naked, "murdering," these most unwelcome cohabitants. It was embarrassing at first, but eventually we became accustomed to it. These sessions were a must to protect our bodies from complete deterioration.

When we arrived, the Masses on Sundays were well attended. One Sunday in September,[6] we were visited by Bishop Josip Srebrnič, a Croatian, who said Mass and spoke briefly to those in attendance. The positive side of this brief and limited visit—as far as I recall the Bishop did not walk around the camp or talk to the prisoners—was our first awareness that at least a few people on the outside knew about the existence of Concentration Camp Rab. The negative side was that he limited his remarks or was forced to do so to religious topics and to a few expressions of solace, but did not offer any words of hope or mention any efforts toward improvement of our status, something we were expecting and hoping to hear. It is also important to comment that Concentration Camp Rab looked its very best for the bishop's visit.

Gradually, there were fewer people present at Mass each Sunday. Even the night prayers in the tents, if they were still taking place, were now only silent prayers; with a few exceptions, they were not heard any more. After the Sunday Masses, attended also by Italian officers and soldiers, the Italians conducted some official ceremonies, always ending with, "Viva il Re, viva il Duce." It did not escape our attention that on one Sunday, after some consultation among the officers, "Viva il Duce" was omitted. As a consequence, rumors of all kinds went through the camp during the following week on the meaning of all this. Unfortunately, on the next Sunday, "Viva il Duce" was back again.

In such complete isolation, with no news from the outside, not even overflights of planes, rumors played an important part of daily life. Our favorite rumor was that the British submarines would come and take us from this island after their crews subdued the Italian garrison. We were not concerned about where the submariners would put ten to twelve thousand people. The rumor sounded so beautiful.

Eventually we received permission to write home, thanks to the Red Cross. The messages had to be short and positive, in other words, no realistic descriptions of the camp or about the situation we were in. Strict censorship existed. To prevent letters from being thrown away instead of mailed, we had to be very careful. Since packages had weight, size, and frequency limitations, we asked our folks at home for condensed food such as roux, flour browned in butter or oil to be added to our daily soup. Because of the fast-approaching winter, we asked for clothes as well. However, we did not want clothes to take priority over our desperate need for more food. In the letters we told our families who our closest co-prisoners were so that the families back home would be able to share the news from several different writers.

Those who came before us and who had families back home able to put some packages together received their packages first. The news about the first packages to arrive spread around the camp at once. The hope that more packages would follow in the next few days now became more realistic. The news that the first recipient died soon after eating the entire contents of his so-eagerly awaited package shocked all of us. We were told that his stomach just could not take all that food. Since dead people were immediately removed, we were not able to confirm this sad news. However, instructions did go around from knowledgeable prisoners, telling us how to deal with sudden infusions of food and how to avoid all kinds of negative intestinal reactions, including death.

Ciril and I received our first food package in late October. We rationed it very well, only half of a spoonful of roux with each ration of soup. I do not recall anything else in the package except roux, but I am sure there were some other food items included. What to send was a problem because things spoiled in transport. Many packages were received partially open with some contents missing.

It came to our attention a little later that packages from the German-occupied territory or from Germany proper were never opened or checked. For this reason and because of our desperate situation, Ciril decided to write for help to our uncle, a farmer in Moos/Blato near Bleiburg/Pliberk in the Southern Carinthia of the former Austria. I was not in favor of this, still thinking that a letter like that sounded too much like begging. However, Ciril thought that Uncle Lojze Milač would be very glad to help out in this difficult situation.[7]

People knowledgeable about the weather conditions in these parts predicted storms and bad weather starting at the end of September. They were right. A big rain and wind storm hit us one night with unexpected ferocity. To protect our bivouac, we had to act in a hurry. The two men in the middle held the two central tent upright supports, while the four of us facing the walls turned on our bellies and held down the pegs holding the tent in place. Rain was pouring down like mad. The wind was so strong that we expected to be lifted off the ground together with all six inhabitants. If I am not mistaken, such storms are called burja or kraška burja. Even though the storm lasted only a little over an hour, we were exhausted. A few of the tents collapsed. In one of the collapsed tents, the six men never woke up; they slept on until the wetness finally woke them up. We had to admit that the Italian military knew how to secure tents; otherwise this storm would have blown away half of the tents and caused even a bigger disaster.

During another such storm with very heavy rain, which lasted only about twenty minutes, large streams of water suddenly poured down from the surrounding hills. This torrent went right through the middle of the camp and through several tents. A panic resulted. People were screaming that the sea was overflowing and that sea water would wash away our camp and us as well. We all got out of the tents and listened to the sounds of the rushing waters. Our sector, on a slightly higher ground, was not in the path of these rushing waters. During the night, with only a little illumination from the guard towers, everything sounded and appeared more dangerous and more threatening. Eventually the flow of water subsided; the fear, however, remained. We did not know if behind those little hills there was a sea capable of sending waves of water into our camp. We had even more concern for the women's and children's camp located at a lower level some distance away. Fortunately, the next day was sunny, and those flooded were able to dry their few belongings, clothes, and tents.

In our tent we were one person short soon after the flood. Why that individual was transferred elsewhere, I do not remember. Soon after, a transport of prisoners arrived from Concentration Camp Gonars on the Italian mainland, one of whom was assigned to our tent. These new arrivals from Gonars were told that they were being transferred to a nicer facility on an island, known in the past as a tourist attraction. When the man was brought to our tent, he could not believe that this was his "much improved" new home. It was already dark when he arrived. We assigned him the best place in the tent, in the middle between the two outside men. Before he fell asleep, he told us that he would protest in the morning because he was promised, as were all others on his transport, special and improved facilities over those in Gonars. There the prisoners were housed in barracks. Next morning, he scolded us because we were not getting up to wash and brush our teeth. In Gonars, he said, they kept clean and washed regularly. We pointed out to him the direction to the washing facilities, but none of us was willing to accompany him. With his wash towel over the arm, toothpaste and brush in hand, he departed. None of us said anything when he returned, unwashed, teeth not brushed, just with tremendous disappointment. It took only a few days before he joined us in our daily cleaning and killing of lice and other pests. We also realized, after he told us a few things about Concentration Camp Gonars, that our situation was worse; actually there was not even a comparison. It became even more difficult to avoid the nightmare, during the nights and during the days, that this camp was intended to put an end to our existence.

As a rule, we did not have to work. We were too weak for that. Occasionally, however, the capos came and selected people to assemble for work assignments near the main entrance. One day it was my turn. When I was standing in line about to be counted, a person in front of me asked what was my profession. Hearing that my friend Tone and I were students, he advised that we say that we were *zidaro*s (masons), otherwise we would suffer greatly during the work day.[8] It was just bad luck that Tone and I were assigned as one team and not each one with a real *zidaro,* which is what we were planning to arrange with the two *zidaro*s standing in line in front of us. On top of that, we were assigned to a corner section of the barracks under construction. On the job we observed others, trying to imitate as best we could. The real *zidaro*s were secretly laughing and at the same time encouraging us in our efforts. An hour later, the Italian man in charge of the construction, seeing our work, started screaming, "voi niente *zidaro,*" and that was the end of our masonry experience.

Our well-meaning advisors were right. The next job was really tough. First we delivered bricks to the masons. When a truck dumped new bricks, we had to load them on wooden platforms and then run with them to the designated areas; two men for each platform. The soldiers were after us, threatening us with rifle butts, forcing us to run. This activity continued until all bricks were delivered, which took more than two hours. How many teams of two were involved, I do not remember exactly; between eight and ten would be a good guess. We were completely exhausted. After that, we were assigned to digging the foundations. This place was a little cooler, and we were deep enough that we were not easily observed at our work. Tone and I again had a common assignment. A soldier kept appearing from time to time to make sure we were working. One time, seeing us resting, started to yell at us to get back to work. A few minutes later he came back and asked us how much we were being paid per hour. He seemed very surprised hearing the truth. He then told us to rest as much as we wanted and promised that he would give us a sign whenever a supervisor was approaching. Thanks to this soldier we had a relatively easy afternoon. It became clear to us that the Italian firm in charge of the construction was telling soldiers that we were well paid and that it was their duty to see that we earn our lire. The prisoners who were really masons went to work more often. I do not know if they received any compensation for their work or some extra food. The truth was that this was a chance, even though only a very slight possibility, to get in touch with the outside world and arrange for the acquisition of additional food items. What items were used in exchange or who possessed anything to exchange in the first place was not clear to me, but I knew that some black market activity was going on in the camp. Therefore, on return to the camp, the Italian guards searched returning prisoners at the main gate; not all of them of course, but many.

Dysentery was the main cause of death in the men's camp. Starting with the month of October, more and more people died from this disease. It was heartbreaking to see how fast people with dysentery deteriorated. There simply was no way to help those infected. A person with dysentery was not able to keep any food in his system; everything passed through in a matter of minutes or even less. The victims of dysentery walked around—if they were still able to walk—half dazed, not hoping or even caring anymore. They were aware that they were dying. The epidemic was most visible at the latrines. There was almost as much blood as excrement on the boards of the latrines. In addition, because of wasting from starvation, many prisoners suffered from wounds on their hips from long hours of lying in the tents on the rough ground. The initial delivery of straw had long since ceased to serve its purpose. On one occasion I observed a man squatting next to me cleaning pus out of open wounds on both sides of his hip bones with his bare fingers. The only way for him to rest or sleep in his tent was on his back. He was not optimistic anymore about the possibility of survival. The latrines were now already overflowing at one end, something that caused problems during the night. Dysentery does not wait. While trying to reach the latrines in a hurry, some people missed the boards. I saw one man slip on the boards; he sank with his left leg into the stench up to his knee. Where this unfortunate man spent his night and how was a big question; he certainly did not sleep in his tent.

By early December, the camp reached a state of complete disaster. In our sector, those unable to walk were brought their soups by their tent mates. Our soup distributors allowed that, since by this time they knew almost everybody by name. The only control, saying the name, was sufficient when presenting the second mess can. In desperation, in a few cases, people did not report a dead prisoner at least for one meal distribution and ate the dead person's portion. We did not walk around the camp anymore; we were too weak for that. We only got up for the two daily musters; the rest of the time we rested in our tents.

One day the capo came running into our section saying semi-confidentially that a collection of shoes was available and that he needed a person from each tent to bring the shoes to the camp for distribution. I was selected for this assignment from our tent as the most fit of the six. The capo collected about 20–25 people. As we dragged ourselves toward the assembly point at the main gate, we tried to guess where the shoes were coming from and what kind to expect—probably Italian military boots, used, of course. We were taken via two trucks a short distance away. There, instead of shoes, we faced a mountain of coffins. Even though we were fully aware of the multitude of deaths each day, this huge pile of coffins was still a tremendous shock and another rude awakening to the reality of our situation. For a while we just stood there, looking and saying nothing. The capo made some attempts to apologize for his lie, explaining that he had to produce porters for these coffins in a hurry. The distance we had to carry these coffins was not long, maybe two hundred yards. We were weak, however, and the coffins were very primitive and very heavy. I was assigned to the front, left position. With my co-undertaker on the front right side, I exchanged a few words. He kept insisting that each coffin contained more than one dead person, which was why these coffins felt so heavy. Looking at my partner, a skeleton, I could not avoid thinking that his turn for this last journey was very near. It is quite possible that similar thoughts also went through his mind when he was looking at me. Our team of four had to take several trips before the job was done. We just dropped these coffins at the assigned area and left without a prayer or any kind of funeral ceremony.[9] I do remember that from the place we dropped these coffins, we had a good look at part of the coast and of the sea. Needless to say that on return to the camp and to our tents not much explanation was necessary. Nobody believed anymore that something positive would ever happened here. The number of one day's coffins was not a symbolic but a realistic indication of the things to come for all of us in the not-so-distant future. . . .[10]

Part II

Early in December, around the time of St. Nicolas's Feast, a substantial number of Italian soldiers came to our sector and, under the command of officers, started searching selected tents. In a few places they removed the tents and dug with bayonets into the ground. After half a day's work they left, finding nothing as far as we were able to observe. We were kept in our own areas, waiting to be searched. Our tent was not one of those selected for scrutiny. Soon rumors circulated that photos of our camp appeared in the newspapers in Switzerland.

Around the middle of the month we received some distinguished visitors: sixteen officers, eight in Italian military uniforms, eight in other uniforms including that of the Red Cross. If they examined the prisoners in the entire camp, I do not remember. In our sector we were ordered to stand in front of our tents, waiting for examination. When my turn came, one officer squeezed one of my cheeks, gave me a soft, friendly slap across the face, saying something like, "You are still O.K." The officer checking me was an Italian; the others were standing by. Everybody in the group took a lot of notes. Their isolated comments gave us no clue what they were searching for.

The lowest point in this camp was reached on Christmas Day 1942. On that day we observed the removal of the most dead prisoners in a single day. The situation was very scary. Was the end that close? Yes, we were fully convinced that our end was just a question of time.[11]

Around this time Ciril became sick with dysentery. Whether the cause was the general deterioration of health, the hygiene situation in the camp, or the slight mold on the top of his roux would be difficult to guess. He started disintegrating at a fast pace. One of the prisoners, Mr. Ukmar, who had friends in the kitchen, brought him grounds from the fig coffee, the only treatment available in such cases. These grounds did not help. Everything he consumed came through almost immediately. He had to spend a lot of time at the latrines. I often accompanied him there to prevent possible accidents in case he might faint. Ciril suffered without expressions of grief or pain; he became fully resigned to his fate.

The day after Christmas brought the first signs of hope. A few prisoners were notified they would be returning home; a few others, mostly those in severely deteriorating condition, were selected for transfer to other camps on the Italian mainland for recuperation before release, they were told. Maybe that special committee of sixteen officers who visited us in the middle of December did recognize what was going on in this camp and recommended changes. Hopes were raised after we realized in the next few days that the first releases were not isolated cases. That week and the next, several prisoners were released.

On 6 January 1943, I was standing next to my tent in the mid-morning, when our capo came to me and said, "You are going home." My initial extraordinary happiness almost immediately changed to disappointment, because Ciril was not included in this happy message. In the tent, after some consultation, we decided that Ciril should go home instead of me. Everybody was of the opinion that his turn to go home would come soon and because of his worsening health, he should go home first. Ciril objected at first but eventually consented. Our capo would have to be convinced that this switch would be acceptable to him and that nothing would be mentioned to the Italian authorities. Fortunately, late in the afternoon the capo came again and announced Ciril's release as well as the release of several other prisoners.

Those who were not to be released yet kept coming to our tent to give us messages for their folks at home. We tried to memorize the names and addresses of their families and relatives in Ljubljana.[12] The man from Gonars had special instruction for his family. So did the navy lieutenant who was assigned to our tent only a few days before when someone was transferred elsewhere. The lieutenant wanted to make sure that I would not forget what he wanted to tell his wife about his illegal imprisonment at Concentration Camp Rab, so that she would be able to take some action. As a Yugoslav navy officer, he was entitled to a different kind of imprisonment. All these instructions were given mostly to me, because Ciril was too weak to pay much attention to these messages or to retain all this information.

The last night in the tent was long; we did not get much sleep; we were full of anxieties that the authorities might change their minds. Daylight finally came. There was nothing to pack. It was cold and we were shivering even though only a month before we received our Hubertus coats in the last package. We said good-bye to our co-prisoners, promising that we would do everything possible for their release. There were no tears; nobody had any tears left.

After we assembled near the main entrance and went through many checks and double checks (I realized then that a swap between Ciril and me would not have succeeded) by our section officers, who carefully examined each individual and compared the information with their papers, we finally left the camp. Many prisoners watched our departure and kept calling, "Do not forget us!"

But we were not free yet. The next step was a stop at the quarantine, where a complete delousing, removal of hair, washing of bodies and clothes took place. We went through this procedure completely naked. When we came out of the shower, the last of the many stops, and exited at the other end, we had to approach a young girl, also a prisoner, in our naked state, fully aware of our deteriorating bodies and all their parts. It was embarrassing. The young lady, who handed each one of us a blanket for warmth and gradual drying while we were waiting for our clothes, dealt with this situation very well. She did not appear to notice anything. We then stood around her, covered only with blankets and listened to her reports about the recent departing transports. When we got back our clothes, most of them had large burned spots, because the heat had to be very high to kill everything we brought with us from the camp.

The Italian army trucks took us back to the Rab harbor. This time it was late morning, cloudy and cold. Our mental state was such that we did not pay much attention to the place, much less admire the surroundings even though we realized that this place and its people had nothing to do with what had happened to us during the last few months. Then the Italian navy took over again. We were fairly gently lowered into the ship's dungeon, a familiar place. At least this time there was room to sit down.

When we arrived at Rijeka/Fiume harbor, the sailors took positions on both sides of the ladders and lifted us first out of the dungeon and then to the upper deck. We were too weak to climb up by ourselves. Apparently the sailors already knew that. The same procedure took place when they lifted us off the ship over a slight incline to the main harbor place. Many people stood around and looked in disbelief. A few of them were crying. I do not know if they were Croatian or Italian or a mixture of both. The Italian sailors did their job with tact, efficiency, and careful handling of each individual.

We arrived in Ljubljana late in the afternoon. There were only a few minor procedures involved before we were escorted through the main exit of the very familiar Belgijska kasarna to our freedom. The last thing the Italian officer asked were our names. I had to help Ciril correctly state his name as Milač Ciril di Giovanni, the Italian version of the name.[13] Now we were free, with release papers in our hands.

From the Belgijska kasarna to our home in Bežigrad was a long way. With no hair, no head cover, and burned and wornout clothes, we presented a terrible picture. Ciril was so weak that he had to lean on me; therefore our progress was slow.

This was a Sunday afternoon, a cloudy, miserable day; not many people were on the streets. However, when here and there pedestrians spotted us, they came over to us, asking where we were coming from; many women embraced us. It became very clear to us that people did not know much, if anything, about Concentration Camp Rab and the conditions there. Those who had relatives in camp Rab were shocked, and many burst into tears. They inquired about several individuals imprisoned on Rab, but we, unfortunately, did not know any of the persons named. Seeing the reaction of the people, especially those who had relatives on Rab, we tried to sound a little more encouraging and positive by saying that the situation now seemed to be improving there, even though we were not very convinced about that ourselves.[14]

On the overpass over the railroad tracks on the former Tyrševa cesta, a schoolmate of mine from the Classical Gymnasium in Ljubljana, Ms. Spazzapan, saw us. At the sight of two such deteriorating figures, she just stepped back and, with tears in her eyes, asked us where we were coming from. She promised to inform everybody in the school of our return. We were almost home when our neighbor, Mrs. Tomažič, spotted us on the Vodovodna cesta on her way to relatives in another part of the city. She embraced us again and again. Mrs. Tomažič told us that at home they did not know anything about our release.[15]

Then there were only ten more minutes, and we were ringing the doorbell at our home.

CHAPTER SEVEN

Days at Home

January 1943–June 1944

❧

At Stalingrad the situation of the German Sixth Army deteriorated day by day. Against the advice of military commanders who were in favor of strategic pull-back, Hitler ordered his troops to stand fast. In November 1942, the entire German Sixth Army found itself surrounded by Soviet troops.

In the West, Hilter ordered on 8 October 1942 the execution of all Dieppe commando prisoners.

The British break-through at El Alamein started on 1 November 1942. On 12 November the Eighth Army entered Tobruk, on 20 November, Benghazi. Operation Torch, the American invasion on the French West Africa, which started on 8 November 1942, all of a sudden presented Germans and Italians in North Africa with a second front. The end of the war in Africa was in sight.

In Asia, British and Indian troops entered Burma, December 1942.

Mother opened the door. I can still see her. Her face, full of deep and rough traces of suffering caused by the events of the last three years, lit up and in a split second wiped away her terrible memories. She embraced us again and again, with tears of happiness running down her face. Although we were still dazed, we knew now that we were finally home. Marija, hearing something unusual happening at the front door, came running downstairs from the upper floor. Seeing us entering the vestibule, she called Father, who was resting upstairs. In a minute, in the middle of the vestibule, we were together again, all five of us.

Ciril's serious health situation had to be explained first. Both of us had to dispose of our outfits from top to bottom. Although we did not have many extra clothes at home because of the war, everything we came home with was of no use anymore. After a shower and some soft food, not too much at the start, we both went to rest in our room. Ciril was now properly equipped for any intestinal abnormalities and was therefore able to rest in a more relaxed fashion. Since we were both very tired, we provided only the basic information about our sudden and unexpected release. That first evening, Father took me into my parents' bedroom and there I saw my books and notes of my Latin assignment exactly as I left them on 28 June 1942 when the Italian military took me away. Father did not permit the removal of my school work from that small table, insisting that these materials had to stay there and be ready for my return.

The next morning, Mother, Ciril, and I took the city bus to downtown Ljubljana. Though we were then dressed in our best, our general appearance shocked everybody on the bus. As on the previous day, all those with family members or relatives in the various Italian concentration camps were very much concerned. We tried to assure them that, according to our last days' experiences on Rab, there was reason to believe that improvements were in the works. Ciril was admitted to the hospital because of his serious intestinal problems. There were no visible or immediately detectable negative signs in my case except the consequences of starvation; therefore, I was not admitted to the hospital. At the Classical Gymnasium, which I visited after the hospital, they registered me into my class and suggested that I stay home for at least a week for recuperation.

During the following few days I visited all the relatives of my co-prisoners on Rab who had provided me with names and addresses. In addition to questions about the well-being of their loved ones, most people asked on what kind of petition I was released from the concentration camp. I was able to provide only a few guesses but nothing definite. When I finally located the wife of the Yugoslav navy officer who was assigned to our tent on Rab a few days before our release, she told me that I brought her the first news that her husband had been transferred to Camp Rab.

My return to school was not a success. I was very anxious to catch up with the others, since I had missed more that half of the school year already. One very embarrassing problem was that as soon as a class session started, I almost immediately fell asleep; professors and students just let me rest and sleep. After three days of trying, the authorities decided that I was not yet fit to attend classes, and I was sent home for an additional three weeks of recuperation. It was not until the beginning of February 1943 when Ciril, who was released from the hospital after two weeks, and I returned to our respective schools on a regular basis.

A year before my difficulties started, I had been transferred to another class of the same grade at the gymnasium and as a consequence did not have sufficient opportunities to develop any close friendships. My best friend from Bishop's Gymnasium, Tone Ravnik, who returned from Concentration Camp Gonars a few months before,[1] was unfortunately in another class. My absence from classes for more than half a year made me feel almost like a stranger. Few, if any, classmates asked questions about my experiences of the last few months. I should add that I was one of the last in class released from a concentration camp; all others returned before me. So my story of the concentration camp was not a novelty anymore although my classmates did not realize that Rab was entirely different from the concentration camps on the Italian mainland. Why there were no questions about my experiences with the partisans was a slight puzzle for me.

I also saw sharp political differences among my classmates. These were the results of split between the students who were active in Catholic organizations and congregations and those who sympathized or participated in the Liberation Front activities. This, of course, is a simplistic point of view or description of the situation. What disturbed me the most was, that the ideas of 1941, when we were almost as one determined to work toward the defeat of the occupation forces, of the foreigners occupying our land, had been lost somewhere in the struggle between the left and right. The people were split as to what kind of system we would prefer to live under after the war, a western type of democracy or the Soviet system. Although these lines were not always clearly defined, stated, or advertised and were very often intentionally disguised in order to cover the true goals, it became more or less clear from what was happening in my classes that polarization was now extreme and the bridge between the two groups destroyed. Here and there during break periods, fist fights broke out between the supporters of the two groups.

A few weeks after my return home, I was approached by my own underground group to go back on active status. At first I was very hesitant to get involved again, partially on the basis of what I had learned and experienced the last few months. However, eventually I consented. The key argument in favor of rejoining was my liaison's conviction that even the most minimal information about enemy troop movements would help the Western Powers in their efforts to liberate Europe, including Yugoslavia. In the spring of 1943, this point of view had strong credibility.

Around this time it was already generally known that the Liberation Front declared itself the only "legitimate" organization in opposition to the enemy. All other groups, organizations, and underground efforts were declared illegal. Whoever organized or participated in any underground organization outside of the Liberation Front activities would be considered a traitor and dealt with accordingly.[2] These kind of declarations were not taken seriously by the majority of those not associated with the Liberation Front. Who gave the Liberation Front the authority for such decisions and on what grounds? The Yugoslav government-in-exile was in London and did not give the Liberation Front any kind of authority or representation. Even to the average person it was clear at the time that many underground organizations were in existence and had different programs and goals. Since all activities had to be conducted in secrecy, mostly by personal contacts, detailed goals of the various clandestine groups, including the goals of the Liberation Front, were difficult to verify. The fact is that I did not fully realize at the time that pro-Soviet, pro-communist sentiments were strong and getting stronger.

I had difficulties catching up with my studies. There was so much material to master, and new assignments were added daily. In science, where I experienced the most difficulties, my friend Tone Ravnik came to help. He sacrificed his time to help me through these difficulties. My professors were, in general, understanding and willing to wait until I was ready. That was not the case with chemistry. On the first day of my return, I was called to answer difficult questions and immediately received a failing grade. After that, this professor just ignored me though I went to him several times explaining that I was ready to answer questions on material covered in the current year. I could never understand why this individual treated me in such a fashion. He was new at the school, never saw me before, and he knew that I came from Concentration Camp Rab. Finally, a long-time friend of my mother's, Dr. Angela Piskernik, who was on the faculty at the school, intervened on my behalf, and I was given a chance to take another exam. I must add that all questions asked on that occasion were very easy; this problem was finally solved.

I also resumed piano studies with professor Anton Ravnik at the Academy of Music in Ljubljana. I immediately realized that my piano classmates had made a lot of progress during my absence. With determination and hard work I tried to bridge the gap. One day, while walking through the city with a new book of piano technical studies, my next challenge, I met my classmate from the Classical Gymnasium, Vida Lajovic, who also studied at the Academy of Music. When I proudly presented her my new assignments in piano studies, she told me to my great disappointment that she had just completed these studies. I realized then that I had a long way to go.

Professor Anton Ravnik was a great teacher. Every step of the way he opened for me new doors to understanding music, to understanding the secrets of what is beautiful in music, of the intricacies and individual idiosyncrasies of each composition. In addition, Professor Ravnik encouraged me to attend as many concerts as possible—standing room for students in concert halls and in the opera house was still very inexpensive—and discussed these concerts with me, thus providing me new insights into this wonderful art.

My parents were always very supportive of my music although they were somewhat worried as to how I would make a living. My father often said that as a pianist I knew enough already. To convince him otherwise, I invited my classmate Fedor Ražem, a star pianist at the Academy of Music, to my house to play a few pieces from his rich repertory. My father was very impressed. On another occasion, by accident, I caught my father leaving the Academy's concert hall where

each Friday afternoon students were performing. I was delighted to see how interested he was. When we were walking home, he admitted that I had some distance
to go before being equal or close to the others. Without a question, piano and related music studies were most dear to my heart.

While we were in Concentration Camp Rab, the Italian military surrounded
Ljubljana with barbed wire to exercise better control over the traffic in and out of
the city. They completed this task on 23 September 1942. From that day on it was
very difficult to get permission for travel outside the city, which, in turn, resulted
in additional food shortages. It took skill, connections, and bargaining experience
to acquire some extras even before the enclosure, because the land owners south of
the city were, from the beginning of the war, often visited and pressured by city
folks to sell or to trade food for money or other valuables. The food we purchased
on the allowable rations was hardly sufficient for day-to-day needs.

After our return from Concentration Camp Rab, we also learned about another new development, the establishment of the Village Guards. They were established in the Italian zone for the protection of homes and villages. The Italian
occupation forces, either unable or unwilling to provide the required protection,
most often reacted in their countermeasures not against the partisan intruders,
who needed food and other supplies for their existence, but against the villages for
helping the visiting partisan forces. After such intrusions, the partisans retreated
to their more secure and defendable areas in the woods and in the hills. On such
visits the partisans also dealt in various ways, including executions, with their real
or imagined enemies, actions which brought fear into many isolated locations.[3]
The villagers, therefore, took protective action into their own hands. This, however, was possible only with permission and assistance of the occupation forces.
Thus, the nucleus of an internal armed conflict at the time of occupation came
into being.

During January 1943, we looked for as much information as possible about
the Eastern front, about the life and death struggle for Stalingrad. Except for the
battlegrounds in Africa, where the front lines were moving back and forth for a
while, the German defeat at Stalingrad was the first sign that the Germans could
be stopped and eventually pushed back. Losing an entire army, thousands of men
and all the armament, was a defeat of major proportions.[4] We had to rely primarily on German and Italian sources for information; however, there were also ways
to get the strictly forbidden radio reports coming from the BBC and the Voice of
America. A few months later, the following May, came the capitulation of German and Italian forces in North Africa, a defeat of a disastrous consequences for
them.[5] When the Allied Forces, British and American, landed in Sicily on 10 July
1943, the first landing by the Western Forces on the European continent, it must
have been clear even to the disbeliever that the fortunes of this war were turning
in favor of the Western and Soviet alliance.

During the month of August, Ciril and I received notices to report to the terrain. We were ready to go, but our parents were very much against it. In their opinion, there were just too few details, how, with whom, or where we were going. Ciril and I had to decide: Should we go without the approval of our parents or wait for further information and clarification? Except for our liaison, we knew only two other persons in the organization, for security reasons, of course. One young man, Bogomil Jakus, who resided nearby, told us that he decided to go. He left at 11:00 A.M. on the day we were supposed to depart at 2:00 in the afternoon. Our departure, however, was postponed, because the link to the group on the terrain was cut. Bogomil Jakus's group was the last one leaving the city during this period of recruitment; then our link was closed.

The sudden and unexpected arrival and passage through Ljubljana of strong German Armed Forces Units was a major event during the last week of August 1943.[6] The presence of German troops offered a more interesting job for us in the underground. For the first time we were now collecting information about the German Armed Forces, their insignia, their numbers, their strength, armament, and the direction of their movements and travel. This was much more interesting than collecting the seldom-changing information about the Italian Forces stationed in the city or observing and describing a person or persons coming or leaving this or that house without even a hint of why this kind of information was important for the war effort.

The first week of September 1943, the people from Dravograd in our house received an unexpected visitor in German uniform. He was a very young soldier from the same village where our female resident was born. Though he was a native Slovene from a strong Slovene family in Aich/Dob, near Bleiburg/Pliberk, he was, to our great surprise and disappointment, thoroughly indoctrinated and fully convinced that the German Nazi philosophies, war plans, and war objectives were right and just. He had no doubts about the German final victory. Counterarguments meant nothing to him. We could see how a thorough indoctrination away from home and family circles succeeded in producing an entirely new kind of citizen. He was not allowed to reveal what his assignment was while in Ljubljana. He would only say that he was commanding a small machine-gun group.[7]

On 8 September 1943, Italy capitulated. In the very early morning hours of the next day the Italian military facilities near our house were already surrounded by small German units strategically placed at each entrance/exit of these facilities. With machine guns pointing at the entrances, they disarmed every military person leaving the place. Observing these activities from a safe distance, we noticed at the main gate our visitor of a few days before, firmly in command of his unit and doing his job efficiently and calmly. The German helmets were hiding his and his troops, youthful appearances very well. There was no resistance on the part of the Italians to disarmament procedures. The Italian soldiers were otherwise free to come and go. The officers retained their side arms. That was also the last time we saw our acquaintance from the village of Aich/Dob. Where he went after this assignment in Ljubljana or whether he survived the war, I never found out.

Later in the morning, I was on a city bus going downtown. The bus was stopped by a German patrol, and all Italian military were ordered to exit. Outside they were immediately disarmed in a not-too-friendly manner with cool, dry commands. Observing all this from the bus, we almost felt sorry for what was happening to this still-proud military, despite the fact that they had been occupying our land. The German units in the city during these initial days were small in numbers and hardly noticeable among the population in comparison to thousands of Italian military, who were now departing south toward Italy as best they could.

The temporary break of authority, the partial interregnum after the announcement of the Italian capitulation, resulted in some important and consequential developments. The city was still surrounded by barbed wire, but the exit/entrance blocks were no longer guarded. Naturally, the traffic in and out increased immediately; after all, this was a rare opportunity of uncertain duration. Indeed, in a day or two the city control points were again guarded and the departures were no longer possible.[8]

We, the former refugees from the German zone, had to accept with anxiety and also fear the new reality of coming under the German administration. The protection we had had in the Italian zone of Slovenia would no longer exist. What the Germans would do was now the question.

Many of us, maybe even the majority of the population, in our naiveté or wishful thinking, were expecting an Allied landing anywhere on the Northern Adriatic coast, either on the Italian or the pre-war Yugoslav territory. That seemed logical since the Italians were now on the side of the Western Alliance. The actual events in our own land took another turn, however.

The first depressing news that reached us in Ljubljana was the defeat of the Slovene National Clandestine Resistance Forces[9] at the village of Grčarice. These forces were encamped in Grčarice expecting reinforcement by the Serb units from not-so-distant Gorski kotar. Instead, they were surrounded by strong partisan units, which secured for themselves the help of the Italian artillery crews and their equipment. Pounded by the Italian artillery, the Slovene National Clandestine Resistance Forces at Grčarice were, after a three-day battle and after running out of ammunition, forced to surrender.[10] For most of us it was hard to accept this news. Most depressing was the information that during the battle Bogomil Jakus had been killed by the Italian artillery, together with several other defenders. It also became very clear that Ciril and I would have been part of the group at Grčarice had we departed on that afternoon when Bogomil left in the morning. The surrender at Grčarice with all its consequences took place on 10 September 1943.

Only a few days later more disastrous news reached Ljubljana. The partisan brigades, again with the help of the Italian artillery crews, forced the surrender of the *Vaške straže* (Village Guards) and a few other anti-communist units at the castle of Turjak.[11] Thus, the partisans successfully eliminated two of their most active opponents. With their fast and, as it turned out later, murderous actions, they secured for themselves a strong position in case of an invasion by the Allies into the territory of Slovenia. They also confirmed that there was no possibility for any kind of joint action among various resistance groups against the enemy. With the acquisition of the Italian armament and elimination of most of their domestic opponents, the partisans became much stronger in many areas and the talk about the "liberated territories" became more realistic.

The castle of Turjak fell on 19 September 1943. A few days later, when walking home from downtown Ljubljana, I heard artillery activity coming from the castle. As I found out later, the defeated Village Guards and some remnants of the Slovene National Clandestine Resistance Forces were fleeing before advancing partisans to their only possible refuge, the city of Ljubljana. They had to turn themselves in to what was supposed to be their real enemy, the German occupation forces. The sight of these defeated, wounded, raggedy individuals walking through the city streets after the surrender was depressing, as a friend of mine told me later that evening. The old Roman saying *vae victis* applied in this particular case to the fullest.

The defeat of the anti-communist military forces by the end of September 1943 was a major disaster. For the communists it was a sweet victory full of cruel vengeance. In a war, unexpected and cataclysmic changes usually have far-reaching consequences. This was the case in Slovenia in September 1943.

We waited with apprehension for what the new authority would bring. Fortunately, Germany was no longer at the height of its power. In the second half of 1943, Germany already suffered three major defeats or setbacks—at Stalingrad, in North Africa, and with the loss of its Italian ally. It was probably due to these serious setbacks that the Germans allowed the formation of a new anti-communist force, the *Domobranska legija* (Home Defense Legion), later renamed *Domobranci* (Home Defenders). The core of this new force were the soldiers and officers of the *Vaške straže* (Village Guards), who sought protection in Ljubljana in September. The approval date of Home Defenders forces came at the end of September 1943.

The goal of this initially strictly military organization was to defend and protect towns and villages in the former Italian zone against the military arm of the Liberation Front, the partisans. As before under the Italians, this was possible only with the support of Germany, which retained control over the Home Defenders through select German liaison officers. Home Defenders, however, were not obligated in any way to assist Germany in its war efforts. Nevertheless, they did indirectly aid them because the Germans were able to limit their military actions and protection to the most vital railroad and other communication links while they left the rest of their newly occupied territory to the care of the Home Defenders.

With the encouragement and assistance of many (mostly conservative) groups, the Home Defenders soon achieved substantial recruitment gains, especially outside the major centers. Thus, a strong and well-led military force was soon in place. Not much later, a move into the political arena followed. Consequently, two authorities came into existence. Home Defenders held the authority at the daily operations level; the Germans, primarily through the actions by the Gestapo, exercised control on the highest level. It did not take long before certain-age groups of men started receiving call-up letters from the Home Defenders to report to active duty. Pressures also came from acquaintances and friends to take sides. My closest friend, Tone Ravnik, joined during the first recruitment drive.

These pressures persuaded Ciril a few months later to join the Home Defenders as well. I understood his decision was made after much inner searching and difficulty. We were now in two different camps, both of us restrained by a certain confidentiality required by our group loyalties. We realized that we were heading in two different directions and away from, what had been up to then, our inseparable life.

The disasters at Grčarice and Turjak greatly affected our underground organization. However, activities resumed soon, and for a while it looked like we were making a contribution to the Western Allies in Italy with the information we collected. At least that was what I was told by my liaison person. The invasion of the Allied forces in the North Adriatic territory seemed less and less likely because, in our impatient view, the progress of the British and American forces in Italy was much too slow. The Germans were still very strong, though they were fighting on two fronts and expecting a third one.

At the beginning of October 1943, the so-called Kočevski process took place. The captured leaders of Grčarice and Turjak were put on trial; of the twenty-one leaders, sixteen were condemned to death and five to forced labor. I was especially hurt upon learning that my childhood guardian and friend, Lieutenant Drago Tomažič, captured at Grčarice, was among those executed in Mozelj on 12 October 1943.[12]

There were more and more arrests in Ljubljana. The popular opinion was that those arrested by the Home Defenders still had a slight chance for release. This, however, was not the case if people were arrested by the Gestapo. One day the news reached our family that Dr. Angela Piskernik, my mother's friend, was arrested and waiting in jail for the next transport to a prison camp in Germany. My mother went to plead for her release to the director of the Ljubljana police, whom she knew from the time of the Yugoslav administration of the Carinthian plebiscite territory, 1918–1920. Her pleading was unsuccessful; mother came home very depressed that day.

The new authority, trying to convince the younger generation why the communist system of the Soviet Union would not be beneficial in our country, introduced in all high schools a new subject, commonly referred to as "Lectures about Communism." At the Classical Gymnasium in Ljubljana I enjoyed these lectures. They were not anti-communist propaganda but explanations of the various ideologies of the nineteenth and twentieth centuries with some emphasis on Marx and his philosophies. I was very much impressed by the broad knowledge of these law-trained professionals discussing the different trends and philosophies of the nineteenth- and twentieth-century philosophers, economists, and thinkers who laid the foundations for the formation of our contemporary society.

Calls to join the Home Defenders were frequent. Among others, I was invited to volunteer for the officers' school in the region of Primorska. The pressures were on the rise from various sides. A setback for the Home Defenders in the spring of 1944 was the German demand that members take an oath of allegiance, the text of which contained these words: ". . . that I will . . . in joint battles . . . against bandits and communism, as well as against their allies, carry out my responsibilities faithfully. . . ."[13]

I was glad that Ciril did not take this oath; his unit was not selected to take part. I felt pain and despair that day, knowing that many of my friends, acquaintances, and schoolmates who participated had no intention of pledging any alliance to the Third Reich nor did the majority of those taking part. However, the Germans did not allow any choice. It was agonizing to see a detachment of the SS marching the Home Defenders to and from the oath-taking ceremony, even though we had to admire the parade perfection of the SS troops. This oath took place on 20 April 1944, just before British and American Forces entered Rome on 4 June and only a few days before the greatest day of the war, "The Longest Day," as it is now referred to, the Allied Invasion of Normandy, which started on 6 June 1944.

I finished my high school studies the first week of June 1944. The "maturity" examination we all had to take in addition to the completed curricula work and exams went surprisingly well. It was obvious that our high school professors were very pleased with our accomplishments. The Director of the school, Marko Bajuk, gave a warm and encouraging farewell speech. With our class administrator, Professor Kopriva, who guided us during the last year through some interesting but difficult works of Greek classical literature, we enjoyed the customary dinner, where according to tradition, we were privileged to include a little wine as well. This "maturity" dinner was a memorable affair. We were together at a friendly and cordial evening for the last time. There were several parallel classes in the last year in gymnasium, but our class had the fewest students. In the class photograph, in addition to Professor Kopriva, there are only nine students.[14]

The days after graduation were days of concern. I was still undecided whether to enroll full time at the Academy of Music or to try for an academic career at the university in one of the humanities or in law school. I still had time because registration and other procedures took place in the month of September. I was undecided even though my heart was taking me in the direction of music. Some of my classmates had made their decisions a year or two before and were now looking with great expectations into the future even though the war clouded every day of our lives. The dangers were everywhere: what would the future bring?

For me these uncertainties were suddenly interrupted during an intermission at a concert. A member of our underground, K. Ž., brought me the message that we would depart to the field the day after next very early in the morning to join one of the units of the Slovene National Clandestine Resistance Forces in the region of Primorska. He gave me the names of a few others who were scheduled to depart at the same time. My parents reluctantly accepted my decision since at that time it was clear that sooner or later I would be recruited into something, willing or unwilling. We departed on the train in a southerly direction. Our leader apparently had the proper documents for all of us; we passed all controls without difficulty. At the city of Postojna we left the train and went to a civilian authority, where we signed some papers. I was very hesitant to sign, suspecting the possibility of joining something I did not really wish to join. I was told that these papers would be destroyed as soon as we left for the field; the papers were necessary during our stay in the city. The waiting in an uncertain situation was very unpleasant. There were strong German forces stationed here guarding railroad and other communication links toward Trieste/Trst. We could not move around. Night and day, one could hear rifle- and machine-gun fire. We were wondering if there was really a place in the hills for more and more military formations. Everything seemed to be ablaze twenty-four hours a day. One night a small group of partisans advanced undetected almost into the middle of the city, where (allegedly) a high-ranking partisan was imprisoned. During the fierce battle that followed, the partisans had to retreat, but everybody became aware that the city was in reality surrounded and thus constantly exposed to intrusions. The Germans in the city did not get involved in this kind of skirmish unless they were directly attacked.

After almost a week of waiting to join the Slovene National Clandestine Forces in the region, some of us were instructed to return home, not as a group but one by one, to wait for further instructions. Our forces in the hills apparently left this area for strategic reasons, therefore, joining this force at this time was no longer possible.

I returned home by train one afternoon without difficulty. When I left the railroad station in Ljubljana, I noticed a schoolmate of mine, M. K., walking on the other side toward Hotel Miklič just across from the railroad station.[15] I waved to him. He either did not see me or did not want to see me at that moment.

The following day a member of our underground brought me a British pistol with the explanation that each of us will hide it for one night until we give it to our military groups in the field. I accepted it and took it, covered with a newspaper, into my room upstairs. . . .

CHAPTER EIGHT

Gestapo Prison

June 1944–September 1944

❦

Arrest! Need it be said that it is a breaking point in your life
a bolt of lightning which has scored a direct hit on you?
—Aleksandr I. Solzhenitsyn, *The Gulag Archipelago*

The news on 2 February 1943 was the German defeat at Stalingrad, the loss of an entire army group. Most people in Europe felt this to be a decisive turning point of the war for two reasons. First, the supposed invincibility of the German armed forces was gone forever, and second, the tremendous loss of men and material and the demoralization that must have overcome the German nation could not have been without negative consequences.

On 26 April 1943, the Katyn Forest massacre of the Polish officers was discovered near Smolensk. It is now established that the executioners were the Soviets. This massacre brought some initial disharmony to the Allies-Soviet relations.

The Axis forces were defeated in North Africa on 12 May 1943. Less than two months later, on 9 July, American and British forces invaded Sicily and on 3 September the Italian mainland. Italy capitulated on 8 September 1943.

The Tehran Conference with Roosevelt, Churchill, and Stalin started on 28 November 1943. Not only wartime but post-war issues were discussed, and several long lasting agreements were reached.

In 1944 it became clear to most people that in Europe the Allies had the initiative. On 22 January, the Allied forces landed at Anzio and on 4 June entered Rome.

The long-expected invasion of Europe, Operation Overlord, started in the early morning hours of 6 June 1944 by air and sea from the bases in England. An armada of immense size in all categories was directed toward Normandy on the coast of France to achieve the liberation of Europe.

The door opened; the light went on; I woke up and I saw a well-dressed man in a dark business suit enter my room. Behind him was my mother and two more men. The first thing I heard was the statement in German, "You are arrested in the name of the Third Reich." I lifted myself up from my primitive wooden bed, dressed for the night only in boxer shorts. I was told to get dressed. One of the three men immediately took my bed apart, finding nothing; another saw a pamphlet next to my bed with a picture of a hammer and sickle on it and grabbed it with great satisfaction. The third man said something to him and the man threw the pamphlet back on the small table. I was asked if I had any arms and ammunition. I pointed to the bookshelves, where three Italian hand grenades were behind the books, carefully secured with wire. He took the grenades without a comment.

The night before, around midnight, I had a strange feeling. I got up, took the British pistol from the table, and went downstairs. Outside the house there was a huge pile of corn husks. I dropped the British pistol behind that pile and went to bed. When the Gestapo men entered my room it was 3:00 A.M. on 29 June 1944, the time of my arrest. As the three men continued to search my room, I was granted permission to wash up in the bathroom located between my bedroom and my parents'. Going out, I saw my father standing in the darkness behind his bedroom door. In a split second I told him about the British pistol, its hiding place, and about the next day pick-up arrangement. Then I stepped into the bathroom just in time as one of the Gestapo men came after me, realizing that there was a possible escape over the balcony into the garden. He then stood next to me until I was done. What my mother was asking these unwelcome intruders, I do not know. I was hoping that she was talking to them as little as possible.

When I left my bedroom accompanied by these men, I stepped toward my parents' bedroom to say goodbye to my father. The Gestapo men maintained a respectful distance at that moment. When we were embracing, my father said only, "Don't tell them anything," and then we shook hands. These were the last words my father ever said to me. Downstairs I embraced my mother; she couldn't stop crying. We then went out of the house into the doubly unknown darkness. The Gestapo men put me in the back seat of a very nice limousine; one of them was seated next to me, and off we went. Unfortunately, I did not understand what they were saying among themselves. This comfortable ride did not last very long; soon the limousine stopped at the main prison gate in the center of Ljubljana.

Unceremoniously, I was registered, turned over to a prison guard, a German, and led upstairs through many locked doors until we reached the second floor, the first room on the right, room 147. The sound of the turning key in the middle of the night, the uncertainty of what was behind that door, how long I would be there, or whether there would be a way out, all this went through my mind while the guard was busy with his keys. The door opened with a harsh sound. In the interior, lit only by the corridor lights, I immediately noticed an unshaven person lifting his head, staring at me with great surprise. The cell was a single with a single prison bed. What would the two of us do there? This uncertainty lasted only a split second, because the guard just pushed me into the room and locked the door behind me. There was no place for me to lie down, so I just stood there trying to orient myself with the help of a little light that came from above the covered prison cell window. Then I heard an unexpected question, "What are you doing here?" At that moment, despite the darkness, I recognized the man. It was Dore Matul, a railroad official and the conductor of the men's singing society "Ljubljanski zvon." My brother Ciril was an enthusiastic member of that choir. I had met Dore Matul a few times but only for brief moments. Matul, realizing this impossible situation and the shock I must have been in, moved over and invited me to share his bed. He almost immediately fell asleep again, something I could not do at all that night. I got up two hours later and tried to rest on a chair. In the early morning hours, two prison helpers brought in a mattress and threw it down under the window. This was to be my resting place from then on.

With no previous experience of prison life, I nevertheless sensed that one does not ask a co-prisoner questions about reasons for his arrest. I told Dore what happened during the night but no other details. He was equally terse in telling me, that he was turned over to the Gestapo by the Home Defenders, his previous captors, who accused him of greeting one of their prison guards with a raised fist, a recognized communist salute. Dore gave me a few pointers about day-by-day prison life, what to expect, and who were the people in charge. He also said that in a few days I would probably be questioned by the Gestapo, to be mentally prepared for it.

Fortunately, the first day was uneventful; I learned the daily prison routine: the house helpers first emptied the stinking toilet pot, brought new water for washing and drinking, and then during the day we received meals, prison meals. Mid-morning one of the German guards brought around one of the local newspapers, which we were permitted to purchase. The guard never provided any change; he took whatever amount one handed to him. Although the newspaper brought the only echoes of outside life into the cell, it was important to us. I had some small change with me; Dore had already spent his.[1] On that first day especially, every time I heard that big door to our floor open, my nerves went out of control, thinking my turn was coming.

The next morning, when the guard was replacing our toilet pot—he happened to be the chief of the Slovene staff in the prison—he pointed to the pot while looking me straight in the eyes. Inside was a small note giving me the name of the person I should reveal as my liaison in the underground organization in case I found myself under extreme pressure. I knew the person listed. However, in situations like this, one could never be sure whether the information is genuine or planted. I tore the note immediately into the smallest pieces possible. By the time of the next use of the toilet pot, this information was safely disposed of.

My greatest worry, tormenting me night and day, was the situation at home. Did the Gestapo return the next day to search the house? Did my co-conspirator arrive and remove the British pistol on time as promised? Did the Gestapo question my parents or perhaps even arrest my father? There was no way to get any information in or out of the prison. It was a high-security institution.

In the afternoon of the second day, another prison worker whispered to me to put my ear against the wall in the back of the cell as soon as I heard light tapping. I had heard that the resident in the next cell was a woman. Later in the evening when the regular prison life quieted down, I heard tapping on the wall for the first time. At first I had difficulties hearing through the very thick prison walls. However, after a few tries I developed the necessary skill for almost normal conversation through the wall. The woman in the next cell, when I told her my name, told me that she knew about me. When she gave me the exact location where she usually stood at symphony concerts and with whom, I also recognized her. She added the name of the person who invited me to work with this underground organization, which convinced me that her statements were truthful. From her I learned that all the cells on this side of the second floor were occupied, unfortunately, by our own members and why.[2]

Mid-morning the next day a German guard opened the door and called me. He took me outside the cell, and there, inside the iron gate, two men were standing. The older, around forty years old, bald, short, very well dressed in a dark suit asked me in German why I was arrested. The young man standing next to him translated. Without any hesitation, looking straight at the distinguished visitor, I answered, "obveščevalna služba." The young translator immediately responded, "Nachrichten Dienst."[3] With a pitying glance, the man just said, "Danke sehr," turned around and signaled to the prison guard to let him and his translator out of the floor. To this day I never figured out who this man was, why he came to ask this question, even before I was questioned by the Gestapo. There is no doubt in my mind that he was a member of the Gestapo in a high position. Who else would receive permission to get that far into the prison right in front of my cell to ask a question? It seemed to me that he was not a hostile visitor but was curious and wanted this information for some reason. However, when one is in prison, waiting for the next unpleasant thing to happen, one's judgement is obscured, and one is always tempted to turn events in your favor.

The anguish over what might happen next kept me awake at night though the mattress on the floor was quite comfortable. I realized that this time my situation was considerably different than in the past, when I was just one of many. This time I was a direct target with certain guilt listed on the Gestapo files. How long before my turn for interrogation would come? How much did the Gestapo know? Who did they interrogate thus far? What did they found out? There was no way to prepare for the interrogation. From time to time we heard screams during the night, which certainly did not help our mood.

My neighbor, Milojka, helped me to prepare for the day of interrogation. She was surprised that my turn did not yet come. When she was arrested, she was immediately taken into the basement where her interrogation took place. Her description of the torture she went through was, on the one hand, useful information; on the other, it put more fear into my mind. Milojka had her hands tied behind her back, and the rope was then led through a hook on top of a wide door opening to the interrogator's desk. The moment she refused to answer a question or tried to avoid a direct response, the interrogator pulled the rope so that she was only touching the floor with her toes. This caused excruciating pain in her shoulder joints. To increase the torture, she was from time to time lifted from the floor until she fainted from pain. Then she woke up on the floor. They gave her some water and, she thought, also some brandy, forced her to swallow, and up she went again. She did not remember how many times this procedure was repeated. She did not tell me what kind of questions she was asked. It was better to know as little as possible. In most cases, no one who ever went through hours of interrogation liked to talk about the details. Everything she was able and willing to tell me prepared me for the future.

Finally the day came. It was probably a week after my arrest when a young Gestapo man came and took me to the cellar. On the way downstairs he was talkative and almost friendly. He already knew that I spent four years as a student at Bishop's Gymnasium at Šentvid near Ljubljana. He added, that he escaped from a similar institution in Germany to join the Nazi Party. In the basement we sat facing each other, and an interpreter was at the table on my right. I noticed right away the torture set-up as Milojka described it, a wooden stick, and a pistol on the interrogator's desk. The room was otherwise bare except for the typewriter on the table in front of him. First, we established that I did not speak German, then the interrogation started. Fortunately, I knew enough German to understand the questions and, therefore, I had some extra time to think about the answers. The interrogation lasted over two hours, and, surprisingly, my nerves held out so that I did not tremble. At that time I did not know anything about interrogation techniques. My investigator was at times almost friendly. Then, all of a sudden, he would start threatening me by pounding on the table with the stick, pointing the pistol into my face, and asking me if I knew what the hook and the rope in the ceiling were for. "Do you wish to hang?" he added. I do not remember what I mumbled in response, but I was very scared. In my great anxiety, that British pistol came to my mind again, and I became concerned that I would not survive this interrogation without breaking down. However, the British pistol did not come up. My other worry was my father, whether they connected him with my underground activities, but nothing of that nature came up either. The name of my liaison to the higher level was the most crucial issue, and I must admit that after severe pressures, pistol swinging, pounding with the stick, and the translator's repeated conviction they would get that information from me one way or another while he was pointing to the hook, I uttered the name provided to me via the toilet pot. I must admit that to this day I feel very badly that I did not resist to the end. To my great surprise, the Gestapo man then told me that the man was already in prison, which was not the case.[4] In a disdainful tone he then told me that I was just a little fish, unimportant, and that he was not even interested in knowing if anyone in our underground organization reported to me.

Somewhere in the middle of the interrogation, another man came in from the adjacent room and asked the interrogator who I was. This man was in civilian clothes, thin, especially in the face, by appearance and personality a person I would not like to deal with. He made a comment about me with a sarcastic expression; however, I did not understand the exact meaning of what he said. I was glad that he left right away.

Two things about this interrogation remained in my mind. First, the Gestapo man told me that they had infiltrated our underground organization long ago and that they knew about our activities and our naive hopes that the British and Americans would invade the Continent near our land.[5] The second point he made was that we did not know the British as the Germans did. If we thought the British cared about us, we were severely mistaken. Naturally, I did not believe his statements, but it was interesting to hear such comments from one of them. Of course, I would like to have known who infiltrated our clandestine organization. I was in no position, however, to ask questions and I would certainly not have received an answer.

I had to sign the typed report of my interrogation without really knowing what the man put down on paper. Again, that was a sign of my complete inexperience in such matters and also my desperate desire to get out of that basement as soon as possible. When the interrogation was over and I had filled out a postcard for my family stating what kind of clothes I needed, the Gestapo man suddenly turned to me and said that there was only one way out of prison—that is, to join them and work with them for a better Europe. Through the interpreter I answered, that I was convinced, if the situation were reversed, that he would not agree to work with us. This was probably the only courageous thing I said the entire two hours or more. He did not take this as an offense; he just said that I was right.

I was then turned over to a German guard and returned to my room. I started shaking the moment I stepped into my room; I had to lie down and was not able to speak to my concerned roommate. The whole interrogation went through my brain again and again in pieces, in distorted order, and fraught with worries that I had told them something that would hurt others in prison. It took me two hours before I was able to control my trembling. The first question I asked Dore was, if in his opinion, I would be interrogated again—a stupid question, indicative of the state of my mind at that moment.

That evening I reported to Milojka a few things about the interrogation with certain reservations. I could not repeat questions about our organization or reveal details to my co-prisoner for my own and for his protection. The fear of cross-interrogation was always there. Milojka's name was not brought up during my interrogation. From my description of the interrogator, Milojka and I were not able to establish whether the same person interrogated both of us. Her fear was that her turn would come again after everybody in jail had had his or her turn. Dore did not wish to know any details either; he only asked whether I was tortured. I was not, and neither was he when he was interrogated, long before I joined him.

Since I was in the first cell on the floor, No. 147, I was often able to observe who was coming and going through the huge gate. This was possible only if the house staff, while going by, opened the viewer on the door; they had to flip the cover into the upright position. Thus, I was able to send information down the line, from wall to wall, as to who was taken downstairs or who was coming to the floor. This very limited, small, and only occasional view of the "outside" world, was nevertheless quite helpful. On one such occasion I observed two guards dragging one of our members back from the basement and past our cell to his room. He had obviously been tortured even though, with my limited view, I was not able to establish his general condition. Surprisingly, almost immediately after the door of his cell closed, he started singing. I had heard his great voice before. Thus, we all felt better right away. Milojka told me later that he had been interrogated for the second time and that he had probably been hanging on the rope a long time. I was not able to find out why he could not walk.

On occasion, the German prison chief came to visit. I never saw this person but will forever remember his harsh, extremely loud voice every time he entered the prison. What he was yelling about and why was a puzzle to all of us. It was probably his way of trying to scare the inmates, a technique not uncommon with Germans in certain positions of authority. I must say that he was partially successful, since we all hoped never to see this guy face to face.

Milojka and I became very good friends. We exchanged views on many things not associated with underground work. I learned a lot about her life, her hopes, ambitions, and about her family. In return, I shared with her everything that was on my mind. This was a great friendship; some would characterize it as a strange friendship of two persons who never actually saw each other. She was older than I, certainly more mature and better educated. She grew up in a family with three brothers, one of them was in a cell on our floor.[6] I must admit, that of all my friendships, men or women, she was my closest, most dear friend. I often think of her, especially about her later life and the circumstances of her death. I do not know how Dore tolerated our daily discussions, but he was more than tolerant and encouraged me to have these conversations on the ground that these exchanges were of interest to him as well.

Milojka was helpful to both of us as a messenger. In prison we had two privileges: to send out our clothes for wash or exchange and to get extra food from home. Milojka somehow acquired sewing supplies. In the hemline of her underpants she skillfully hid tiny messages. Thus, our families were informed that Dore and I were sharing a cell, that we needed small change, a lot of it, to be able to purchase the daily newspaper, and that they should alternate food donations since we shared everything. The shipments of clothes and food were, of course, carefully checked by the German prison guards. The two guards who had access to our floor brought our packages. It was often obvious that some parts of the contents were missing. One day I had the opportunity to observe through my viewer one of the guards happily eating out of one of our packages. We were aware of such minor irregularities of our guards. In this prison our German guards, who were under the control of Gestapo, were in general fair or at times even good to us. For these reasons we did not complain via our families about any irregularities. The guards would have been punished and removed from their jobs since the Gestapo were touchy about the behavior of people under their control. Their own rights, behavior, and actions were, of course, a different matter.

My mother received permission to visit me a month after my arrest. She was visibly relieved at finding me in good shape. When we were together in the visitors' room, a Slovene policeman in uniform stood right next to us listening to our conversation. At first I did not know how to get away from him. I tried to move to another corner but he followed. Finally, I asked him why he was standing next to us and listening, since I was a Gestapo prisoner, not one of theirs. That helped. He apologized and went away. Mother was now able to tell me that the British pistol was picked up later during the day of my arrest, that the Gestapo people never came back to search the house, and that nobody made any further inquiries or asked for my father. Thus far, the family was still doing reasonably well. Mother also told me that when she knocked on the door at the Gestapo headquarters in Ljubljana, my schoolmate, M. K., who often visited our home and whom I had seen walking toward Hotel Miklič across from the Ljubljana railroad station, opened the door. For a moment they were both speechless; then my schoolmate invited her in.

The prison privileges normally included a daily courtyard walk, a shower once a week, Sunday church services, and library books. These privileges were denied to Dore and me. So we had to compensate for these privileges on our own. We arranged routine one-hour walks inside our cell twice a day; it took a little planning to find enough room to follow each other in that narrow space. Each of us had on alternate days the right to use up what was left of the washing water—there was not much of it—after our essential needs were satisfied. On Sundays, we listened to the people walking to and returning from church services. Most of all, we wished to go to the courtyard to see who else was there. Lacking all this, the newspaper was the only entertainment. One day, when I saw a large map on the front page of the newspaper which the German guard just handed to me, indicating with arrows the sudden break-out of the American tanks in a southerly direction from the previously almost-stationary battle lines around the Normandy beaches, I jumped for joy. The guard probably guessed why I was so happy, immediately reacted, and yelled at me saying that if such behavior happened again, there would be no more newspapers and I would be sitting in the basement dungeon. I apologized to Dore for my stupid and inappropriate behavior. Those newspapers were so important to us; we went through them to the last word every day. Crossword puzzles took some extra time; we did them together. I still remember one that gave us the most trouble on one or two lines. The text came from a Latin proverb. When we finally solved that puzzle, we both recognized the Latin text behind it written in hexameter: *Guta cavát lapidém non ví sed saepe cadéndo* [The drops of water make a hole in the stone not by force but by continuous falling].

Dore Matul was very well versed in Slovene choral music. I learned a lot from him about his experiences with choral conducting and also about the difficulties amateur choral groups present. The conductor depends on the willingness of the singers to achieve his performance goals. He told me about interesting foreign tours and what he learned there. We avoided domestic politics, however. Dore knew, in general, in what direction my hopes were heading, and I knew that he was at least sympathetic to the Liberation Front, if not more. These differences did not interfere in any way with our daily life in this small, crowded space. We were always able to reach an agreement on any kind of problem.

During the month of August, Milojka and I found out that more former Yugoslav army officers were arrested and brought to prison. Milojka managed to get in touch with one of them in the cell just below her. How long they stayed in the prison or where they were taken afterward, we were not privileged to learn. The news also reached us that the British decided to switch all their support to Tito's forces, that they discontinued their support and removed their military missions from Mihailovič. Soon after, the Americans and Soviets did the same. That was another blow to our cause. Our hopes were vanishing at an alarming rate.

Some men on our floor managed to climb, with the help of co-prisoners' shoulders, above the covered windows in the evenings. Because we were on the second floor, they were able to look over the prison fence to the city street and observe the people walking there. One of the outside guards noticed that, and punishment soon followed. The prison workers arrived, removed the window cover, and boarded up the window completely. Now we were in almost complete darkness day and night. Dore and I were lucky. We pulled a little money from our pockets and persuaded the carpenters to give us one of the wooden boards which had a removable knot in it. The fellow even adjusted it a little, so that we did not have too much trouble removing and replacing it as needed. That little stream of light meant a lot to us, and we used it sparingly, always ready to replace the piece in a hurry. It was strange that the German guards kept coming with the newspapers even though it was dark in the cell. Apparently that extra money they usually collected was all that was important to them.

The Gestapo interrogations on our floor ceased after a month. Neither Milojka, Dore, or I were called again. I do not remember seeing any of the others taken down to the basement. No doubt Gestapo agents were going over interrogation statements to arrive at some decisions. We had already been sitting in the cells more than two months waiting for the next step.

Then it came. Milojka was informed that she would be leaving with a transport in a few days. She was allowed to notify her family as to what she would need for her trip. She was not allowed to take very much. Soon she managed to find out who else received notification for the same transport; I was not one of them. All others on the floor, except I, were in the group and probably a few from other sections of the prison. I was heartbroken on the day of her departure; I was losing my dear friend and communicator. When Milojka departed, I saw her through my window viewer, opened for me by the guard who accompanied her from the floor with her modest bundle. At the big floor gate she turned around and waved. That was my first and last eye contact with her and that only through the prison door's smallest viewer.

Now I felt doubly imprisoned. She was gone. No more pleasant conversations, no more encouragement, no more discussions of things that burdened either of us. I kept thinking how hard it must have been for her after her interrogation, going over every word she said. She often shared her thoughts and worries about many details. I tried to console her. However, I had my own interrogation on my mind all the time; so my attempts at consolation were probably not very convincing. Milojka was gone and the period of interrogations was probably behind her. Dore tried to console me by saying that her departure definitely removed her from further interrogations and torture and out of the local Gestapo hands.

Three hours later I heard Milojka's voice again. Dore and I looked at each other. What was going on? We heard the key turning in the adjacent cell; Milojka was back. I called her at the first opportunity. It turned out that she was the only woman selected for this transport and that was the reason she was sent back. However, she had had the opportunity to meet her brother, her closest friends and associates in the assembly room; it was a most happy reunion, she said. Her disappointment at not going with them was great. Milojka's pleadings with authorities to let her depart with this transport were in vain. She guessed that the people assembled for this transport were the higher-ranking people of our clandestine organization. The man in charge half-jokingly told her that there would be many more opportunities to join a transport in the not-so-distant future.

Unfortunately for both of us, she received a roommate that same day, a very young girl. Our conversations had to be much more reserved because we did not know why Milojka received a roommate at this point. One cannot be too careful in such situations. We had to limit our conversations considerably, and we were forced to scrutinize our topics with great care.

Ten days later, the chief of the Slovene workers in the prison informed me about the date of my departure. He also gave me a postcard for my family so that they would have time to send me the most urgent supplies and clothes.[7] There was no information as to where I would be going. A few days later my mother visited me for the second time. She had the courage to inquire at the Gestapo Headquarters where I was to be sent, but she received only a general reply—across the border, out of the territory of the former Yugoslavia as a forced laborer, and assigned appropriate work there. My mother was under the impression that I would be working somewhere in the former southern Austria. I was very glad that she received permission to visit me. The goodbye, however, was difficult and emotional for both of us.

The day of departure eventually came. It was already September, after almost three months of imprisonment by the Gestapo. I was very pleased that the Gestapo did not pay me another visit. What was on those papers the man typed during the interrogation was constantly on my mind even though I was aware that no revisions were possible. This was a closed case. Now I was given the orders for the next step, where and to what I did not know. During my last conversation with Milojka, I learned that she was not included in this group either; she would be left behind and that hurt her tremendously. I had such hopes, after her return to the cell, that we would go together into the next phase. Milojka, on the other hand, was concerned about my future, and being aware that I did not know any others in the organization who were in prison, advised me to ask for Hinko. She seemed quite sure that Hinko would be on the same transport as I, because he was not included in the first group.

With a heavy heart I had to say goodbye to Milojka. She expressed hope that we would have a chance to meet after the war. God willing. I also said goodbye to Dore Matul, thanking him for being such a pleasant companion. He, with a smile on his face, said that I should help him if our side won, and he would do the same for me in case his side was the winner. This statement was as close as we ever came to declaring our allegiances. I wished him successful survival of the war. From the outside of my cell, I said goodbye to Milojka once more, for the last time.

There were many people in the downstairs assembly room; energetic conversations were going on among many groups. My guess was that there were over a hundred people of both sexes assembled there. I looked around to see a familiar face without success. Were all these people members of our clandestine underground organization? There was a crowd but I felt isolated, not knowing anybody. Well, that is the way life goes. I then asked one person if he knew Hinko. Fortunately, I asked the right person. He pointed to a tall, sporty-looking fellow not too far away, who was deeply involved in conversation with two good-looking young ladies. I hesitated for a while before I approached him and timidly told him what Milojka advised me. His reaction was more than cordial. He introduced me immediately to a number of people; in turn, my depression lifted right away. I would have companions from now on.

Soon after, we boarded a train. It was after the curfew when we were taken to the railroad station, a normal practice when prisoners were removed from the city during the war. This way, there were no onlookers, family members, or demonstrators present. I recall that it was around midnight when the train left Ljubljana railroad station, this time in a northwesterly direction toward Kranj, Jesenice, and was scheduled, probably I thought, to cross the border into the former Austria, where I assumed we would be put to work somewhere. That was the message I received from my mother, who had inquired at Gestapo headquarters in Ljubljana. We were placed into regular open passenger cars, not in cattle cars as in the past.[8] This fact in itself offered some hopes. I was sitting next to a very young man, who, after learning my name, told me that he had been in the Gestapo limousine late at night on 28 June 1944, when they were looking for me but could not find my street. After he was dropped off at the prison late at night, the Gestapo probably checked the city map again and found my street. Would the British pistol have been sitting on my desk if the Gestapo had located my street the first time around? I got goose pimples thinking about this possibility. The fact that I was born on the feast of "Guardian Angels" must have had something to do with this lucky coincidence, was the thought that went through my mind.

A little later, still during the night, a tall man came to me, introduced himself, and told me that he, as the highest-ranking officer among our group of prisoners on this transport, would be responsible for all of us as much as circumstances would permit and that I should turn to him with questions or for help. He also told me that, out of approximately 130 people on this transport, about a third were members of our organization; the others belonged to the Liberation Front group. Therefore, I should not discuss my prison experiences with anybody, until we were able to establish who was on this transport. He added that we would try to work together with members of the other group; in the eyes of our captors, we were here for the same reason, for opposing German occupation forces.

We were heavily guarded at each end of each car. One of the guards had an attaché case, probably containing the information about us inmates. How nice it would have been to go over those documents. But the man did not sleep, and if he did, someone else held those files.

We arrived in Villach/Beljak early in the morning before 7:00 A.M., and received permission to get off the train. When we were all assembled in the open on the railroad station, all 130 of us, a strong, husky man, also a prisoner, stepped in front of the group and started singing. The whole group then joined in; our singing reached out in all directions and soon we had a large audience. Nobody applauded but many listened with obvious interest. Why authorities who were present did not stop our performance was a slight puzzle. Singing in Slovene was certainly not welcome in this part of the former Austria, now Germany; it may have even been specifically forbidden. We were singing at least half an hour, song by song, the audience just standing there and waiting for the next song. When we were ordered back on the train, it crossed my mind that the Germans might possibly use this concert as proof of how happy we were at the prospect of going to work for Germany. There were no cameras around as far as I was able to observe, but who knows?

The train just did not want to stop anymore. Yes, it did stop again and again for reasons of the train schedules, but not for us. We kept looking at the signs of the railroad stations to see where we were. We passed Klagenfurt/Celovec, Leoben, and were surprised to notice eventually signs for Vienna. Where are we going? We became even more concerned when we crossed into occupied Czechoslovakia. The further away we went from our home-land, the fewer guards were watching us. They were replaced two or three times. However, nobody considered jumping off the train. I doubt that the guards would have even noticed a missing person. We were apparently all resigned to the fact that we would spent some time in Germany, as many others who preceded us on similar journeys were doing. We kept hearing in our heads the German official reminders, repeated again and again, "If you try to escape, you will be shot." No doubt they were serious about that.

The first signs telling us that we had arrived in occupied Poland, appeared, if I remember correctly, on the third or fourth day. We became convinced that we would be taken to the Eastern Front area, probably to build German defense lines or something similar. Why were they taking us so far from our homeland? We became really concerned; all optimism disappeared. Looking at the signs, there were some arguments as to whether this was Poland or Czechoslovakia, but the reality was there—it was Poland.

Then we were in the open again in an almost-deserted land. The train seemed to be picking up speed. There was nothing to see, except land, not cultivated land, just land, left and right of the train. Where were we going? Where were they taking us?

CHAPTER NINE

Forced Labor Camp Auschwitz

September 1944–January 1945

❦

An assassination attempt on Hitler by Wehrmacht officers on 20 July 1944 was unsuccessful and had disastrous consequences for the conspirators. One of these was Field Marshal Rommel, though Hitler gave him a chance to poison himself to avoid the political difficulties of putting Rommel on trial.

The Warsaw uprising of the Polish Home Army started on 1 August 1944. Though the Soviet troops were not far away on the other side of the Vistula River, they did not intervene. Even the re-supplying efforts of the RAF, who needed Soviet airfields to refuel for their return home, were approved by the Soviets only after long, time-wasting negotiations. The Polish fighters had to surrender to the Germans on 2 October 1944.

Romania, the German satellite, surrendered to the Soviets on 23 August 1944.

The most memorable event during the summer was certainly the liberation of Paris by French and American troops on 25 August 1944 . Fortunately, Hitler's order to destroy the city first was not carried out by the German commander.

The German fortress began to crumble when the opposing forces were approaching its borders. Now the German news media reported mostly the destruction of communication lines, railroad tracks, and bridges to help troops in their retreat.

Part I

In the distance, in the middle of nowhere, something gradually came into view. There must be a town there, we thought; maybe even our next break from the long train travel. The closer we came, more surprised we were. After entering this

place, we were in the middle of a huge settlement with no visible end in either direction. When the train passed through a huge door in the form of an arch, with
a sign supposedly greeting newcomers,[1] we looked around and observed a multitude of activities and a crowd of all kinds of people either walking, carrying, or
pushing materials alone or in groups. Our greatest surprise was the sight of many
people in strange uniforms, dark gray with wide stripes, that resembled heavy pa-
jamas. People of both sexes were dressed like that, differentiated only by various
signs on their arms and on their backs. All of those we were able to observe
seemed to know what they were doing or where they were going. Another, immediately noticeable characteristic of these people was that there was almost no
talking, just silent motion, almost a *perpetuum mobile*. This must be a strange
place, we thought; it looked like a sophisticated prison-work establishment run
by automatons.

Soon after we rode into this strange place, the train stopped at what looked like
an official train station, not an elaborate one but ready to handle people and/or
various loads of material. When the train came to a halt, we heard a loud command, "Alle aussteigen,"[2] a command which everybody understood by that time.
We grabbed our bundled property and left the train. An officer, probably a Gestapo man, dressed in black, ordered us to form a three-deep orderly line in front of
him. He then walked down the first line, looking at this assembly, observing what
was standing there in front of him. By some coincidence, I happened to have been
in the first line, certainly not my preferred place.[3] The officer then asked who spoke
German; many hands were raised. He then asked one of them, a young man, to accompany him. He went from person to person standing in the first line and asked
almost exclusively about our education and profession. I answered, "abiturient,"
which meant that I just completed high school. His comment after this initial survey was that we seemed to him a little different from the sort of people he usually
received in this camp. He would see to it that we got jobs according to our abilities,
since many kinds of employment were available in these camps and were much
needed to help Germany to the final victory. He did not forget to include that important phrase, "If you try to escape, you will be shot." Except for that statement, I
have to admit, he did not display any kind of hostility.

The rest of that first day was more-or-less routine. We went through registration, where several secretaries, all very well dressed and with perfect make-up,
gave the impression of a life in another world. They questioned us in detail about
our background, family, education, skills, and experiences; everything was carefully recorded. All went on in an almost cordial atmosphere. These procedures
lasted nearly all day. To our great surprise, one of the secretaries in these offices
(there were several) spoke fluent Slovene. She was very good looking and very well
dressed. When she heard we were from the Slovene lands, she came around and
helped where translations were necessary. She asked many questions about where

we came from, our last residence and so forth; however, she would not disclose anything about herself. From her almost non-existent accent and pronunciation of the Slovene language, we were not able to place her into any particular region of Slovenia. We did not know if she was there as a regular employee or as a prisoner. This young lady did not hesitate to speak Slovene right in the middle of the German office.

When we were later taking showers at a large facility, one of the fellows uttered his doubts that water would come out of the openings in the ceiling; he was immediately yelled into silence for even thinking of such things. We were then issued IDs and led to the various forced labor camps scattered all around this strange settlement.

Never in my life, even in my dreams, had I seen such huge facilities. Looming over this place was a heavily guarded I.G. Farbenindustrie Plant, which, according to some estimates, was seven kilometers long and almost that wide. The entrance(s) to the plant was under heavy guard day and night; without proper ID, there was no admission. The high and impressive-looking chimneys emitted not-always pleasant fumes. Around this plant there were camps, many camps, mostly on the western, southern, and eastern side. No resident of the forced labor camps was able to get around often enough to take a count of these various camps and figure out who the inmates were. Our attention was first drawn to the I.G. Farbenindustrie plant facilities, what was going on there, what was being produced. There was no doubt that something very important and vital to the German war effort was produced at that huge plant.

The first night I spent in a pre-fab in *Lager* II.[4] At five in the morning an unpleasant voice lifted me out of bed; it was one of the civilian capos, undoubtedly a prisoner doing his routine job. We were led around like cattle from one minor task to another. Not being familiar with daily routines makes life more difficult, and one is immediately willing to learn more and to learn fast. Finally, six of us were selected, apparently for a special assignment. We were led to a water pond, where six men in striped uniforms stood almost motionless next to fire-fighting equipment.[5] This was one of the few times that I came close to the concentration camp prisoners. We received warnings right at the beginning not to approach, to talk, or, especially, to offer any assistance or food to these prisoners. Any such action would result in an immediate transfer to one of the concentration camps with all its consequences. The six men standing there were in a very deteriorated state. I could not help but think back to Concentration Camp Rab. The visible difference was that these prisoners were in striped uniforms, which made them at least from a distance look a little better. On the Island of Rab, toward the end of the year 1942, almost all of us were in miserable-looking rags. However, the expressions of these six men standing next to the fire-fighting equipment, their starved bodies, and their deeply-set eyes told very clearly of a life of suffering, starvation, and despair.

A little distance away another man, also in a striped uniform, was laughing and exchanging cigarettes with two Gestapo men.[6] After ten minutes or so, this man, apparently a capo, came over and started shouting commands. The six men went through the fire-fighting drill with military precision and unbelievable speed. A second demonstration followed. Then it was our turn. None of us understood any commands and we had no pre-assigned positions. The result was complete chaos; we were falling over each other trying to drag the equipment to the water hole while the capo yelled and cursed. Five tries completely exhausted us. Only then did the first team receive orders to instruct us. From this point on each one of us had a specific job to perform. After a few more tries, we came close to performing this exercise in an acceptable manner and speed. The proper storage of the fire-fighting equipment had to be done with equal care and minute detail. The six men then left with their capo. We did not try to exchange any words with them or among ourselves. There were no other Slovenes among this fire-fighting group, and I was wondering where the others went or what kind of jobs they received.

Soon after the fire-fighting training was over, I received orders to report immediately to *Lager* III. *Lager* III, the fellow who took me to my new place told me, was a camp for women, which worried me right from the start. What would I be doing there? My guide did not know. At the entrance to the camp, a Russian woman prisoner in civilian clothes asked for our permission to enter the camp, just glanced at it, and directed us to the center of the camp, to the main office, a modest but neat facility. There I found a group of Slovene men from our transport already waiting. The commander of the camp came and spoke to us. A lady from the office, a middle-aged woman from Zagreb—the office manager as we found out later—served as translator. His speech and his instructions were very strange for a German camp commander. He more or less said that we would have to work together, fulfill the responsibilities expected of us, and be extremely careful in our behavior at this camp for various reasons. He did not specify. He then said that observing the rules to the letter was the only way and our only hope of surviving to the end of this war. Almost apologetically he added that any infraction of the rules or misbehavior would force him to turn the rule-breaker over to the Gestapo, something he was loath to do. He was counting on us to do the job right. After instructing his office manager to give us further details, he welcomed us to his camp, turned around, and left. We stood there in silence for a moment and so did the lady from the office. We noted that the man had a slight limp when he walked away. He was approximately forty years old, possibly wounded in the war or placed here for political reasons as many other Germans were.

The Croatian lady then described the situation to us. This camp consisted of two different women's sectors. One third, separated from the rest of the camp, was for the German and the Volksdeutsche women who held various positions either

in the factories or in the camps. The camp was their residence. There were no restrictions on their coming and going except they had to be back in the camp by
10:00 P.M. The German part of the camp had a separate entrance and exit, very inconvenient for them because it required walking all around the camp from the
main road. The other two-thirds of the camp was occupied by women who were
brought here from the occupied Eastern lands; the majority came from Poland,
the Ukraine, and Russia, but other nationalities were represented as well. The
women from the Eastern Block were not permitted to enter the German territory
of this camp and vice versa. The Eastern Block women were also free to come and
go at any time, but in the evenings after work, they had to pick up a permission
slip in the office, a *propusk,* in case they were stopped during the darkness by various patrols in this huge settlement. The key issue for this camp was that men, except those with special written permission and deliverymen, were not allowed to
enter either the German or the Eastern block sectors at any time. No visitation
permissions were issued. The same rules applied to women trying to enter men's
camps.

Then came a slight or disguised warning. There were many changes in the administration of this camp from its initial days when women were first brought
here to work in the factories. The Croatian lady was not here from the start but
had heard a lot about those days. Self-administration came later; it had existed
now for almost two years. Most of the forced labor camps had some kind of self-
administration when we arrived, but the arrangements varied considerably from
camp to camp, depending on the camp commander and/or where the prisoners
came from. When self-administration was first approved, the jobs assigned to us
were first given to the women in this camp. This arrangement did not work because of so many antagonistic feelings among various ethnic groups, especially
between the women in the German and in the Eastern Block sectors of the camp.
The women themselves wanted male prisoners to take over these responsibilities.
We were, allegedly, the third group of men assigned to these jobs. The other two
groups had been removed for not performing as expected. The last group had
been removed only a week before our arrival. They were all Croatian men, and the
lady said that she was very sorry about their removal. She would not specify the
reasons behind their discharge. What were these men doing now? She only said
that misbehavior and breaking of the rules by a few resulted in the elimination of
the entire team.

Our assignments, she told us, would include: (1) staffing the entrance as door-
keepers at both sectors of the camp 24 hours a day, 7 days a week; (2) fire-fighting
preparedness and fire-prevention supervision in the camp; (3) constant checking
of the physical facilities and reporting of malfunctions to the camp's office; (4) en-
forcing the clean surroundings in the camp with special emphasis on health and
hygienic conditions; (5) assuring every night that blackout *(verdunkeln)* rules were

observed by every barrack. Then she mentioned another rule: During air attack warnings, people in the camp were encouraged, actually instructed, to seek protection from the falling anti-aircraft shrapnel fragments in the not-so-distant woods south of the camp. This privilege was not granted to us because of our fire-fighting responsibilities.

These jobs were physically not difficult at all, even though it would include a lot of walking outdoors in the harsh winter. Nevertheless, we did not like the nature of the beast, having in a way to control our co-prisoners. To our question of whether we had any other choices in job assignments, the Croatian lady responded with a slight smile that she would not recommend even thinking about it; the alternative would immediately be a striped uniform.

They took us then for a tour of the camp. The inhabitants were not very interested in us; most were at work anyhow. The reactions from the women at the entrance checkpoints were more positive. They already knew that we were scheduled to take over the next day at noon, and they were pleased about that. At every step, office, kitchen, washrooms, the question of our native language came up. Nobody ever heard this language—no, it was not Slovak; it was Slovene. The guess was that we were assigned these jobs because we did not belong to any of the ethnic groups represented in this camp.

The office manager then assigned us on the basis of established and tested schedules to various slots and times at the entrance checkpoints and to the roaming responsibilities in the camp as they were practiced up to that time. We were offered the opportunity to change individual assignments, if agreeable to all concerned; any changes would have to be reported to the office before they would go into effect. We soon realized, that we were actually under the command of the Croatian office manager from Zagreb.[7]

I saw the official commander only twice more during my stay in the camp as he was walking through the camp; however he never approached or spoke to us again.

We were assigned to a barrack in the southeast corner of the camp, a standard accommodation in the camp, with beds on two levels to jam more people into each room. In the German sector there were no double-level beds because the women there were not prisoners but employees. A one-level arrangement added considerably to the comfort. I do not remember how many beds were in our room; however, availability of space was a problem and it took some time to achieve a *modus vivendi*.

In the barrack, on the first night, I encountered another enemy—*Cimex lectularius*—or in common language, bedbugs, not one or two, but an army of them. The moment we turned off the lights for the night, they attacked, attacked in force. At first I did not know what was happening, I had never seen these creatures before. In a few moments they were all over me: legs, arms, neck. I jumped up and started removing and killing these intruders the best I could. That blood, that smell, their determination, their presence, all this brought an attack of nausea. I was not only sick; I was also desperate. One person in the room immediately recognized these attackers and explained their habits. Not everybody in the room was attacked. The men on upper beds suffered much less. My case was the worst. For the first night we agreed to leave the lights on. That should help we thought. After several attempts to try to get some sleep without success, I finally decided to sleep on a bench right under the light. This was not a comfortable arrangement since the bench was very narrow, but there were no enemy attacks there.

The next day I reported all this to the office, thinking that the health conditions were one of the high priorities in the camp. There I heard that this problem could not be easily solved because everything in the camp was old. Someone did come and sprayed around the room. I also received another mattress. All this did not help much. For the time being I had a bed, but I slept on that narrow bench under the light.

No matter what the job, one learns from experience. We were actually without any direct supervision. In the second half of 1944, Germany needed all their men on various fronts. There were almost no German men in the forced labor camps. The operations were set to run in a routine way. There were spot-checks, however, as we soon discovered.

In the Eastern Block area, where most of our responsibilities were concentrated, we soon encountered two problems. At the end of September and during October, when it was still relatively warm, many men from forced labor camps some distance away, most of them further west, often assembled on the road outside the main entrance to our camp. They sang folk songs in impressive and carrying voices and waited for the women to join them for an evening walk. On my first night there, I enjoyed listening to them and tried to understand the words or at least the nature of each song. I did not know at the time whether the songs were in Russian or in Ukrainian; they certainly were in one of those languages. A few of the men, probably under the influence of alcohol, then tried to enter the camp as a group. There were no gates there; the entrance was always wide open so that delivery trucks and the fire-fighting equipment could get through. Unable to speak Russian or Ukrainian, all I was able to say was "verboten," and "propusk." But the men kept pushing me back and gradually entered the camp proper. Luckily for me, a few women near the entrance of the camp persuaded the intruders to leave. I was very grateful to them for their much-needed assistance. The only other solution would have been to report these men to the office. I knew and the women knew, too, where the matter would end, if the Gestapo were called. On another such unpleasant evening when I struggled with a few men and tried to persuade them to leave, I heard from behind me a loud yelling and saw a man in a black uniform approaching from inside the camp—he had probably entered through the German sector—telling me in an unfriendly manner to be more energetic and to do the job right. I did not understand everything he said, but I realized I had been severely reprimanded. By the time he joined me at the entrance, the men had already gone down the road. Obviously, they had no intention of encountering him.

The man was very tall, robust, and rough-looking. He told me that he controlled all labor camps to see how the directives of self-management were carried out. He told me to tell the others that we could expect him in the camp, with the proper authorization in hand, at any time, day or night. He stayed around for a few minutes and after a while became a little more civil. He even asked what my native language was and added that knowledge of German would be a must in the years after the war. The problem of forced or illegal entry by men eventually subsided, thanks mostly to the women in the camp. We soon established good working relationships that helped them and us.

The other problem in the Eastern Block area was more sensitive. The barrack where the restrooms were located was some distance away for most of the inhabitants. So the temptation was to go behind the barrack and urinate there rather than make the long trip to the proper place. For health reasons, that kind of behavior was strictly forbidden. Getting caught in such a situation was embarrassing for both parties. We tried to solve the problem by talking repeatedly to barrack chiefs, who were elected by their roommates. It helped a little but never really solved the problem. Neither action, to ignore behavior or to remind someone on the spot, was correct or satisfactory. I followed the first approach, thinking that the awareness of being caught was sufficient warning, but not everybody felt that way.

We were not required to be concerned about the interiors of the barracks. That was the responsibility of the barrack chief. In most cases, the women worked very well together; I do not remember any unhappy cases in this respect.

Watching these women going to work, some starting at five in the morning, was depressing. Their clothes were old; many had no stockings; their legs were reddish-blue from the cold; to keep warm they were dressed in all kind of nonmatching attire; they marched to their posts and work assignments diligently day after day, six days a week, to earn a bare living.

With the exception of entrance control, we had no other responsibilities in the German sector of the camp. Sitting or standing at that entrance—both entrances had small booths with an open front window—was boring except during the rush hours before and after work and around 10:00 P.M., gate-closing time. The parade of women walking by the booth, exchanging greetings with most but not all of them, were the highlights of the day. Some of the women resented our presence there and our "authority." In turn, we also developed a dual standard for dealing with these few unpleasant souls. Fortunately, very rarely did men try to enter the camp from this side. At night the gate had to be locked; women late-comers had to be reported to the office. At first we just opened the gate for those coming late and then asked for ID. This did not work because some women re-fused to identify themselves. Later we asked for ID to be handed to us through the openings in the gate, and then we admitted the person. This way we were able to record the person's name and ID number and note how late she returned to the camp. In most cases we did not even report to the office those who were less than thirty minutes late. However, we were much stricter with the hostile women. Most often the women came to the gate accompanied by men, who occasionally threatened us. On one occasion an non-commissioned officer pulled his pistol. I walked away and refused to open the gate until the woman persuaded the man to leave. She was very apologetic, and we parted with a friendly goodnight. She came back two days later when I was on duty and thanked me for not reporting her to the office. We, of course, exchanged information among ourselves about unpleas-ant individuals and difficult cases. It was difficult to find the right balance between leniency and strictness. Either one could backfire. The Croatian lady in the office, with a teasing smile on her face, once mentioned that she was very pleased that the women in the German sector were so much more regular in com-ing back to camp on time since our arrival.

It did not take long for the Eastern Block women to get to the point of under-standing that we were no different from other workers in the camp, either in the kitchen or in the office. Except for minor incidents, we had very good relation-ships with the women in both sectors of the camp. The barrack chiefs were also cooperative, taking reminders very well. The learning of other Slavic languages was one of our top priorities, but we soon discovered however that the Slavs here borrowed from each other and were in the process of creating a common Slavic "Camp Esperanto."[8]

There was little direct news of how the war was progressing, but enough to know that the Eastern Front was not a great distance away and gradually coming closer.

Near our camp the people in the striped uniforms were sorting a huge amount of lumber. We observed one day one of them hitting another mercilessly with a wooden stick; about five or six others, were just standing there, observing. The man, who was so cruel, most likely their capo, was wearing the striped outfit. After the beating was over, the work continued. How the beaten man was able to work after being beaten so badly was a real miracle. The next day some of us were walking during our free time down the road next to that lumber site. We were talking loudly as usual. Suddenly we heard a few words in Serbian asking us from where and when we came here. We first walked away a little further down the road and then came back to roughly the same location. There we stopped and formed a circle to give the appearance that we were talking among ourselves. We told the man in the striped uniform that we came from Slovenia only a few days before and that we were in the forced labor camps. He was from Belgrade and had been in the concentration camp for already over a year. At this point we had to continue our walk because other people were approaching. Fortunately, his capo was not present, permitting that brief exchange.[9]

Occasionally we received very small round pieces of dry cheese as part of our food rations. We started saving those pieces. At night in complete darkness we threw these pieces of cheese into the pile of lumber. These pieces were the only food small, hard, and heavy enough that we were able to throw that far. It was not much, but we hoped that it helped the concentration camp prisoners a little. Our repeated attempts to get the attention of the prisoner from Belgrade again were useless; he was either working somewhere else, or the presence of his capo prevented any further communication.

On our walks we and all other prisoners kept to the main roads; going anywhere else was dangerous. I am still convinced that one of the camps east of us was for British prisoners of war. Some survivors of Auschwitz dispute that.[10] The camp where British prisoners of war were allegedly kept was too far from the main road to see if the inmates wore British uniforms. Rumors circulated that these were British officers, who were not required to work; for this reason they were not seen at any other location of this huge settlement. Further to the east were concentration camps for men and women, the Monowitz (Monowice) camps. We were repeatedly warned by various people not to walk even on the main road close to these camps; it was very dangerous and a good place to get arrested. We usually turned back before coming too close to these two concentration camps.

My new friend Hinko was not in our camp. As a medical student, even though he completed only one year of medical studies before his arrest, he was assigned to an ambulance center some distance away. The center was for prisoners of the labor camps only, not for any other groups. Class systems were everywhere. On his free times he often visited me and brought the latest camp information, including all the rumors that were circulating.

The various technicians and repairmen who came around from time to time were mostly German and French. I once asked a German why he was in Auschwitz; he replied that he had stepped on the wrong train. Many of these prisoner-technicians were well educated, doing their assigned jobs as required. Those Germans capos were of a different brand; rumor had it that they were criminals. From their cruel and merciless behavior, it was not difficult to accept the story that they had been drafted for their positions because of their criminal past.

In addition to the forced labor camps and the concentration camps at Birkenau (Brzezinka) and Monowitz (Monowice), there was a Hitler Youth camp very near the town of Auschwitz, an Italian camp, and a French camp. What kind of arrangements the Italians had with the German authorities, we did not know. They most likely enjoyed a better status than the forced laborers. The French, however, were an entirely different matter. I befriended one of their electricians who often came to our camp to do repairs because I could speak a few words of French, and that pleased him very much. The French, even though working for the Germans, were completely independent, were well organized in their strongly protected and isolated camp, and did not allow others to visit their residence. They were organized into military units with a strict hierarchy or military command structure. My new friend, the electrician, did try to explain to me why they were seemingly voluntarily working for the Germans; however, I did not fully comprehend his explanations. To the best of my understanding, it was an arrangement between the Vichy and the Nazi governments, which prevented forcing the French to serve as German auxiliary military units on various fronts.[11]

My French friend invited me to an evening of entertainment in their camp; he told me that it would be something special. This friendly invitation required some logistics since I could not possibly get permission to enter their camp. However, my friend arranged for everything. The most important factor was his assurance that even if we got caught, they would not turn me over to the Germans; the worst that could happen would be to be expelled from their camp. He brought me into the camp by an irregular route. In the big hall I was the only stranger among Frenchmen. They were very friendly and greeted me as one of their close friends. I do not know what my friend told them about me, but I felt like an honored guest. The entire performance was something out of another world. The group of entertainers came directly from Paris to give their compatriots so far away from home something from their homeland. The variety show lasted over two hours. The spoken words went over my head with some rare exceptions; everything else I enjoyed tremendously, from the classical music to the short sketches appropriate for men working in this kind of isolation. I was so grateful to my friend for providing for me a look at another world. I parted from these men with great happiness in my heart.

The forced labor camps were not entirely without entertainment either, but it was provided by the local talent. For the folks from the East, the accordion, Russian style, was the main (most easily accessible) instrument in supporting a variety of activities and performances. There were always individuals who had something to offer, for example, the young, beautiful, and talented Tamara and her group. The dining halls served these kind of activities very well.

In *Lager* II, in the dining hall, there was a piano in a relatively good condition. With the help of an interpreter, I asked the camp commander for permission to use it for short periods during my daytime off-hours. I received permission to practice during those hours when the dining hall was not in use. The commander, a civilian, also asked the kitchen workers if that would be agreeable to them. Most of the kitchen workers were from our camp, so there were no objections. At first I could only play what I still remembered; later I found piano music, mostly of popular nature, in a drawer nearby.

Music brings people together even in very strange surroundings or unusual circumstances. Soon after I started playing in the huge hall, a woman from the kitchen came to me with a booklet of Russian folk songs in her hands. She was a piano major at one of the Soviet academies of music. I immediately got up from the piano bench and asked her to play. To my great surprise, she told me that she would not touch a piano until her country was victorious. I thought that such a decision was too great a sacrifice and counter-productive, since playing her favorite instrument would help her overcome her trauma. Because of the language difficulties, I was unable to share my thoughts and remained silent. Her husband was a major in the Soviet Army; she had no idea where he was, whether alive and well or wounded or killed in action. She urged me to learn a few of the songs in the booklet and said that she would be delighted to hear me play these songs. The booklet was her gift to me. She seemed well educated but deeply depressed because her great expectations and promise had been denied as was the case for thousands of others during those years. At the time she was probably around thirty years old, very reserved and very dignified.

On another occasion a German soldier came into the dining hall after hearing the piano. He introduced himself, saying that he had been a piano student before being drafted. He did not hesitate to play for me. I was just amazed at his technique. He played a Liszt composition which I did not know; I believe it was one of the Hungarian Rhapsodies. I saw him only once more. That time he played almost an entire recital, a great performance. He also brought me some music he bought when he had a few days leave. I never saw him again and often wondered what happened to that talented young man.

Only once I almost got into trouble. I was playing the song "Hej, Slovani," when someone approached from behind, strongly pressed his hand on my shoulders, and in a commanding voice told me to stop. The word "verboten" came across loud and clear.

Playing the piano in a different camp actually brought me a little closer to the prisoners in my camp. Thus, I was invited one Sunday afternoon to a Russian barrack to hear new Russian poetry. When I arrived there, a little unsure of myself and what I was going to hear, I was introduced to a giant of a person, a Russian poetess, who had been writing her poetry in this camp for a number of years already. I sat there, the only man among approximately twenty-five to thirty women, listening to poetry in a language in which I missed almost all meaning, but I remember the soft sounds of the language, the expression on the poetess's face, and the smooth flow of the words. The women in the room were very silent throughout the reading and gave the poetess hearty applause and praise at the end. I am still sorry that I did not ask at least for a copy of one of her poems on that day. One often thinks "I will do this another day," but that day never comes. . . .

All these are some of my positive reminiscences of the camp, of the men and women working there, and of a few individuals who became closer to me. However, the dark clouds and the realities of Auschwitz were not too far away.

Part II

One evening, a Ukrainian woman, Vala, who was working in the kitchen, told me how she came to this camp. After the Germans occupied the Ukraine and destroyed almost everything, they assembled in the villages the remaining population, mostly women, and offered them employment further west. These women had no alternative except death by starvation; therefore, they accepted. Vala and the other Ukrainians in the camp were now worried about some papers signed before they were taken west. She did not know what she signed. Now they were very much worried what would happen to them when the Soviet Army reached the Auschwitz camps. They wanted to go back to their homes but feared possible severe punishment for signing those papers[12] which would prove that they had volunteered their services to the German Reich.[13]

Next to our camp were Polish prisoners. They appeared to be under much stricter control than forced labor camps but not under military guard. Though there was some distance between our camp and theirs, we were able to communicate as much as our language problems allowed. The Poles had been in prison for years. Those men that we talked to must have been imprisoned at a very early age as in 1944 they were not much more than twenty years old. We tried to find out from them a little about the Auschwitz camps history. Being prisoners they did not have much information; their status and severe restrictions of movement prevented adequate observation. However, on one occasion, one of them said that since 1942, transports of people had been arriving almost daily, but there were roughly the same number of people in the camps throughout the years. This information did not seem logical or reasonable. We thought that he was just trying to scare us. He would not say anything more even though we were urging him to explain. Nevertheless, we became concerned.

The Germans had very extensive anti-aircraft guns set up all around the factories and further away from the camps. We avoided places where these guns were set up; these places were off limits. In addition to guns, there was smokescreen equipment everywhere that would cover the entire area with smoke to protect the factories from air attacks. The smokescreen equipment was placed around the factories, all camps and some surrounding territory. Under very windy conditions (many days were windy), the very high chimneys often gave away the location of the I.G Farbenindustrie plant. One of our colleagues came too close to smoke-making equipment. As a result his warm winter coat disintegrated in a few hours. Because he was able to speak German, he decided to request a replacement coat. The rest of us were not convinced that complaining about such an incident was a good idea.

It came as a surprise to all of us that his request was granted. He was directed to a barrack far away from our camp and came back with a very nice-looking and warm winter coat. At first he was not willing to talk; his behavior, however, was strange. Several hours later, after being pressured repeatedly, he told us that in this particular barrack, there was a mountain of clothes, shoes, boots, sorted only roughly by general categories. When he was taken into this place and saw all that was stored there, he was shocked and scared. The prisoner who took him inside did not say a word and pulled out a coat of the approximately correct size in a hurry. Our colleague had to sign a paper and that was all. We kept questioning him how much was there. Mountains of stuff, he answered. It looked like all those rumors surfacing here and there were not really rumors. What happened to all the people? There was just too much clothing there to ascribe it to any normal sequence of events, even a severe epidemic. In an epidemic, the clothes would have been destroyed in any case.

The truth came out only piecemeal and gradually; it was conveyed in whispers and only after a person-to-person confidentiality had been firmly established. Talking about these high secrets, or even knowing about them, was in itself almost a death sentence if caught by or reported to the authorities. But there was no way to verify the truth of what was so secretly circulated.

Our attention was initially directed toward the fact that there were no cemeteries in Auschwitz. "Look around," our informants would say, "Do you see any?" The cemeteries could have been located some distance away as was the case on the Island of Rab. The mortality rate in the concentration camps, although not in the forced labor camps, was very high due to malnutrition, sickness, mistreatment, and frequent executions of prisoners for any reason or no reason at all. The Nazis apparently set up crematoria for quick disposal of corpses and to keep the number of victims a secret. Many informants thought no records were kept.[14]

In a very short time, we, the prisoners in the forced labor camps in Auschwitz, became fully aware that in comparison to our daily life and work assignments, the concentration camp was not only a hell of pain, cruelty, and starvation, it was also a place where chances for survival were minimal. Indirectly, this awareness of the concentration camps kept everybody in the forced labor camps under firm and constant control simply by creating an ever-present fear of the possible next step. There were only two punishments for minor or major infractions of the rules or for disobedience: (1) transfer to a concentration camp or (2) immediate execution.

The location of *Lager* III, our place, was far away from the Auschwitz camp's railroad station and railroad tracks. We did not have the opportunity, even during our walks, to approach the railroad areas and to observe the traffic and activities there. Neither were we located next to the main road leading to the front lines in the direction of Cracow (Kraków). Thus, we were unaware of the amount of traffic coming and going in and out of Auschwitz, what was being moved and when.[15]

However, what that Polish prisoner implied, the unexpected discovery of the mountain of clothes in the storage, and the whispering about the mass killings in the past years made us aware that this place had many different faces, some of which were not to be discussed under any circumstances, were not to be believed, and had best be erased from our minds or records forever.

These mass killings and deaths apparently took place before we arrived, at least that was what we were told by a few of those who had been in Auschwitz for several years. We did not know that killings were still going on while we were there.[16] Neither did we know at the time that certain groups of people were specifically singled out for extermination.[17] We were told that those considered most dangerous to the Third Reich were the primary targets for elimination.

For all these reasons, we started reminding ourselves constantly to avoid in every way possible getting into difficulties with the authorities and, as a consequence, being arrested and then transferred to one of the concentration camps, the first step to the final punishment. A cloud of fear and nightmare was hanging over us. All these pieces of information came to our attention from people outside *Lager* III. I have serious doubts that the women in the Eastern Block sector of our camp had any idea of what was going on. That may not have been true for the women in the German sector of the camp. However, there was never, never, the slightest rumor coming out from the women residing there.[18]

A shock came one day when we heard that one woman from our group of the transport from Ljubljana had been arrested by the Gestapo, when she was caught giving a concentration camp prisoner some food. Apparently, this prisoner came from time to time to the office where C. J. was working. He had special technical skills which were in demand in that part of the factories. The chief of her department pleaded desperately with the Gestapo to let her go, claiming that he needed her very badly for the operations in his department, which were so vital to the entire production in the factories. Fortunately, thanks to him, C. J. was saved from the worst. It was a great relief and also a serious warning to all of us.

We Slovenes usually gathered evenings around a few tables in a corner of the dining hall for discussions, for occasional singing, or just to be together. Among us was also a woman from Ljubljana with two beautiful daughters. This lady always looked so sad and worried. She was especially concerned about her daughters, so concerned that it seemed a little unusual. Once I was sitting across from her at the table, examining my booklet of Russian songs; most of the others already left. Her two daughters were at the other end talking to a few women there. When

I looked up, I saw tears running down the lady's face. I tried to console her by say-ing that our situation was not that desperate and that we had a good chance for survival. She just looked at me for a little while. Then she confided her worries and the reasons for her constant and deep concern. Her husband had been ar-rested by the Gestapo for the single reason that he was Jewish. She had no idea where they took him; she had never received any message from him or about him. Now she was very concerned about her two daughters because they were half-Jewish. What would happen to them? Were they in serious danger? She did not understand why she and her two daughters had been selected for our transport, since the rest of us were political prisoners. I was slightly aware at that time that Jewish people were a special target under the Nazi regime. I did recall hearing on the news about the *Kristallnacht*[19] of 1938, and about what was happening in Vienna after the Nazis occupied Austria in 1938. This information came to us from people who reported how the Nazis were searching for Jews in Vienna, ar-resting them and confiscating their property. However, we also knew that the Nazis were doing the same to their political enemies of any other ethnic group on a large scale, including their German and Austrian opponents. We were con-vinced that the same would happen to us, and it did, after they occupied our land.[20] I did realize that evening that the good mother's tears were indicative of great despair, a despair she did not even share with her two daughters.

At one of those evening gatherings, we were surprised by a special visitor. We did not know at first the identity of this man in a black uniform with short, stocky build and with an impressive belly. The black uniform immediately reminded us to be careful. The man took a seat at our table and told us that he was in charge of all camps in Auschwitz; he was not specific about what he meant by "all." A person from our office came by at that moment and greeted him by saying his title and his name. I do not remember either. He just sat there for a while, looking us over and asking where we came from. The information did not seem to register with him, and we thought that he had no idea where our land was on the map of Europe. Since we were singing softly before he approached our tables, he must have heard us. We, of course, stopped singing as soon as he came near. After a while, because the conversation did not go anywhere, he urged us to continue singing. At first we were a little shy, but our courage did come back. This man in black uniform was sitting there and listening. He seemed to be deep in his thoughts, almost absent from the place where we were. Then came a great surprise; he asked if we knew the song "Kje so tiste stezice?" ("Where are those little footpaths?"), a Slovene Carin-thian folksong. His pronunciation of the song's title was rough, almost difficult to understand, but it was clear that he knew the song and probably much more about our land and people than one would have thought at first. We sang several verses. Soon after that he got up and left, saying "Gute Nacht" (Good night).

After he left, we guessed that he was probably an Austrian from the Carinthian province, southern Carinthia most likely, where a large Slovene minority remained after the Plebiscite of 1920 when the borders between Austria and Yugoslavia were set after World War I.

This man came four or five more times and every time we had to sing and to include "Kje so tiste stezice," usually as the last song of the evening. However, we also became a little suspicious about his intentions, because every time he came, he tried to join the two beautiful young sisters. The two were either twins or very close in age, around seventeen or eighteen years old. When the man approached, the two girls immediately left their places and ran around the tables while he chased after them. The man never gave the impression that he wanted to catch, touch, or harm them in any way. However, we were in Auschwitz. Attention to any individual was something to worry about. After they ran around the tables three or four times, the chase was over, and the involved parties took places at different ends of the tables. The entire situation was rather funny; it looked like children at play, but the underlying consequences were of concern to all of us. Now the poor, terrified mother had an additional major concern.

Cold weather arrived early in the fall, with strong winds, often mixed with rain and even with a little snow. The night duties became more difficult. Usually we put on everything we had just to keep warm. One of the men from the Ljubljana transport volunteered to take night duty at all times if we relieved him from other responsibilities during the day. We gladly agreed to that, since our turns at night thus came up less frequently. We were a little distrustful about his reasons for this. The man was older than most of us, around 45 to 50 years old, with a pleasant personality and speedily learning Russian.

I started suffering from frostbite on the toes of both feet because of the cold weather. At first it presented only a small irritation but soon reached a painful stage. No matter what I did or what I inserted into my boots, the situation deteriorated rapidly. Now that the cold had almost but not entirely eliminated the bedbugs, the frostbite set in. Toward the end of November, however, I received a package from my relatives in Carinthia, a pair of used hiking boots, a size bigger than what I normally wore. Who thought from so far away in Carinthia that a pair of boots would be so welcome? Even though my own boots were in better shape, after a few days of wearing my new, slightly oversize boots, my frostbite was almost gone. Those boots were like a miracle and certainly saved my feet from a serious problem. Who was the previous owner of these boots? I suspected that they belonged to one of my two cousins, who were before 1938 Austrian, and after that year, German citizens, and as such were drafted into the German Army. In 1942, they were both killed at different locations on the Russian front.

On one of these very cold nights, when I had the duty at the main gate, sitting in the adequately warm entrance shelter, two women from the camp came to me at

3:00 A.M. At first I did not understand the reason for this nightly visit. After they stepped into the booth, I noticed that the young girl was pregnant, very pregnant, I thought. Her older companion informed me that another girl from the same barrack already gone to the office and that a rescue car would take this pregnant girl to the hospital. I had never seen any pregnant women in our camp, so this visit came as a great shock. The older woman then told me that she could not stay, because she had to go to work at five in the morning. The pregnant girl was twisting in pain but smiling nevertheless. I begged and begged the older woman to stay. "What will I do if the real thing happens?" I kept saying but to no avail. The woman left wishing me luck. I did not have the slightest idea how this process went. However, the young girl was in pain. During those times that the labor pains subsided, she kept saying in Russian, "Mitja, don't worry, everything will be alright." Many Russian folks had problem with my name Metod; therefore, occasionally they called me Mitja, claiming that Metod in Russian is Mitja. The girl kept laughing at my extremely nervous state. Would I have to assist her in delivering the baby? She tried to assure me that the baby was not coming yet. She was in "my custody" for almost two hours before that primitive ambulance arrived. I wished her good luck. There were no babies or married couples in our camp; she was probably transferred after the hospital stay to another camp. In the morning, when the women went to work, they kept asking, jokingly, about my baby delivery.

A few times when we were on duty at the main gate late at night, the German army patrols (or maybe they were SS troops) came down the road. Although we received the password every evening just in case, the commanders of these patrols did not like to be asked to identify themselves. After a while, when hearing many footsteps approaching, we did not even step outside; what were we supposed to do? We let the patrols pass our camp without interference. We were afraid that these very tired and heavily armed troops would react in an unpleasant or dangerous way. Fortunately, we rarely saw organized military nearby, except a few individuals who were off duty and trying to visit the ladies in either sector of *Lager* III.

Part III

The distant thunder, hardly noticeable at first during the months of November and early December 1944, gradually became more audible. There were no doubts in our minds that the Russian front was coming closer and closer. You could sense some nervousness among those in command around the camps. Most people (not all) realized by then that Germany would be defeated sooner or later. The important goal, constantly on everybody's mind, was to survive. A lot could happen when the front lines approached, when one authority departed and another took over. What would it be like when this huge wave crossed over? There were great concerns about what the Germans would do before their retreat to the thousands of prisoners. Would we find ourselves right in the middle of the battlefield, and what could we expect from the approaching frontline Soviet troops? Nobody considered at the time the possibility of a cessation of hostilities before the front reached the Auschwitz camps.

However, the Soviets, even though very close to us at the end of 1944, were not the only force approaching Auschwitz. The American and British air forces were now as far north (American) and east (British) as occupied Poland.

When the American (and British?) air force planes flew into the vicinity of Auschwitz,[21] the sirens started blasting, and the protective smoke filled the air to hide the entire Auschwitz complex. Whoever was in the camp at the time was directed toward the nearby woods south of the camp to seek protection from the hail of particles from the exploding anti-aircraft grenades. Actually, nobody told the people in our camp to seek protection. The women's camp was too close to the factories, less than a quarter of a mile away, not a safe place during an air attack. Everybody was running as fast as possible to reach the partial protection of the woods. When I first broke the rules and ran into the woods, I experienced first-hand what the women had been telling me about. That heavy rain of fragments was very scary; it sounded like a severe hailstorm, the pieces falling and falling without a pause. The thickest and tallest trees offered the best protection. Which side of the tree was better had to be decided by the location of the branches and how many branches were above you. One felt like an animal being chased from all sides. Almost no one possessed any adequate head covering. The total time spent in the woods was usually a little more than an hour; air attacks normally lasted around 20 to 30 minutes. Occasionally, the planes in the vicinity caused an alert status but didn't bomb our location. On the one hand, these planes brought us hope for an end of our imprisonment; on the other hand, the bombs were very often too close to our camp for comfort. During one attack I was standing next to a Russian prisoner who was in great excitement, screaming and praising our Allies, the Americans. Then a bomb fell very close to us; the air pressure was tremendous. My Russian co-prisoner grew pale and yelled with a raised fist at the departing planes, screaming unprintable oaths.

During one heavy direct attack on the factories on 18 December 1944, I was standing and observing the approaching planes from a grenade-shaped concrete structure, a free-standing bunker, inside our camp.[22] The small openings in the front of the structure offered a clear view of the factories. From this point, well protected from the falling shrapnel, although not from a direct hit, I was able to see how the planes approached, descended slightly still in perfect formation, and then released their bombs. The strong winds on that day uncovered the chimneys and the higher buildings in the factories, thus providing a clear target for the attacking planes. The earth was shaking; the explosions were deafening. The bombs fell in clusters, one cluster after another. When the planes turned around instead of departing, a few of us Slovenes and a group of young Polish women ran toward a shelter built from bales of pressed straw. All of a sudden, the air pressure threw us at the straw shelter, and then, in a split second, an explosion followed. No one was hurt, fortunately, and we rushed inside the protective structure. Many people were already there. We squeezed together because the darkness prevented better use of the space.

In such situations, when the bombs are falling all around and you expect to be hit at any moment, every person lives with his or her own fear, thoughts, hopes. It helped to hold onto the person(s), man or woman, next to you. Since we entered this protective structure with a group of young Polish women to seek protection together, we were a little surprised at their not only gentle but here and there aggressive touch. Was that fear only or something more? This togetherness offered some comfort even though you had never seen the person or persons next to you ever before in your life. A natural instinct created at that moment a determined willingness in each one of us to assist each other no matter what the future would bring. It felt as if one's heart stopped during each hit nearby; the nerves in one's entire body were brought to a breaking point.

When the threatening sounds of the airplanes gradually diminished and the shells of the anti-aircraft guns stopped exploding, the sigh of relief was sensed inside the shelter although at first nobody moved. We started looking around, trying to decipher in the dark whom we were leaning on or who was squeezing our hands or attempting an embrace. Slightly ashamed of our fear and our display of general weakness, we exited from the shelter one by one. Not far away, maybe hundred yards, was a huge crater, where the bomb that lifted us off our feet hit. Fortunately, the terrain there was very soft and mushy, and the exploding bomb did not scatter its deadly particles around.

During another large-scale attack, we abandoned our positions and ran into the woods with other people from the camp. On that day two bombs hit our camp. One destroyed half of our residence barrack, the other a barrack in the middle of the Eastern Block camp. When we ran to see the damage, we heard a voice calling for help. One girl had crawled under the her bed when the bombs started falling in the vicinity. She survived without a scratch even though her barrack was almost flattened. It took a little time to get her out. We were all relocated to other barracks. The attacking planes did not use incendiary bombs during the attacks on Auschwitz; otherwise our camps would have gone up in smoke. Our fire-fighting equipment would not have been able to deal with any major fire in spite of the training some of us received.[23]

In those cold and very windy December days, a group of about twenty to twenty-five French women were brought to our camp. The rumor had it that they were released from one of the concentration camps, something that was hard to believe. Their looks confirmed an extremely rough life though; they were skinny and undernourished. In civilian clothes of all varieties, they looked different from the others in *Lager* III. We wondered if their clothes were from the storage area. Their behavior was strange as well. They kept to themselves, never exchanged any words with anybody else outside their group. That complete silence surprised us and confirmed that the so-called rumors of concentration camp life were not just rumors. We recalled our first observations of the "striped" prisoners, who, although working together, almost never exchanged any words. These French women were in our camp only a few days. Where they were taken after that was not known in the camp; one hopes they went back to France to at least partial freedom.

The problems resulting from the consumption of alcohol, or something that was supposed to be a drinkable alcohol product (illegally produced of course), were known to us as soon as we began working in *Lager* III. The men waiting in the evenings outside the camp often had bottles of this poison in their pockets. They tried to force us to drink their product, the sight of which alone raised severe warnings. It looked like a soap mixture; how it tasted I don't know since I successfully avoided allowing any drop of it to go down my throat. Needless to say, refusing a brotherly drink greatly offended those who were offering. Telling them that there was no drinking permitted while on duty did not have any meaning or did not register. It also came to our attention that this home-made alcohol had very damaging consequences for some individuals.

One late evening in the mid–December 1944 during very cold weather, we were called to an Eastern Block barrack where the women were desperately trying to prevent a very drunk and violent man from entering their residence. How and where this man entered the camp was a puzzle to us until the next morning when we found a part of the defensive fence destroyed in an area far away from the main road. This man was completely unaware of where he was and what he was doing, except he was determined to enter the barrack. It took several men and a few strong women to drag this man to the main entrance, where we finally pushed him into the arms of other men who were standing and laughing there. I had never experienced so much power in any single individual. Those more knowledgeable than I in these matters kept explaining that drinking the special alcohol mixture produced and distributed around the camps caused this wild behavior. Fortunately, the men standing outside dragged this unfortunate and very sick soul away.

Throughout December, everybody realized that the days of Auschwitz were coming to the end. That thunder, at first heard only as a distant storm, was now clear and distinctive. We could hear heavy artillery fire and other kinds of loud explosions. It was obvious from ever-louder sounds of thunder that the front was approaching. When Christmas came, in spite of all that was going on in our vicinity, there was even in the forced labor camps a special meal that evening. After all, the Feast of Christmas had to be celebrated; our eyes were simply closed to everything that was happening all around as we did so. Our group assembled in the hall after the evening meal to exchange Christmas greetings and wishes for freedom in the coming year. It was in a way a festive occasion; our thoughts went back to our homes, to our land, to our dearest. My mind traveled back, against my will, to 1940, the last Christmas in Dravograd; to 1941, that terrible winter during the first year of occupation; to 1942 in Concentration Camp Rab; to 1943, to the disasters and executions after Grčarice and Turjak; and then back to Auschwitz, so far away from home: I was facing such an unknown and insecure future. A few Christmas songs helped a little, but deep concerns were there, many deep concerns.

The air attack on 26 December was especially strong, with many waves of planes. On this day the factories were clearly visible and exposed. The planes were attacking and attacking. When we returned from the woods, another case of breaking the rules, one thing was obvious—we had no heat. Apparently the main source of heat in the camps received a direct hit. Without heat we were going to have a difficult time: We learned that the heating would not be restored for some time, if at all. We started collecting all available mattresses to pile against the cracks in the windows and walls. Fortunately, the kitchen was still able to operate, and from there a little warmth escaped into the adjacent hall where we consumed our meals. We wore all our clothes, as many layers as possible, to keep from freezing and from getting frostbite. Sleeping at night was most problematic; we woke up often because of the cold. Even though I kept them covered during the night, my boots were frozen in the morning; I had to warm them with my feet. The women in the camp still maintained their working schedules; they were frozen to the bone in the morning on the way to work. Many said that they had heat at work and that helped them to get through on those cold days. How much damage was done to the factories was difficult to guess; operations seemed to be continuing.

During this attack we thought that one of the attacking planes had been hit. It separated from the formation and experienced difficulties keeping proper elevation. The sounds of its engines were different from what we were used to hearing. From our limited view, we did not see any parachutes or see the plane descending. All signs, however, indicated that one of the attacking planes did crash; a few persons claimed that they heard an unusual explosion a distance away.

Because the Eastern Front was so close to Auschwitz at this point, we started receiving visits from the Soviet planes as well. The Soviets came only at night, mostly during the evening hours, one plane at the time. These air raids were more nerve-wracking because of the darkness and the mosquito-like circling strategy. We waited in fear. A flare being dropped was a sign that the next bomb would be hitting in a few seconds. These single attacks lasted roughly an hour; the plane kept going around again and again, even over the camps near the factories. Not much damage was done with a bomb here and there, but these lengthy visits affected everybody's nerves. I'm certain that the Soviets were fully aware of the existence of the factories and the many camps around them; maybe not the ground soldiers on the front lines but the local commanders must have known about our existence and presence.

The Soviet planes, one at the time, visited us almost daily. They did not drop bombs every time but often enough. No doubt, we were now very close to the battlefield. Sounds of fighting were heard around the clock, and we could already distinguish artillery fire from other explosions. Sometimes we thought that we heard even machine-gun fire though we could not tell whether the sound came from the front or from the patrols circling around the camps. We never saw any SS troops in action or passing by our camp. In my entire time in Auschwitz I saw only one SS man, who came to the camp entrance trying to visit a woman in the German sector. I noticed on his uniform the insignia of the NDH (*Nezavisna država Hrvatska*—The Independent State of Croatia) and asked him what he was doing so far away from home. Even though he was very talkative, trying to arrange for permission to enter the camp, he did not clarify his assignment in Auschwitz. However, we were told again and again by other prisoners that the SS troops were stationed here, that they were in charge of the concentration camps, and that they might have the last say in what would happen before the arrival of the Soviets.

The big question at the arrival of the new year was whether 1945 would bring peace. We knew very little about the Western Front and almost nothing about the war in the Pacific and Asia. We also heard occasionally about the so-called new developments in the German war industry, something we could not completely ignore. However, the situation around Auschwitz at the beginning of January was more or less decided. The week after that great attack by the western Air Force planes and the destruction of the heating system, we tried to cope as best we could. Those of us not working in the factories were wondering how much damage the latest major American air attack and the attacks by the single Soviet planes caused inside the factories. Not much information came from the people working there. They were always taken to their work places by the shortest way possible and did not have a chance to look around. The toughest assignments, we were told, were given to those concentration camp prisoners who were forced to remove unexploded bombs. The rumors circulated that many assigned to this kind of work died when the bombs exploded. I did not witness, and could not confirm, that such work and such accidents took place.

I saw my French friend for the last time early in January. He told me that they were preparing to move west as soon as their command reached an agreements with the German camp command. A move was expected soon, he told me.

My friend Hinko visited me more often during those days. His instructions covered the evacuation of the ambulance corps, where he was working, on short notice. As he had several times before, he tried to get me a job in his ambulance to help him during the move but he was not successful. His superiors were sympathetic to his requests but not willing to get involved in such matters. Nobody really knew where such requests were decided and who was making decisions, so it was safer not to get involved or expose oneself to more scrutiny.

It was either on 15 or 16 January when I woke up around 3:00 A.M., not because of the cold but because of the sudden complete and deadly silence. After weeks and days of constant thunder and bombardment, this sudden terrifying silence was unexpected and very scary. I woke up another colleague, who, according to his story, had been arrested by the Gestapo while serving as a sergeant with the Home Defenders. Together we walked around the camp. Uncomfortable peacefulness surrounded us. There were no movements; nobody walked around; we did not even find the night-roaming guard except for our colleague standing at the entrance with visible fear on his face. We thought that at any moment the Soviet soldiers would come down the road or emerge from the surrounding woods. The German military probably retreated during the night, we thought, and new forces would take over. Why else would there be no firing and fighting? That, of course, would have been an ideal takeover. Two hours later, the first women were on the way to work, also wondering about the reason for the depressing silence. It was strange that this silence had such a negative effect on us. It probably introduced a new dimension to our situation, a dimension we had not been used to over the last two months. This silence was a predecessor to something never before experienced, a major cataclysmic happening. That day marked the beginning of the end of that notorious place known in pre-war times only as Ošwięcim and from 1940 on and forever by the German name of Auschwitz.[24]

Some of the workers in the factories were told to go back to their camps and wait for further instructions. Men and women from the same village were trying to get together in anticipation of an evacuation or something else. Deliveries to the kitchen were still made; however, there was fear that supplies would stop coming. The office had no information; they seemed to be more confused and worried than anybody else in the camp. The Soviet planes were still coming every night and dropping bombs, although not as often as before. At night we could not seek protection in the woods; it was even more risky than staying in the barracks. If any places outside the factories were hit by the Soviet planes, I did not notice. Our camp was spared even though it was so close to the factories.

The worst evening was 17 January 1945. It was cold and miserable, dark as always, with slight precipitation. That Soviet nerve-wracking mosquito was above us again; it just did not want to go home. An older Russian woman became hysterical, knelt in the middle of the camp's main road, prayed loudly, and cried that she would soon be killed. She kept saying "pomiluj, pomiluj" (have mercy). Because shrapnel was falling, we tried to get her off the road to the nearest barrack but she fought us madly. When a bomb fell in the vicinity of the camp on open ground, the earth shook as always during the bombardments, and she finally agreed to be moved to the ditch, where she continued her praying and crying. It struck me on that occasion that older people might be more afraid to die than younger ones. Probably older people realized that death could have come at any moment, while young folks avoided such negative thoughts or did not fully comprehend the seriousness of the situation.

While we were dealing with this hysterical and terrified woman, we heard a great commotion from the main road in front of the factories. Because of the darkness, we were at first unsure about what was happening. Then the Soviet plane circling above dropped a few flares at intervals, but fortunately did not drop any bombs. A very long, slow-moving column of exhausted concentration camp prisoners was on the road, accompanied by many armed guards, probably from the SS prison detachments. This column of prisoners was heading in a westerly direction; they must have come from the men's concentration camp, Monowitz, east of our camp. How these people were able to walk, when so poorly protected from the wind and cold in their striped uniforms and caps, was nothing short of a miracle. Where they were being taken, nobody could guess. We were aware that the march was probably only the beginning of a long journey. Here and there a prisoner would collapse next to the road. Because we also heard pistol shots, we assumed that those unable to continue were shot on the spot. We noticed many who fell on the side of the road and never stood up again. We were not able to determine if any of the prisoners were executed, because we did not dare to leave the camp to see from a better vantage point what was happening. The entire column was very long, and hours passed before that death march crossed our camp's boundaries.

The next day, 18 January 1945, Concentration Camp Monowitz for women was evacuated. The same scenario was repeated. Because the evening was not as dark as the night before, we had a slightly better look at the column of these desperate individuals. Here as well, those who were unable to continue fell down at the side of the road. What was the destination for these prisoners? How would they get there, and how many would survive?[25]

Mid-morning of the next day, I noticed a few of our women taking material out of the office; most of them carried various supplies and office files. I did not realize that during the night or early morning those who had worked there had left via the entrance in the German sector, including the Croatian women from Zagreb. How and why this happened was not clear to me. Of course, these workers often went in and out of the camp, so it did not alert the person at the entrance to anything unusual. One of the women leaving the office had in her hand several card files and was waving one at me. She had my office record with my photo on it in her hands. I ran after her and pleaded with her to hand over my card. She refused. In anger, I tried to pull the card from her hand, but she turned around and squeezed the cards between her knees. When I made the attempt to get what I thought belonged to me and nobody else, she suddenly made an obscene offer. This woman did not have the best reputation in the camp. Her offer scared me a little; I released my grip on her and ran to the washroom to wash my hands. I myself was not quite sure why I did that. But I am still sorry that I did not get a look at what was inscribed on that office index card.

During that day and the next many people left the camp and did not return; the German sector was almost completely empty. Some of the German and Folksdeutsche workers had probably been secretly evacuated. Then the rumors found fertile soil. Variations were impressive: (1) The Germans would depart and allow us to remain in the camps; (2) We would be evacuated like everybody else; (3) The SS troops would go through the camps, execute whoever they would find there, and burn down the camps.

In the afternoon, a civilian official arrived and told us—we and the barrack chiefs were now the only "officials" in the camp—to count the people in the camp, to try to convince the kitchen help to provide meals, and to wait for additional instructions. We did not know who this official was, but we followed his instructions. Actually, we had a fairly nice and friendly community now. Men were coming into the camp to look for their friends. When we were going from barrack to barrack to count people, we saw many couples warming themselves under the blankets. We kept only one person at the entrance just in case other instructions came or supplies were delivered. In truth, we were expecting to see the Soviet advance troops emerge at any moment.

What to do next was a big question. Most of the people from the Soviet territories were thinking of remaining in the camps or in the vicinity—a few already had connections with Polish families in the area—and waiting for the arrival of the Soviets. The women in the camp, those that we knew better, were saying goodbye, wishing us a safe and happy future and thanking us for our friendship. We exchanged small gifts, in most cases only small pieces of paper with a few warm words. At this point rumor had it that SS troops were no longer around, that they left when the concentration camp prisoners were evacuated. There were also no other signs that the German authorities, what was left of them, cared one way or another about the prisoners in the forced labor camps. The women from the Eastern Block group more or less decided to either stay in the camp, move to other camps to be with people from their home areas and vice versa or to seek shelter with the Polish families in the Auschwitz neighborhood. The only connection to the authorities was that civilian man, who from time to time stopped in the camp to assess the situation and to review the amount of food on hand.

Late Saturday afternoon this man came with orders for evacuation. The last meals under the control of the German authorities would be on Saturday evening and Sunday morning and noon. After that, we had permission to take food supplies from storage. He commanded us to assemble Sunday toward evening at a specified location for evacuation purposes. This order applied to all forced labor camps. However, this time there were no threatening remarks added about what would happen if we decided not to follow evacuation orders.

We explained these orders to the barrack chiefs. By mutual agreement we decided that those who were part of the evacuation would take from storage two loaves of bread each; there was still plenty on the shelves. The rest of the food would remain in camp for those who were planning to stay or go into temporary hiding in the vicinity. Except for the loaves of bread, that German tough, vinegar-tasting military bread, there was not much else to take. The opinion was that those evacuated would soon receive additional food and those remaining would receive food from the arriving Soviet authorities. How this was handled in other camps, we had no chance to observe. In our camp there were no arguments regarding distribution of the remaining food supplies. The Germans at this point did not care one way or another; however, they made it clear that no additional supplies would be delivered.

When we left the camp, there were still quite a few women there. They assured us that the kitchen would be operating, and the people would be fed as best they could. Many tears were shed at our departure. In those few months of togetherness, we established not only good working relationships but many friendships as well. Most people from the Western territories, however, but definitely not all, decided to join the evacuation group. From our original transport, several people, those arrested as sympathizers of the OF, the communist-controlled Liberation Front (Osvobodilna fronta), decided to wait for the Soviet troops, but again this was not unanimous.[26]

We assembled toward the evening on Sunday, 21 January 1945, thousands of people from all parts of Europe, organized in columns of four or five across, and waited, again under German armed escort, for orders to march west away from Auschwitz.[27]

CHAPTER TEN

Auschwitz: Evacuation and Escape

January 1945

❧

The first V-2 rockets, one of the new German weapons for winning the war, were directed toward England on 8 September 1944. These V-2 rockets were the precursors of techniques for space exploration developed after the war.

Belgrade was liberated by the Soviet forces on 20 October 1944. The Red Army thus established a firm base in Yugoslavia for a further push west and south.

The news about Roosevelt's election to a fourth term on 7 November 1944 spread around Europe instantaneously.

The last major offensive by the German forces began on 16 December 1944 in the Ardennes. After the German initial success, the superior Allied forces repulsed the enemy; casualties on both sides were heavy and costly in human lives and military equipment.

The assembly center for the evacuation of the forced labor prisoners of both sexes was closer to the town of Auschwitz than our own *Lager* III. Prior to departure and on the way there, we Slovenes tried to make sure that we departed as a group, even though we had been residing in different labor camps in that huge compound. The German organizers of the evacuation and their military escorts were letting people assemble according to their wishes as long as searching for one's own group did not cause confusion and delays. Nobody knew the exact time of departure although we were told that the march west and south would start that evening or during the night. Slowly, the Germans got us into organized columns; I do not remember if we were four or five abreast. I happened to find myself in the front row of our block of around 50–60 men and women. In the best of military tradition, we stood there a few hours, often running to the nearby latrines for the necessary relief.

In addition to the two loaves of German bread taken from the kitchen supplies, most of us also carried two wool blankets. We rolled these tightly and carried them over the shoulders and across the body; this way they were secured and also provided extra warmth, much needed in those cold and penetrating January days and nights. We also tried to take with us all our other possessions. I had a wooden, box-like small suitcase, which my father bought in Krakow during his First World War military service. If this suitcase would have had a memory, it would have been very surprised to return during the Second World War almost to its origin. Although not very convenient to carry—I strapped it on my back—it also served as a convenient seat or even something to lean on during the long stops. Among those assembled, I also spotted the woman who took my index card from the camp's office. She had a huge bundle on her back, really huge. I considered approaching her once more for the return of my papers but then changed my mind. Even if she were willing to reconsider, how would we find that little file, if it was still there, in that huge bundle and in that darkness. Also, she looked at me with such fierce and unfriendly eyes that I lost my courage.

The sundry items those half-frozen and by-then very hungry people had in their possession, either for their survival or as possible trading items, were worthy of detailed description, and at the same time they made it clear how much we wanted to protect ourselves under those circumstances. There was, however, at least one exception to all these attempts to carry as much as possible. A Croatian friend, nicknamed Braco, known to all as a skillful trader or, as some would say, successful black-market operator, stood there dressed as if going to an evening opera performance; nice winter coat, impressive hat, warm gloves, good leather boots, a perfect gentleman. Asked how he planned to survive without blankets or anything else, his answer was philosophical and simple: "If I survive, I will acquire everything I need again, if not, what good would all this stuff be to me?"

One had the impression that the entire European continent was represented within this group of forced laborers. People from the East were there as well; if there were any Soviet citizens among us, I do not know, but Russian, Ukrainian, and Polish were heard in addition to Czech, Slovak, Serbo-Croatian, French, Italian, German, and a few others. Though we did not know what the situation was on the Western and South European fronts or whether the war was almost over or not, the main hope for all of us in that column was to get home or close to home as soon as and by any means possible. Survival, as always, was constantly on our minds.

The order to move came exactly at midnight on Sunday, 21 January 1945. We were doubly relieved; the long and nerve-wracking wait in the cold night was over, and there existed at least a half-realistic hope that the next stop would be slightly less exposed, closer to home or, by some miracle, even home itself.

The German guards—there were quite a few of them—were certainly not SS troops or front-line soldiers but were armed nevertheless. Their responsibility was to accompany or drag these people away from Auschwitz to a new workplace in some kind of orderly fashion and with minimal problems. These guards looked as tired as we were, and they were most likely more than displeased with their assignment. A few individuals who tried to get something useful out of them were told in an unfriendly way not to bother them. They were walking next to the column on both sides, often in the less-trodden section of the snow-covered road, which made their march even more tiring.

The night was dark; any illumination came from reflections on snow on that flat land. The sky was covered with clouds and not much help, if any at all, came from the stars; but we got used to the darkness and marching fairly fast warmed our bodies a little. For a while the people in the column moved almost in complete silence, in a kind of mysterious stupor, which emphasized the uncertainty of our situation. Constantly on our minds were the Soviet airplanes that had been destroying our nerves in recent days. Should they spot us, would they know who we were or would they mistake us for German troops in retreat? How much visibility can a pilot get from a plane with only Christmas tree-like illumination? But we did not hear any airplanes near or in the distance; all we could hear were our footsteps—many, many footsteps.

A few months before, when our train was approaching Auschwitz, we saw almost no settlements or houses on that final stretch of land. Now we were on a parallel road, and we saw only here and there an isolated house; naturally, we could not see into the distance because of the darkness. These few houses we passed were small and looked poverty-stricken.

We were completely unaware of how many groups were ahead of or behind us. However, we guessed that there were that night close to sixty thousand or even more people on the road. Instead of evacuation, the correct term for this move should have been "retreat." After all, the Soviets were coming and we were moving away from them, each group probably for a different reason, but moving away nevertheless. From time to time we had to get off the road to provide free passage for German military trucks heading in the opposite direction, toward the front lines somewhere in the distance behind us. We also saw a few artillery pieces going to the front but no tanks. When the yelling started to get off the road, the soldiers guarding us became very nervous, looking over this mass of people running off the road. For our own safety, we had to clear the road in a hurry. Those vehicles moved fast with no intention of stopping for anything. But no German military unit of any kind overtook us going in our direction.

After about one hour of marching, the entire French contingent, members of *Le service du travail obligatoire* (Le S.T.O), caught up with us and passed our column in a very fast and efficient way. Those Frenchmen were in uniform, dressed to perfection, with identical backpacks and no extras hanging from their bodies. They were organized, I believe, in groups of approximately one hundred, or so it seemed, each group with a commander. We were admiring their discipline when they passed by, unit by unit. The entire move to get ahead of our group took about twenty to thirty minutes. They were moving fast, almost running around us, while we still walked at our own pace. I tried hard to spot my French friend among them, an impossibility, of course; I am sure he was there heading toward home. Observing this speed and efficiency, we wondered why these capable people lost the war in 1940 so quickly.

The items too heavy to carry were now being thrown away. A march in the snow on a slippery and messy road takes a lot out of a person. The last warm soup-like meal was already history. Some folks were falling behind, going to the end of the group or joining a slower-moving one behind us. We had been on the march about two hours when it started to get much colder; fortunately there were no strong winds that night. I exchanged only a few words with those next to me from time to time, words of encouragement, not much else.

It was probably a little after 2:00 A.M. when we caught up with a wagon transporting eight older women, a wagon pulled by two oxen, therefore moving very slowly. I immediately recognized the man in charge of this unusual outfit, who was identified as an official by a large Red Cross band on his sleeve. It was Hinko, Hinko Špendl, the ambulance attendant. He was extremely happy to see us. We had lost contact with him for the last two days but assumed that he had departed ahead of us with his ambulance unit.

When he spotted me, he approached the nearest guard and requested that one person be released from the column to help him care for these women who were unable to walk. Hinko, almost fluent in German, was tall, had an impressive personality and knew how to approach those in charge. The guard seemed to have no objections—nobody actually knew how many people were in this entire column; it did not really matter one way or another—so Hinko grabbed me by the arm and pulled me out of the column. I called back to my friends that we would catch up with them later. Hinko apparently did not forget Milojka's wish that Hinko and I should stay together.[1]

I was welcomed by the eight women resting on the wagon, covered with everything they had and keeping close together to stay warm. My suitcase was placed on the wagon, but I had kept important personal items and provisions with me, including the crucially important blankets. We waited until two more groups passed, then continued our journey as soon as the first break between the retreating groups offered an opportunity. Hinko was with the oxen most of the time; I walked next to the wagon.

The ambulance unit, where Hinko had been working, had departed Auschwitz late on the previous afternoon. It was clear to all that a wagon pulled by oxen would delay the advance of the entire ambulance unit. Those in command, therefore, asked Hinko, because of his language dexterity, to stay with these women and do the best possible for them. He readily agreed. Hinko had a good heart for the less fortunate. His travel progress was slow though, and the necessary stops consumed a lot of time. The women helped each other though they spoke at least two if not three different languages among themselves. Hinko told me that all night groups of all sorts of people passed him. A few passers-by even joked and asked him how far he was planning to go to find a home for his oxen and how he planned to greet the Soviets when they caught up with him.

This column of retreating humanity apparently did not have an end. Group after group passed us during the next hour. Because of the increased cold, the women asked if we could stop at the next house to warm up a little. Knocking on a strange door at that hour of night was not a pleasant or safe thing to try, but Hinko was willing. We pulled our wagon to the side of a house. Somebody opened the door even before we approached the entrance. When Hinko explained the situation with the help of a Polish-speaking woman, the couple in the house cordially invited us in. We did not know at the time that the women in the wagon already had some discussions among themselves and decided to remain somewhere and not to continue this, for them, impossible journey. When asked about his opinion, Hinko told them what they wanted to do was their decision. After a short discussion, all eight women voted to stay somewhere provided a temporary shelter could be found for them. Hinko and the Polish interpreter then talked to the man of the house and his wife. In exchange for accepting these unfortunate women, he would turn over to them both oxen and the wagon with everything on it. The family was extremely happy with his offer. They promised they would get in touch with their neighbors to place these women in several houses in the vicinity and that they would share the newly acquired property with those who were prepared to help. Hinko then described this transaction on a piece of paper in German just in case other "authorities" would show up and try to confiscate what had been turned over to this Polish couple. The women were visibly happy about the arrangement. We were sure when we departed that the two oxen would not see another day. It was really the only way to secure this property for the benefit of the people for whom it was intended and for those who would now have additional hungry folks in their care. Hinko and I decided to depart immediately. All women on that wagon wanted to embrace Hinko, thanking him for his care and concern. "Haroshi hlop" (a nice man), they kept calling after us when we left the place.

Reaching the road again, we were right away pushed into the passing column by the armed guards. They asked no questions; Hinko's Red Cross insignia meant something. We did not inquire who these people were, but from their looks we guessed that they were forced laborers. Our attempts to walk faster in order to catch up with our own group were not successful because the guards would not allow us to go ahead. We decided, therefore, to use the next opportunity and get out of this column and out from under the German control. Another reason why we decided to escape were the guards themselves. Their behavior was rough, and in our opinion they were capable of anything, not a healthy situation from a prisoner's point of view. Thus, when we had to leave the road the next time, we walked a little further into the darkness than the others, covered ourselves with snow and waited. Nobody missed us when the order came to continue the march. We stayed in the snow for a while. Three more large groups passed until there was a lull in the traffic. We then went back on the road and proceeded in the direction the rest of the folks took, at the same time listening carefully in case any other group approached us from the rear. However, because we were walking faster then most of the groups, the chance that other groups would catch up with us was minimal.

This sudden apparent freedom brought into our hearts a special feeling of happiness but also concern and fear. What now? If stopped or questioned, one of our answers would be that during the night we lost contact with our group and became stragglers; as such we were trying to rejoin the group as soon as possible. The other variation, when further away from Auschwitz, would be to claim that the authorities released us from the forced labor camp, and that in Auschwitz they would confirm that fact.

Gradually, daylight came. We could now see and appreciate the struggle prisoners had experienced during the long, cold, night march. Both sides of the road were full of items people had thrown away to lighten their loads. It was not easy in the darkness of the night to take out of the bundles and carrying cases the more precious items important for survival. We could almost tell at which place during the march there was sufficient light for sorting. Those areas were full of discards. Those discards also served us as markers, telling us that we were still on the road others took.

Around seven in the morning Hinko suggested that we stop and get something warm into our stomachs. He knocked on the door of a small house by the side of the road, and a skinny man appeared. He did not seem too happy to see a stranger standing there, but after Hinko's explanation, he let us enter the house.

We realized right away that this was not a place for begging. As I recall, the entire living space was very small; more than that, two pleasant goats had their own place at one end of it. Two small children, both girls, poorly dressed and looking very hungry, came and stood next to the table, when we started to open our bundles. Hinko grasped the situation immediately and told the woman of the house, standing at the small fireplace and preparing something for breakfast, that we would appreciate a little warm water, nothing else, to remove the chill from our bodies. We certainly did not want to take and consume that modest amount of goat milk standing in a glass on the fireplace even though the woman had sincerely offered it. The man said very little. From his starved face we could easily deduce that theirs was a life of misery and deprivation. We took out a loaf of German military bread and started cutting off narrow pieces. After warming these pieces at the fire, we all had a very modest improvised breakfast, consisting of pieces of bread and warm water. The little girls received in addition a half glass of goat milk each. It was hard not to look at one of the girls who, with her big and beautiful eyes, kept staring at us and silently telling us, I am hungry, very hungry. The younger one was shy. After she received her piece of bread, she turned around and consumed it in complete privacy.

Hinko tried to explain to both parents who we were, from where, and what our intentions and hopes were. When the man, not as old as we originally thought, finally started talking, he said that we were lucky that our homes were somewhere far from this place. They suffered a lot during the war years. Right then their main concern was what the Germans would do during their retreat, how in this interim period he would provide for his family, and what the new authorities would be like.

When we were ready to depart, Hinko intentionally left the loaf of bread on the table. The woman, however, picked up the bread, brought it to him and said that we will need the bread more than they. Hinko took the bread without a word and then handed it to the older girl standing at her mother's side. The girl did not say anything but pressed the bread to her chest; her eyes, however, told us more than we wanted to know.

The road was empty, no more marching groups, no armed guards, nothing. For a while that gave us a strange feeling. Where were we? The important thing, however, was to keep going. Where were the others, would we ever catch up with them or should we? There was no easy escape from the road if we encountered the wrong kind of people or trigger-ready armed units. Running off the road would be very suspicious, we thought. We decided to proceed in the same direction and take our chances. There really was no alternative.

Because we walked at a fast pace, we soon started catching up with stragglers. Not much news came from them. All of them were completely unaware where they were, where to go, what to do. To the best of our own ability, we gave them some advice in which direction to go to seek help.

The daring idea to try to reach our homeland came to us only gradually. At first it seemed an impossibility to even think how to cross such a distance under those completely regulated and controlled circumstances on every road and on any corner. We realized that sooner or later we would encounter one authority or the other. On the other hand, why try to get back to the detachments of forced laborers and work for the Third Reich now that we had at least a chance to go home? To reach home, we would have to get out of occupied Poland, cross occupied Czechoslovakia and annexed Austria—and finally pass through a considerable part of occupied Slovenia. There were police, border controls, military patrols, and Gestapo men everywhere. At this stage of the war it was also difficult to guess where would one get support, shelter, and food or where one might be immediately either reported or turned over to the Gestapo. One minor advantage in our favor was Hinko's language skills. In addition to German, he was well versed in Czech, two factors we thought would help us first in Czechoslovakia and then in Austria. We knew we were near the Czechoslovakian border, how near we were not sure.[2]

We were on the march all day, here and there munching on the dry, sour bread and drinking water from the melted snow. There were more and more stragglers on the road. Three of them were young guys under seventeen years old. When they heard us speaking Slovene, they approached us and asked for permission to join us. They were Croatian, and to me it is still a puzzle how they got there and why they were not under someone's care. The oldest of them was their spokesman, the youngest probably not more than twelve or thirteen years old. They promised to help in any way possible while traveling with us. Hinko immediately agreed; now we were five. The boys wanted to get back to Croatia. In addition to the three Croatian boys, we picked up during the day three more people from our original Ljubljana transport to Auschwitz months before. All of them either were not with our Slovene group when we left Auschwitz or got separated from the group during the night. There was Jože, Francka, and another man whose name I believe was Karl. Hinko, our leader, now had to worry about a team of eight people.

Late that same afternoon we finally approached a larger settlement. In the cold winter day this town gave the impression of complete isolation and inactivity. In the distance, in the center of the town, we noticed a church steeple. Hinko, always ready with a new suggestion, thought that the church may be able to provide some overnight quarters. Knowing that in the pre-war years I attended the St. Stanislaus Gymnasium, a school near Ljubljana named after the Polish saint and protector of youths, Hinko thought it was my turn to negotiate. I went ahead and knocked on the door of the priest's residence. A female caretaker opened the door and invited me in; the priest was not home at the time. I introduced myself as a former student at the St. Stanislaus Gymnasium and told her that the only thing the eight of us wanted was a roof over our heads for the night, nothing else. She told me right away to bring the entire group in and that the priest would help in any way possible. She also said, with a little smile on her face, that the priest would certainly want to hear all about the St. Stanislaus Gymnasium.

Most happy with the successful mission, I almost ran back to bring the group in. Hearing the happy news, my co-travelers hurried toward the church and the priest's residence. I noticed at that moment that Hinko was a little further back and slowly walking toward me in company of a young, well-dressed man and his son of approximately twelve years of age. When this Polish gentleman learned from Hinko that we were from Auschwitz and trying to get back to our homes in

Slovenia, he told Hinko that the last train from Poland into Czechoslovakia would pass nearby late this evening; after that the rail lines would be destroyed to slow down the Soviet advance. The way to the nearest and the last railroad station on the Polish side, however, was still some distance away and not in the direction the other groups in the column had most likely taken.

At the priest's residence something on the stove had a very appealing aroma. That time the priest was there and greeted us very cordially. In his pre-war years he had an opportunity to visit St. Stanislaus Gymnasium and even remembered one or two names on the faculty. The Polish gentleman now repeated his information about the last train, and as the priest also confirmed that fact, we had to make an on-the-spot decision either to remain there or to try to reach that last train. Both the priest and the young businessman were convinced that this was our last chance to cross the border into occupied Czechoslovakia. The next day and on foot it would be impossible to successfully cross the border; it was too far, too-rough travelling, and too dangerous. We had to make an immediate decision; there was no time to lose. Only Karl decided to stay; the rest of us picked up our gear for another tough march. The Polish gentleman and his son insisted on taking us to the railroad station the shortest way possible; we would never make it otherwise. The last thing the good priest said was that we should come back to his residence if we missed the train. We shook hands with the priest and followed our new friend and his son into the night, leaving a good warm meal behind us. Trying to reach our homes was definitely our top priority.

The Polish gentleman was walking fast and was constantly urging us to walk faster and faster or we would miss that last train. Exhausted from the previous night and all-day march, we were not making much progress. It was dark already and getting darker. Somewhere in that area finally ended the long story of my wooden suitcase, which now attempted to leave the Polish territory for the second time after a side journey of more that twenty years. I tossed it to the side of the path, not having enough strength to carry it any further. While parting from it, I said a few words of thanks for good service on this long and most difficult march. We threw away almost all of our extras just to speed up our progress. In spite of that, the Polish gentleman became more and more concerned that we would not make the train. He, therefore, decided on another action. He ran to one of the houses and either hired or just pleaded for a horse and a sled. In a few moments the owner and our friend had everything ready; we squeezed ourselves on the sled and departed at full speed possible toward the railroad station. It was still about a thirty-minute ride before we got there. We did not arrive a second too soon; our sled and the train arrived at the station almost at the same time. In complete darkness we said our warmest thanks to this most generous man. He did not even want to give his name; he only said that he was most happy to be able to help us to get that far. We boarded the train in a great hurry at the last second.

The Polish gentleman stood there next to the steaming horse, his son at his side, and looked at the slowly departing train. He must have been an important person in the region. To get a horse and sled in a second and at night was not a minor achievement. He assured us while we were speeding with him and as he controlled the horse, that the owner would get everything back and that he and his son would get home without any difficulty. The horse's owner would probably insist on taking both of them home. There was no doubt that without him our future would have followed an entirely different path.

The train was completely dark and full to the last corner. We found some accommodations in the corridors, but even that space was at a premium. After a while we realized that all other passengers were German soldiers, very tired, most of them sleeping or trying to sleep. Nobody talked; nobody asked any questions. The train kept going; only here and there it slowed down a little. The occasional whistle reminded me of that other train ride in June 1942, which ended with an attack on the train. This time we just went on and on. The only other sounds along with the train noises were isolated snoring melodies, confirming that the passengers were human beings.

Though we tried hard to fall asleep, the cold and the uncomfortable environment worked against such attempts. And when sleep does not come, your mind searches for pleasant memories, but instead darker thoughts usually take over. Sitting there in the corner of a corridor, cold and tired, I was trying to guess what happened to my colleagues in the evacuation column. Where were they at this point and where were they heading? Auschwitz was by then already far away, but my thoughts kept returning there again and again. Was the German pull-out without damaging consequences for the people remaining in the camps and in the vicinity? When did the Soviets arrive? Did they bring much-needed help for those who remained there? At that time we were firmly convinced that the Soviets had already liberated Auschwitz and that the crucial and dangerous transition of power and authority was over.[3]

It was early in the morning when the train pulled into a huge railroad station on the Czechoslovakian side of the border in the city of Moravska Ostrava. This was indeed the last train, the very last train, crossing the border from the northeasterly direction.

It was also the final station for our train. The soldiers disembarked immediately and walked in orderly manner through the main building. We had to leave the train, and stationed ourselves on the walkway near one of the several tracks of this multi-track station. Hundred of soldiers were standing on these walkways, kicking their boots to keep warm. We were certain that the main station building was full of people, but at the same time we also knew that the authorities were observing and checking the passengers. Therefore, we remained standing where we stepped off the train, the only civilians among hundreds of German soldiers. I kept urging Hinko to remove his Russian fur cap *(kučma),* which attracted more attention than our entire group, but he was stubborn. The German Military Police walked by several times without even as much as looking at us. The situation, nevertheless, was tense.

After a while Hinko decided to look for help. He left me in charge and walked slowly toward the main railroad building. The impression he tried to give was that of a passenger just waiting for one of the next trains. We, however, stood there looking nervously at each other in complete silence. Hinko did not return; an eternity passed. Our human needs also grew more and more pressing. How much longer could we wait like that? Finally, we saw him coming back at the same slow and relaxed pace. With a simple gesture, he told us to pick up our stuff and follow him. We walked over several railroad tracks, down the front of the building to a small workroom, where two Czech railroad workers let us rest for a while. It was a little warmer in this workroom than in the open and there was room to sit down. The much-needed toilet facilities were close by.

In comparison with the situation in Southern Poland, we got the impression that on this side of the border the atmosphere was less tense, that the immediacy of the Soviet advance had not sunk in as yet. There were, of course, no visible signs which would confirm these feelings, but a person somehow develops a sixth sense and feels a certain difference. Maybe it was the expression on peoples' faces; maybe it was the way people walked around doing their business and their daily routines. Something different was in the air. Nevertheless, we did not dare to enter the main railroad building.

Hinko received information from the Czech railroad workers about which train to take and when to get to our next destination. The railroad men also told him which trains were less frequently checked by German patrols. In the afternoon, therefore, we boarded a passenger train in the direction of Vienna. Up to this point we traveled without tickets; under the previous circumstances, tickets were not necessary. However, this was a regular passenger train. To avoid any suspicion, we had to be legitimate.

We found a nice empty corner on the train. On the opposite side were some Czechs, a family-like group. When they heard our language, they were immediately interested and wanted to help. Since they were regulars on this train, they knew all the particulars and also those who were in charge. They gave us food, probably their lunches, and plenty of advice. At a railroad crossing, I believe the station was either Hranice or Přerov, not far from Olomouc, we had to leave these pleasant and helpful Czechs and go into hiding again. It was a little easier this time, because our new acquaintances gave us a few names in order to find reliable connections; they gave us also their names as references. As a result, the help was readily available, but the train was not. We wanted to go directly to Vienna the shortest way possible. Since it did not look as if we would get a train soon, Hinko finally went a little too far with his suggestions. He wanted to arrange that we would board a locomotive on a solo trip in a southerly direction as if for maintenance work. The engineer, however, flatly refused saying, that if we were stopped, that would have been the last stop for all of us; the risk was just too great.

The presence of the three Croatian boys, who looked even younger than they were, and one woman gave our group an appearance of a family; thus we attracted less attention. The Croatian boys kept together; they never separated. It was nice to see how they helped and cared for each other. Their leader was smart, attentive, helpful, and enjoyed the full confidence of the other two. With Hinko's permission, they went in the evening to the waiting room of the main station to explore the possibilities. There was a watery, warm soup available there, they told us on their return. Hinko then suggested to Francka and Jože to take advantage of this opportunity. Everything went well for them as well. Finally, Hinko and I went in close to midnight. At this time the waiting room tables were all occupied because a group of German soldiers had just arrived. I wanted to turn around; Hinko, however, spotted a table where only two soldiers were sitting, and two chairs were still unoccupied. For me this kind of association was most uncomfortable, but Hinko was always daring. The two soldiers had no objections. We were enjoying our soup almost in complete silence, as did the soldiers sitting next to us. At that moment, two German military policemen entered through one of the entrances on the one side of the room and started checking identification papers. We wanted to get up and depart through the opposite door but had to remain seated when we noticed two other military policemen entering from that side. We were trapped. Silently and very slowly we worked on the remaining drops of the soup. The first two policemen went by our table; the other two were approaching. Thinking probably that the first two already checked our table, they also went by. The two soldiers at the table noticed our nervousness. When all four military policemen finally left the room, and we were ready to depart, the two soldiers wished us good luck for the next such occasion as well.

At around five in the morning we boarded a train for Vienna and arrived there without any difficulties—no controls, no police. In Vienna, there was no connection between the north and south railroad stations. The next task, therefore, was to get across the busy city. We accomplished this mostly on foot; only on occasions we jumped on the streetcars for short rides under the pretense that we took the streetcar going in the wrong direction.

The next destination for us was the city of Maribor in occupied Slovenia, the home of Hinko Špendl. The first part of the trip south through Austria went almost without delay. South of Graz, in Steiermark, the train stopped more often for unknown reasons. It was night, dark, and we tried to get some sleep. While crossing the old borders between Austria and Yugoslavia, we heard from time to time rifle and machine gun fire and also saw flashes from minor explosions. Most of this took place at a fair distance from the train, however. Since the railroad car we were in was almost empty, we had enough room to lie down on the benches and to doze off.

It was still night when we woke up. With great surprise, we noticed that the railroad car we were in and a few others were standing on the side tracks, and there was no locomotive attached. Hinko looked out. He spotted an armed guard in German uniform walking along the tracks and asked him for the name of the station. "Bolšaja štacija, čort znaje što jest" (a large station, only the devil knows the name), was the reply in Russian instead of German. After looking again and again, Hinko suddenly screamed, "It must be Maribor." He decided that we should leave immediately, walk across the tracks, through the main building and to his home even though it was still curfew. We did exactly that. Why nobody, officials, police, or Gestapo stopped us, I still wonder. We walked right by all those officials in the building and exited on the other side into the open, completely empty streets.

On this long trip from Vienna to Maribor, police and other controllers walked a few times through the railroad cars at select stations and stops. Only once did they ask for our identifications. Seeing the name Auschwitz—my guess was that they did not have the slightest idea where Auschwitz was—they accepted our explanation on that single occasion that we were released from the labor camp and were returning home. Why many others did not ask for identifications was a real and most welcome puzzle.

Outside the main railroad station, the three Croatian boys started shaking Hinko's hand, saying, "We know where we are, and we thank you for bringing us here." Though Hinko tried to persuade them to stay with him until he would be sure that they really knew where they were going, they wanted to leave right away and they did in great excitement. We saw them running and disappearing around the corner of the next street. They left us the same way they joined us, suddenly and unexpectedly.

The rest of us walked to Hinko's home. When he finally woke up the family, the happiness of his return was immeasurable.

It was around five in the morning when Hinko entered his home for the first time after an absence of four years.[4] We waited outside until he had a chance to embrace his mother and two sisters, Joža and Nada, his immediate family. Being uncertain that entering Hinko's home was the right thing to do, we hesitated for a while, but the family insisted. As we heard so many times before when seeking help, most mothers would say, "Another mother is probably helping my son right now; therefore, I am glad to be of assistance."

Mrs. Špendl was a tall woman, very thin, and most cordial. She promised us that she and her two daughters would do everything possible to help us out in this difficult situation. It was obvious from the start that the older daughter, Joža, was the mistress of the house. She was probably older than Hinko. Joža held an important position in a hardware store and through her customer contacts met many people, including German soldiers, seeking tools and parts for their own or their family needs back home. People from the small farms outside of the city often brought her various food staples in gratitude for her assistance. Thus, the family did not lack the essentials. The youngest in the family, Nada, a good-looking teenager, appeared a little lost with so many strangers around; she, however, worked hard and with great care to make us feel at home. I never learned anything about Hinko's father. He never mentioned him, and we did not want to pry.

After some sleep and food, it was time to think what to do next. We wanted to depart as soon as possible to reach our homes in the Italian zone; except for Francka, whose home was on the German side but a considerable distance from Maribor. The key difficulty was the strict travel restrictions because of partisan activities. To be caught without proper travel permission papers meant immediate arrest and deportation or even imprisonment with most serious consequences.

I remembered then that one of my cousins on the mother's side was stationed as a German soldier at the main Maribor police station. I hesitated for a while to get him involved and endanger his position, but Joža thought that he might be of some help. Joža, therefore, went to the police station and after she finally located him, invited him to the Špendl's house to meet a relative of his. Though Joža was not sure if he would come, Franz Legat, my cousin, appeared that evening in full uniform at the Špendl's residence.[5] He apologized to Joža that he was not more open when she visited him and reminded her that speaking Slovene was strictly forbidden, and therefore, he had insisted on speaking German, especially in the presence of his superiors.

The idea was that we would get registration forms from the police station in order to apply for residency in Maribor without going to the police station ourselves, where we would be forced to disclose our address right away and how and why we came to Maribor. Having registration forms with us would give us a day or two to find out about other possibilities for the next step. We knew very well that we would have to leave soon; our presence here would be noticed sooner or later. We also had no ration cards for food purchases, a must in those circumstances, and we didn't want to eat the rations of our host family.

The next evening my cousin brought the registration forms. Two days later the happy days were over.

Hinko and I tried to get in touch with a friend of the family to seek advice of how to get out of Maribor and how to get a travel permit. When we turned a corner to the next street, we walked right into the hands of a police patrol. No explanations or forms were of any help; we were arrested and taken to the police station. After several hours of waiting, they took us to an inner office. The police chief and his assistant arrived; such attention did not look good to us. The police chief apparently had received information about us from the Gestapo in Ljubljana, because he told us immediately that he knew exactly why we came to Maribor. He knew of our earlier association with the partisans in the Italian zone. The story of our release from Auschwitz did not impress him at all. During his very loud lecture, his voice reminded me of that Mr. Hertle, who yelled at my mother when we moved into a room in our own house in 1941. That kind of Hitler-like speech is difficult to forget.

As Hinko explained to me later, the police chief wanted to ship us with an armed escort to a concentration camp in northern Germany, far away from the Slovene territories. His assistant, a fairly young police officer, who was standing there during the chief's long verbal attack, had a different idea. He argued that they could not afford an armed escort for such a long trip. Instead, he suggested that we should be sent to the *Arbeitsamt* (Labor Office) in Graz and put to work there. If the *Arbeitsamt* in Graz did not confirm our work assignment there in one week's time, Hinko's family in Maribor would suffer serious consequences.[6] For a few short moments the gray-haired police chief did not say anything. Then he turned around, gave the papers to his assistant and said something like, "Do what you want," and left the room.

We were no longer under arrest. The young police officer gave Hinko detailed instructions and papers for all four of us—he was a little surprised that there were two more in hiding—and urged Hinko to follow instructions to the letter for the sake of his family. Hinko thanked him for not shipping us to a concentration camp. The man said nothing, just handed Hinko the rest of the papers.

We then left, at least partially and temporarily legitimate for our next assignment.

CHAPTER ELEVEN

Hospital Worker— Graz, Austria

February 1945–April 1945

❦

On 26 January 1945 the Soviets liberated the huge Auschwitz complex, including what was left of the Auschwitz concentration camps.

In Asia, US forces started the liberation of the Philippines on 9 January 1945. At the end of the month, on 28 January, the first support for the Chinese came via the newly built Burma Road.

On the Italian Front, the Allies faced many obstacles and strong German defenses. The rough, mountainous terrain did not help. The Allies had to break through three heavily fortified German defense lines in 1943 and 1944: Gustav Line (south of Anzio), Caesar Line (south of Rome), and Gothic Line (south of Florence). Most attention in Italy, however, was paid to the repeated Allied attempts to bypass the famous monastery Monte Cassino which was, after much struggle and bombardment, ascended by Polish troops on 18 May 1944. At the beginning of 1945, the Allies still had not crossed into the Po River valley.

There was not much time left. Joža, when she found out the circumstances of our arrest and the decisions at police headquarters, went immediately to two family friends who had business connections with the *Arbeitsamt* (Labor Office) in Graz. They suggested that we go to the *Landeskrankenhaus* in Graz (the county hospital located in the city) and ask for employment there based on Hinko's status as a medical student and his hospital and ambulance experience. Thus, we would avoid being at the mercy of the people at the *Arbeitsamt* in Graz. In addition, there might be jobs in the hospital for the other three of us as well. This way, we would stay together and probably receive living accommodations in the hospital buildings or nearby. Any hiring or work placement anywhere had to be reported and recorded at the nearest *Arbeitsamt*.

With proper papers and the names of a few people in Graz, just in case extra help should be needed, we said goodbye to the generous Špendl family. It was at the end of January 1945 when the train took us north again; fortunately not too far north.

Hinko's first action after arriving in Graz was to call a liaison person. Hinko pleaded for a telephone introduction and recommendation for himself and for his group to the employment office of the *Landeskrankenhaus* in Graz. As a medical student he wished, even under these circumstances, to stay close to his future profession. An encouraging answer soon came, and we went immediately to the impressive set of hospital buildings some distance away. Hinko took me along to the employment office, to the woman in charge of the hospital administration. I do not recall the correct spelling of her name; however, she was well known by all under the name of Frau Žviržina. Her office was that of a perfect devoted Nazi with more than one photograph of Hitler and many Nazi insignia on her desk and on the walls. She proudly displayed her Nazi Party emblem. Frau Žviržina was without doubt an excellent and efficient administrator. One had the impression that she not only knew every person working in the hospital but that she knew as well the exact place where "her" workers were at any particular moment. The whole atmosphere in her office reflected much more the Germany in 1941 than the Germany at the end of January 1945. Of course, she had not seen anything like the retreat from Auschwitz and probably firmly believed that the new secret weaponry allegedly under development would change the course of the war.

Hinko received an appointment as a medical orderly in the Dermatology Department. For the three of us the hiring process was not that smooth, especially since I was not able to answer Frau Žviržina's questions without Hinko's help. Her comment after my failure was that without an adequate knowledge of German, the only work available for a person like me would be with a shovel and that was exactly what I received. There was clear sarcasm detectable in her comment. Jože and I received assignments in the hospital coal shoveling unit. Frau Žviržina added something like, "Take it or leave it," to her decision. It did not help that Hinko had attempted in his skillful way to get us something a little less strenuous. Francka was assigned to the hospital kitchen. The big advantage of getting a job in the hospital were the living accommodations. In the hospital buildings, the top floors were not in use although furniture had been left there. The floors were empty because possible air attacks made it too dangerous to keep patients there. Hinko and I shared one room; Jože shared a room with another person; Francka had her own room in another building with a few other women. There were other hospital workers on the top floors, men and women, but not many. The conditions, therefore, were far from crowded. Most people did not want rooms on the top floors; the preferred places were in the basement.

After we settled in, we took a look at our places of work and at midday received the first meals in the hospital. I accompanied Hinko later the same afternoon to the Graz *Arbeitsamt* to satisfy the strict orders received at the Maribor Police Headquarters. Hinko informed his sister Joža about everything that took place and told her to stop in person at the Maribor police station to make certain that his family would not suffer any negative consequences as a result of our temporary stay there.

The next day at seven in the morning I had to report to the *Betrieb* (The Hospital Physical Plant Center). The person in charge took Jože and me a short distance along the streetcar tracks to a large open area. A huge mountain of coal was on both sides of the tracks. An open streetcar wagon was standing there, and four men were swinging shovels, loading the coal. Jože and I were assigned to this team. Two things scared me right away. First, the four men standing there looked very big and strong to me, and second, the coal shovels they were using were long and heavy. In addition, the top edge of the wagon being loaded was higher than I was, and the coal had to be thrown into the car with a fast swing of the shovel. How would I survive on this job?

A tall and strong Turk gave me a shovel and assigned me a corner position, considered a better place than the one in the center. There were normally three men working as a team on each side of the streetcar wagon. If all six men were present, a wagon had to be loaded after a certain amount of time. When full, the wagon was pulled by a locomotive to the *Betrieb*. It took about fifteen to twenty minutes before an empty wagon replaced the full one; a pleasant break for the laborers. At the *Betrieb* the coal was unloaded via a chute into the hospital furnace storage. This job was done by a second team consisting of four men. It was considered less strenuous work there than the loading of the wagon cars on the open grounds. Depending on need and demand, workers were on occasion switched between the two units. The coal in the open area assured enough coal supply in case no deliveries of coal came via the railroad. At the time I was working there, railroad deliveries were already irregular due to air attacks on the railroad station and on the nearby areas.

The *Betriebs Leiter* (the man in charge of operations) was a native of Graz and had been on this job for years, even before Germany annexed Austria in 1938. He communicated with the loading gang almost exclusively via the man from Turkey; thus we considered the Turk as our informal leader and representative. The Turk introduced us to the rest of the team which consisted, in addition to the Turk, of a Russian, an Albanian, and a Pole. They were very cordial and welcomed us. If I am not mistaken, the Turk did ask the *Betriebs Leiter* something about Jože's and my ability to do that kind of work. After a brief conversation between the two, the chief left.

Jože and I received a number of instructions important to the newcomers. The first and most important one was to start using the shovel the "wrong way." If you were right handed, you had to start as a left-handed person. On a shift lasting from seven in the morning to five or six in the afternoon, working right-handed only would completely destroy your body and your posture and cause too many blisters. To last that many hours a day, six days per week, working on both sides, was the only way to shovel coal and to survive. The first half a day, I was unable to shovel very much coal, but my co-workers encouraged me to keep trying. It took me a few days to get adjusted to this work, switching from left to right and back on hourly basis. Our co-workers, seeing our willingness to assume our share of the work, were very accommodating and did additional work which would normally have been our responsibility. After two weeks I felt almost fit to do the job although not as well as the old-timers.

Luckily, I was assigned to the side where the Russian had the center position, the most difficult assignment. At the center the coal skidded down on both sides when thrown into the wagon; therefore, it took more effort to keep up with those working in the corners. Gregor, the only name I still remember of the entire team, was very good to me. Whenever there was some final work to be done and there was no room for two workers to do the job, he would take over. The modest Russian vocabulary I had picked up in Auschwitz pleased him very much. He told me that before the war, he shoveled coal in the Soviet Union for eighteen years. For him this job was not a problem. His hands were big and hardened. His shovel flew through the air like a little toy.

Jože was luckier. The *Betriebs Leiter* transferred him soon after we started to another much more pleasant job. For a while there were only five of us, and it took us longer to load each wagon. One day the *Betriebs Leiter* came and started yelling at all of us about our slow work. This was unusual, because in general the man seemed very reasonable and pleasant most of the time. An argument followed between him and the Turk: we did not comprehend it all, but suddenly the Turk lifted his shovel high in the air, ready to split the chief's head in half. We all screamed at him and he lowered the shovel. Shocked and scared, the chief turned around and ran back toward the Betrieb. The Turk did not explain to us anything; his shovel, however, worked at double speed for quite a while. We feared severe repercussions, but nothing happened.

A few days later, the chief brought us the sixth man. If Jože and I were a disappointment to the team because of our height and apparent lack of strength, this man—very small, thin as a rail, and over fifty years old—seemed even less capable. Our leader protested right away. While the discussion went on, the scared new man stood there, saying nothing, just looking around, especially at the mountain of coal. As it turned out, it was the Gestapo's decision that he be assigned to this hard labor, though it was obvious that he would not be able to swing even an empty shovel. What to do with him was now the question. Our leader, after a short consultation with the rest of the gang, decided that the man would do the necessary cleaning and sweeping around the area, which we usually did before the noon break and at the end of the shift.

It took a while before we found out a few things about our new gang member. He spoke French only, a definite rarity in those surroundings, which immediately isolated him from most if not all the people working in the *Betrieb*. My very modest knowledge of French was the only communication link with this man. From my conversations with him and from a few points of information we received from the *Betriebs Leiter,* we learned that in pre-war days the man had been a high-ranking member of the Belgian government, a minister of commerce, someone said. How he got to Graz was a puzzle he could not explain, but there were so many such puzzles everywhere that nothing was a surprise anymore. I do not remember his name, if I ever knew it; for convenience, we called him simply, "Monsieur." He worked very diligently. For questions or explanations he turned first to me and then immediately pointed to the Turk, recognizing him as his real immediate superior. Often I was unable to understand what he was asking or explaining. Because of the language problem, he became very dependent on me not only on the job but also at his residence in the hospital and at the other places, such as kitchen and washing facilities. My first name sounded strange to him, so he called me "mon garçon" instead. The "mon garçon" was not always praised for his help. Occasionally, the man got angry, and I was not able to figure out why. Nevertheless, we spent some free time together because he did not have any one to be with or even to talk with. The Belgian minister, if that really was his pre-war position, was a proud owner of a small electric portable stove, which he gladly loaned on occasions to take the sour taste out of the bread. However, he always stood there, observing the process and took the stove back to his room as soon as possible.

Shoveling coal was very hard work; it never became easy or routine. Occasionally, the hospital administration tried to get more work out of us. Our work days ended at six in the afternoon, not at five. On occasion, the supervisor would come a few minutes before quitting time and order us to work another hour "for the State," as he put it. We had no choice. A Gestapo station was right at the corner next to the hospital. We were told often that we had only two choices, to do what we were told or be turned over to the Gestapo for a trip to a concentration camp. Not a pleasant alternative. Most of the time we met our quotas for the day; occasionally, however, this did not happen and we had to stay until the wagon was full and ready to be moved. We realized that the hospital had to be heated and that a lot of sick and wounded people depended on us.

Under such difficult circumstances and constant pressures, one would expect tempers to flare among workers with accusations that one or the other was not doing his share. Nothing like that ever happened on this team. Cooperation and concern for each other within this group of six men, each of a different nationality, was exemplary at all times.

I cannot say the same about the unloading team. All of us on the loading team were *Fremd Arbeiter* (foreign workers); on the unloading team was an older Austrian worker, the only one left from the pre-war gang. He, of course, had the full protection of his superior. In addition, he very much resented working alongside all those foreigners. Working with him was a big disadvantage. He would push a sizeable part of his section of coal over to your side and then call the supervisor and complain that you were sabotaging the work. I got into trouble that way several times and once they threatened that they would turn me over to the Gestapo if it happened again. No explanation of any kind helped; the Austrian worker was always right.[1]

During a subsequent similar incident with the Austrian man, after he had called the supervisor, who was standing next to the wagon and threatening me, a person approached and called my name. The newcomer and the supervisor engaged in a fairly long conversation a short distance from the wagon; then the supervisor told me that he was giving me a fifteen-minute break to meet with my visitor. I had never seen this man before; the whole situation seemed strange.

The visitor, as it turned out, was from Eisenkappel/ Železna kapla in Southern Carinthia. He came to Graz to visit his son, who had a few days off from his military duty. His son did not have permission to spend his leave at home because he was a Slovene.[2]

When my relatives in Eisenkappel/ Železna kapla heard that this gentleman was traveling to Graz, they gave him some extra food for me; he, in turn, assured them that he would look me up. Because we had very little time for conversation, he promised to visit me in the evening at our living quarters. We had a very pleasant conversation later about my relatives and acquaintances in and around Eisenkappel/ Železna kapla, where my mother was born. He repeated several times that my mother had been the most beautiful girl in that region, and these comments made me very happy. I also sensed his deep concern and fear for his son, who had to return to the Russian front in a few days, but he didn't know where his son's company was stationed.

I received an unexpected side benefit from this visit. From that day on, the supervisor treated me like the rest of the gang members. The others had established their status long before, simply by making sure that the Austrian worker and the *Betriebs Leiter* were afraid of them. The Austrian never tried his dirty tricks and false accusations on me again.

With the improved weather air attack warnings and air attacks greatly increased. Early in the year we left work and went to shelters as soon as the sirens announced the approaching planes. However, because these attacks were now so frequent, the authorities decided that we had to stay on the job until the planes came very close to the city. Thus, our rest periods were cut considerably.

On the hill right next to the mountain of coal we were loading stood a nice-looking building housing nursing students, all women. When these nurses left the house or came back from school or work, we as one stopped working, leaned on our shovels, and tried to get their attention. Only very rarely did one wave to us; most of the time we were completely ignored. We debated among ourselves whether the reason for this coolness was the strict German policy forbidding any kind of association with foreigners or that our appearance and our job assignments were much below their social status. Our appeal to the authorities to let us use shelters in the nurses' building during the air attacks, which were much closer to our place of work than the *Betriebs* shelter (to use the nearest shelter was the general rule), was naturally turned down without any explanation.

On sunny days two little girls, one Hungarian and one Ukrainian, about three years old, often played nearby. We enjoyed hearing their cordial exchanges, each one speaking in her own language. They seemed to communicate with and understand each other without any difficulties.

In the main administration building, Hinko discovered a most pleasant and beautifully furnished library with a rich collection of books not limited to medicine. The doors were not locked even in the evenings, and there were usually no patrons in the library during the late evening hours. After familiarizing ourselves with the rules (no books were to be taken from the room), we learned everyone was allowed to use this attractive room. There was also a grand piano there. At first I was hesitant to touch the keys on this great instrument and attract outside attention. But under constant urging by Hinko, I finally decided to try this piano—in *sotto voce,* of course. My hands were rather stiff from shoveling coal. However, every pianist, no matter on what his or her level, understands the inner feelings and great pleasure of touching those wonderful piano keys.

We visited this library frequently when we were free, always late in the evening. On one of these evenings when I was playing, a woman doctor entered the library, just checking to see what was going on. I immediately stopped and apologized for the disturbance. To our surprise, she only inquired whether we were working in the hospital and where. Then she looked up something in one of the books and left. At the door she turned around, told us in which department she was working and added that the books and the piano are for those who have genuine interest in them.

Sometimes even small, insignificant things help. In the middle of March, I was told at the end of my day shift to return at eight in the evening and work the night shift in the unloading area; Gregor was my partner that night. Apparently there was a coal emergency, and a fast re-supply was badly needed. The other workers would be scheduled as two-men teams for similar double shifts the next few days, we were told.

That second shift went surprisingly well for several hours. At midnight we even received a relatively good lunch from the kitchen, special delivery. Gregor was in a very good mood, singing Russian folk songs while shoveling. A few songs, the most popular ones, I knew at least the tune if not the words, but I could not sing along because Gregor was a real Russian bass, reaching into the deep registers, a *basso profundo*. The coal was skidding down the chute fairly easily; we were pushing it from both sides. When one wagon was emptied, another one standing nearby, was put into place. These extra wagons of coal were brought in during the day from the railroad station, most likely on a rare lucky day for a few extra deliveries.

Soon after midnight, I started sweating more than usual, and my body alternated from chills to fever at regular and frequent intervals. I did not want to tell Gregor about my difficulties, because if I left work, everything would fall on his shoulders. However, he soon noticed my condition and called the night supervisor, who released me immediately. Gregor said that I did not need to be concerned about him, that he would take care of everything.

Hinko awakened when I came back to the room half-delirious. He established that I had a very high fever, probably flu combined with exhaustion, and brought me aspirin tablets. The rest I remember only vaguely, mostly from what Hinko told me later. He apparently went early in the morning to look up the woman doctor who had spoken to us in the hospital library a week or two before. This doctor then admitted me to the hospital ward.

When I snapped out of my delirium, I found that I was lying in a large room with approximately forty to fifty other patients. My fever must have been still very high, because I was very hot and soaked throughout. The first thing I noticed, was a group of about fifteen or more doctors making their routine inspection of all patients in the ward and checking on their current status. When this entourage stopped at my bed that first morning, the chief asked why this *Haus Arbeiter* (house worker) was here. Every patient had his name listed about the bed and the name of his home town; instead of the home town, I was listed as House Worker. One of the doctors answered briefly. The chief then turned to one of the very young women doctors (maybe she was a medical student) and left me in her charge. She stayed behind and checked me over, because there were no records about my status as yet. I was probably brought in only a short time before this inspection tour. She promised that she would check on my recovery daily. After that she gave instructions to a nurse and joined the rest of the team in a hurry. These inspections were done twice weekly and included every doctor in the department. The chief of the department, also a full professor at the Graz University Medical School, assigned patients to the individual doctors, who then reported on their progress or lack of it. These reports were brief and to the point; the chief would not waste his time with long explanations. The chief made all decisions; the others just followed orders, perhaps making some suggestions in their brief reports.

On days when no full inspection took place, doctors with special assignments came around, again as a group and talked among themselves about each case with special attention to a few more difficult cases. After that, individual doctors would visit their patients to check on their progress.

Because my bed was next to a door and a passageway, I had only one neighbor. He heard that they referred to me as "Haus Arbeiter." He also noticed my difficulties with the German language. I, in turn, remarked that the inspection team remained at his bed for considerable time and that discussions went back and forth. The next day, when I felt considerably better, we started talking. The conversation was not easy because he spoke Russian only. He was twenty years old, and his knee had either been damaged in an accident or by a war injury. He told me that he was brought to this hospital because his specific case was something German doctors were interested in; his treatment could probably be applied to their own wounded. In Russia, he said, he would be healed by now or without his leg; here they were still thinking, studying, and debating what to do. The result would most likely end the same way—he would lose his leg. I was not able to find out how he came to Graz or from where. According to him, he had been in the hospital ten or twelve days already with no change in his condition. This young Russian was an interesting fellow; he told me about the defense of Moscow in the winter of 1941. The Soviet soldiers, before they attacked to push back the invading Germans, stripped to the waist to increase their fighting spirit and to show their superiority under those extreme cold conditions. Whether he was there in person or just heard about these battles was not clear to me. As per religion, he had a simple answer; he did not need any. His great wish was to see his home once again.

In a large hospital ward like the one I was in, all kinds of things happen. Some patients were treated roughly, often because of their own unpleasant behavior. Others screamed from pain occasionally, especially during the night, before somebody appeared. The night attendants seldom entered the ward to check. Most depressing were the early mornings on the days when one or more corpses were removed. Many died silently during the night, but not all. Who the patients were, those from the Graz area and others as well, I did not know. As a *Haus Arbeiter,* I was in the hospital by a special privilege or just plain luck. The Russian and I were, as far as I recall, the only foreigners in the ward. The place where we were cared for was definitely not for the upper classes but was adequate, clean, under good control, and efficiently run.

I spent four days in the hospital; the chief released me upon my doctor's recommendation. She, however, saw to it that I received another four days of recuperation after she learned what kind of work I was doing for the hospital. Hinko wrote to both doctors brief thank-you notes. They both very much deserved thanks; they worked with me as they would with any other patient in the hospital and showed sincere concern for my recuperation and well-being.

It was tough at first to swing the shovel again. The technique was still there (you do not lose that for a long time); however, my body lacked the required strength. After a few days and a lot of help from my co-workers, I was almost back to normal.

The air attacks became more frequent now, and the bombs were being dropped closer and closer to the hospital. On one or two occasions bombs fell very close to the hospital on the eastern side. The shaking of the earth when bombs hit—not one but several—was very scary. I was walking early one morning to work when a single low-flying plane flew right over me, and I was able to see the pilot when he made a sharp turn. It was my guess that he saw me as well—a single person on that wide, deserted street; the pilot, however, did not return to have another look. It was probably an observation plane. He did not drop any bombs or fire shots.

If sirens announced approaching planes while we were at our quarters, we ran into the basement to seek shelter. The basement was full of severe cases, patients who could not have been moved fast enough before and during the air attacks. They were permanently quartered in the basement. We usually sat in these areas during attacks in the available spaces among these very sick people. After a while we also noticed that on the floors below our residence, many patients became terrified upon hearing the sirens and asked, some even screamed, for help. Instead of immediately running to the basement for our own protection, we then first ran to the next floor down and moved beds to the lower floors or to the basement. Not only the patients but the hospital staff appreciated that extra help. Many of these people were victims of the air attacks; some were very badly hurt.

After every air attack on the city, the rescue teams delivered more and more victims to the hospital. Some received help immediately and were released; these were the lucky ones. Others were placed into various areas of the hospital, depending on the seriousness of their injuries. I remember a young girl, who at first did not realize, probably because of heavy sedation, that she lost both her legs. The next night when we saw her again, she was completely crushed, having realized what happened to her. We tried to console her the best we could; nothing helped. The day after, she was no longer there, and we were not able to find out what happened to her—everybody was tight-lipped.

We loaded less and less coal at this time because of more and more frequent air attacks. A new order, therefore, came, adding Sundays to our work responsibilities. The shoveling time with Sundays included still did not bring the amount of coal loaded up to the levels of the previous weeks. We, nevertheless, did not like being without a day of rest.

Then came Easter Sunday.[3] The old-timers decided that too much was too much, that on Easter Sunday we would not work. Half of the men on the loading team were not Christians, but they knew how important this feast was in this country. We went on strike. At seven in the morning, regular starting time, we assembled in the *Betrieb* and made ourselves comfortable in the area near the entrance. The supervisor was extremely unhappy and nervous; the supply of coal was getting low. He pleaded and pleaded, first with the Turk and then with each individual, asking us to grab our shovels. "On this festive day we should not be asked to do this heavy labor" was our answer. The supervisor made some telephone calls; who or where he called, we did not know. After two hours, a higher official appeared, again trying to sway us by friendly persuasion. The rumor, according to those coming to the *Betrieb* on business, was that the hospital administration was concerned about other workers joining in. This did not happen, however. In spite of that, we did not move.

At ten in the morning, after three hours, the ultimatum came. Either we went to work or we would be transported immediately to the nearest concentration camp, and an emergency crew from the city would take over our jobs. After a short consultation, the Turk decided that at this stage of the war, it was probably better to go back to work. Our shovels moved much slower that day, but they were swinging, nevertheless.

Hinko and Francka were fairly satisfied with their assignments under the circumstances. In spite of increased air attacks, the city seemed still to function almost at a normal pace. For one reason or another all streetcar conductors, those collecting money or issuing tickets, were removed, and only the drivers remained. Streetcar rides thus became free. However, it was interesting to note how well trained the residents were. They still kept placing the amount of money required for streetcar rides next to the driver, even though he kept repeating that no payments were necessary.

In the middle of the week after Easter Sunday, the supervisor came over to our work place and told me that I was being transferred to another job. I thanked my co-workers for being not only very nice to me but most generous with their help at all times. I almost felt sorry that I had to leave this team (however, not this work). I took over Jože's job. Jože did not come to work that morning, and after some investigation and a search of his room, we realized that he had escaped. None of us had the slightest idea about his plans. We felt hurt that after so many weeks and months of togetherness, from Auschwitz via Maribor to Graz, and specially because of Hinko's unlimited assistance to Jože, that he would disappear without a word to us. But in the evening that day, we were certain that he was gone.

My new job was not physically demanding. I became assistant to the man in charge of delivering food three times a day to various hospital buildings. In between hours we had to pick up dirty laundry or deliver washed bedding. My new boss was a native of Graz who had been working on this job for years. He was proud of his efficient and fast performance. Speed was essential, especially for the delivery of meals. He drove his delivery vehicle fast; I had to jump off my standing platform when the vehicle was still in motion, just before it stopped. Thus, the meals were removed in split seconds after he brought his beloved vehicle to the delivery stations. With laundry, speed was not essential, but our performance standards were, so we maintained the same speed. The man became very annoyed if the dirty laundry was not ready at the specified time; he would complain but mostly to himself. Often, when we stopped to pick up meals, he would go into the kitchen for some extras; however, he never forgot that he had a helper. I really appreciated that.

One special attraction, as he pointed out to me at one loading dock, was a meeting of two lovers twice a week. They were both Albanians; a well-built handsome man and a beautiful woman. The woman worked in the area behind the loading dock; the man delivered supplies from somewhere outside the city twice a week. After he unloaded his truck, they stood on the loading dock and passionately kissed for a long time. The woman waved, tears running down her face, as her man departed. Everybody around this loading dock knew about these meetings, and many people were present on each occasion. The two did not mind. On the contrary, they would say, please come and watch how we love each other.

Discussions about the war became more frequent in the hospital cafeteria and a little more open, but they still took place only between individuals, not in groups. People would look at the available maps and realize that the front lines were coming closer and closer. There were occasional standstills when the fronts did not move for days in either direction. With every new Soviet offensive, it became clear, however, which side was in control on the field. The Soviet advances came in stages. During one of those talks, I heard from an Austrian that the Soviets already guaranteed the Austrian pre-war borders, something that was hard for me to believe at that stage of the war.[4] Where she received this information, she would not say, but probably she had been listening to foreign radio broadcasts, which were strictly forbidden in Nazi Germany and in the occupied territories during the war.

Although the Nazis tried to hide the negative effects of the war—no black attire was allowed to mourn the fallen soldiers—more invalids were seen in the city, especially on the streetcars, where everybody saw to it that they were properly accommodated. We also observed that more people with minor physical problems from the war were joining the labor force. One slightly crippled person suggested to me that I approach the orthopedic clinic in the city and ask for shoe supports, because I suffered a lot without proper arch support. All I needed, they told me at the orthopedic center, was an approval from my immediate supervisor. It took only a few days and I was properly equipped; my feet and hip pains disappeared in a few hours.

The real war now reached Graz. The great exodus from occupied Hungary passed right through the city. This looked like the evacuation from Auschwitz, except that those fleeing were different. In Auschwitz and in Southern Poland, our groups consisted mostly of raggedy, hungry, and freezing forced laborers those leaving Hungary were carrying much or all of their possessions. Many were military personnel, mostly officers with their families, although they were not traveling in any kind of military formations. There were many trucks, private automobiles, wagons pulled by horses, and fewer pedestrians than in Poland. The impression one received was that the departing groups belonged to the upper classes and that fewer ordinary people were participating in this retreat. Those escaping had loaded trucks, cars, and wagons with heavy crates and the like. The columns passed through the city day and night for days.

Everybody realized now that even any possible new German secret weapons under development, so often talked about as being capable to provide in a short time a turning point in this war, would no longer be of any help to the endangered city of Graz. Its time has come. In this city, which so proudly called itself *Die Stadt der Volkserhebung* (The city where the people [meaning Nazis] seized power), and where you could see twice as many Nazi Party insignia as in Vienna in the streets on people's coats, jackets, and dresses, the darkness of the situation and the cruel truth probably entered and burdened the minds of the city folks at this point. You could easily see the depression and fear on their faces. The Soviets were *ante portas*. One hoped that the people still remembered how the Soviet prisoners of war were treated in German hands everywhere, especially in the early years of the war. Now the successors of those prisoners of war were coming.

Hinko's sister Joža came to Graz for a visit and also to discuss with her brother how to get the family together again before the war's end. Even though the cities of Graz and Maribor are geographically not far apart, these two cities would be in two different states after the war.

We also felt that the time had come to try to reach our homes again. The way from Graz to Maribor, the direct and shortest route, however, was in the opinion of many too dangerous to try because of the nearness of the front lines. In addition to Hinko, his sister Joža, and myself, Hinko also asked Francka and an older person from the Slovene region of Gorenjska, the only other folks from Slovenia working in the Graz hospital, if they wanted to join our escape. We worked out an escape route and decided on a very early departure the coming Sunday morning from the *Landeskrankenhaus* and, we hoped, from the city of Graz.

CHAPTER TWELVE

Building a Defense Line

April 1945

❧

A second conference by the leaders of the West/Soviet alliance took place from 4 to 12 February 1945 at Yalta in the Crimea. The agenda included steps to conclude the war and to find post-war solutions.

On 13 and 14 November 1944, first the British and then the American bombers destroyed the city of Dresden. This quasi-vengeance, causing 35,000 deaths, was of questionable justification. There was no strategic reason supporting these attacks so late in the war and with Soviet troops already approaching the city. At this time the Soviets were also close to Breslau and Budapest.

On the Western Front the Allied forces continued their advances. They captured Cologne on 8 March 1945 and crossed the Rhine River by the Remagen bridge.

In Asia on 1 February 1945, American troops were heading toward Manila. The U.S. Marines landing and fierce battles on Iwo Jima, with the memorable U.S. flag raising on Mt. Suribachi, took place between 19–26 February 1945.

It was a Sunday in the middle of April 1945 very early in the morning when we crept silently out of the hospital buildings and out of the hospital area during the first hour after the curfew. We left our rooms in perfect order, even the bedding, and the rest of the hospital property we left on the beds properly sorted and organized for eventual pick-up. That much we certainly owed this hospital, where, in spite of hard work, we had had a fairly regular and safe life. Our desire to reach home and join our families on time, that is, to be there when the battles of this war would finally stop, was the key reason for another escape attempt, even though still at considerable, or maybe even, great risk. It was also very unclear in those days which one of the soon-to-be victorious powers would liberate this or that part of the Central European geographical area.

We headed first toward the railroad station in the city of Graz. In disbelief we observed the destruction becoming more severe with every step closer to the station. On the last stretch we had to climb over piles of all kinds of debris and cement blocks from the destroyed buildings. The sights were depressing. There were no people around on any section of this usually almost-impassable main street. We were not stopped by any persons of authority; they simply were not around. We reached the city of Köflach, west of Graz, shortly after midday. To that point we made good progress because we were able to travel part of the way by train. From Köflach on, such conveniences were not available. We knew that in order to cross over the mountain pass of Packsattel,[1] we would have to go part of the way *per pedes apostolorum* (in the steps of the apostles), on foot.[2]

We left the city of Köflach in a hurry, trying to bypass police check points. Therefore, we stayed away from the main roads and proceeded in the right direction on the parallel streets. Once outside the city, we had to return to the main road, the only road. There was a lot of mostly vehicle traffic going southwest; many of the refugees were Hungarians. All of their vehicles were overloaded, and there was no hope obtaining a ride on their wagons. We therefore proceeded at a slow but steady pace toward the highest point on this mountain range. After crossing the pass, we would have to walk a considerable distance down the other side to the province of Carinthia.

Of the five of us, only the one older person was, in a few respects, new to our team. Hinko, again our undisputed leader, his sister Joža, Francka, and I had been together since Maribor; Hinko, Francka, and I since Auschwitz. We called this older man "Očka" (little father) because he was roughly two decades older than the rest of us, short in stature, and very thin. He was from Gorenjska, a region of Slovenia occupied by Germany. He had nothing good to say either about the Slovene partisans or about their opponents, the members of the Home Defense. Očka was mobilized by the partisans one night, taken from his home against his will. In a skirmish with the Home Defense, according to him, a political commissar stood in the rear of his group of partisans and threatened to shoot on the spot everyone in the front line who left his or her assigned position or retreated. The Home Defense men, by a fast advance, nevertheless forced the partisans to retreat; Očka took this opportunity and tried to escape from the partisans. He hid himself in the bushes and waited for the approaching attackers. Five Home Defense men then surrounded him, and with weapons pointed at him, threatened to kill him. In those split seconds of despair, he spotted nearby a lieutenant in German uniform and screamed in German to get his attention. When the lieutenant came over, Očka told him that he was forced to join the partisans and begged for his life. After a brief questioning, the lieutenant turned him over to another unit and thus saved his life, at least in Očka's opinion. He felt very sorry that he had to turn to the enemy when his life was at stake. Jože, when he first heard this story one evening in the hospital in Graz, insisted that his unit of the Home Defense, where he served as a sergeant before he was arrested by the Gestapo, did not mistreat captured partisans and neither did men in the other units of the Home Defense. Očka, however, was not willing to change any part of his story.

When the road became steeper our advance slowed down considerably. The day, however, was beautiful, just right for a march of that sort. With so many refugees on the road, we were not concerned about any road blocks and controls.

A column of empty German military trucks caught up with us on a steep part of the road. One of the drivers called to Joža and Francka, who were walking a few steps ahead of us, if they would like a ride. They asked him to take the three of us as well. That did not please him very much, but he finally agreed. We climbed on the truck, happy to get this opportunity. We gained considerable time even though this column of trucks climbed at a slow pace up the mountain road.

As we reached the Packerhöhe near the highest point on the road, the truck suddenly stopped. At first we did not realize what was happening, but after we were ordered to get off the truck, reality set in.

Two German Unteroffiziere (non-commissioned officers), members of an Alpine unit, were already talking to Joža and Francka when we joined them. I was the last to step off the truck. Apparently the two Unteroffiziere were asking if we were related. For Hinko and his sister, the same last names, there was no problem. Očka probably sensed that relationships meant something here and quickly introduced Francka as his niece. I did not know what was going on and confirmed, when asked, that I was single. At that moment the second Unteroffizier tried to help by declaring that it was obvious that we were a family and that they had made a mistake. Sensing the situation, Joža tried desperately to convince the two men that I was her fiancé. The Unteroffizier with the higher rank did not budge. He arrested me on the spot, kept my ID, took me away from my friends, and uttered the well-known statement, "If you try to escape, you will be shot." I hardly had a chance to wave goodbye to my companions and friends. With German efficiency, not listening anymore to Joža's complaints, the two men in charge stopped another truck and ordered Hinko's group to take off.

The sudden realization that from now on I would be completely on my own scared me. They took me to a house next to the road, Gasthof Packerhöhe—a restaurant with overnight accommodations before being taken over by the German Army—and assigned me a place on the straw-covered floor right behind the door. The minimum essentials I received included eating and drinking utensils and a blanket. Working equipment would be provided the next day, I was told. They gave me permission to walk around the front of the house but not move any distance away. Standing in front of my new prison house and observing the activities on the road, it became very clear to me that the troops on this mountain pass were looking for workers and that only single men were taken. Well, I was a victim of circumstances.

On the left side of the road, if coming from Köflach, was a small, picturesque village. From here there was a clear view over the distant valley below. Except for heavy traffic on the road in those days, one had the impression that this was an ideal place for those wishing to enjoy tranquility and natural beauty at the same time. The air was brisk, the sun rays strong. I walked back and forth in front of the house wondering what would happen to me next. A few other men were brought in and taken away from their groups; the only reason for the sudden arrest was that they, too, were single men. I was unable to speak to anybody; all my new companions spoke only Hungarian.

Between six and seven in the evening, other prisoners returned from work. They came from the hills above the road, carrying shovels, picks, and other digging equipment. My first impression was that they were not terribly beaten down; the guards who accompanied them were few, and only one officer was in control. At first I thought that they were all Hungarians. Later in the evening, however, one man approached me; he was Croatian. From him I learned a few things about this place, the kind of work they were doing, and the treatment they were receiving. In his opinion the situation was not too difficult to take. The Alpine unit in charge here was from the Austrian Tyrol; they did their job but were otherwise reasonable and understanding of the prisoners' situation. My new Croatian acquaintance felt that the men of this Alpine unit were pleased with their assignment; anything else would be worse for them. The same evening also I met two Dutchmen. Since everybody else spoke Hungarian only, the two Dutchmen suggested that we form a team of four men as required for work assignments here. They promised to suggest that to the officer in charge in the morning.

I slept very little that night, not because my bed was only a wooden floor with some straw over it, but because my mind was with my friends who had had to leave me behind. Where were they? How far did they get? Would Hinko and Joža still be able to get back to their home in Maribor, or was the city already changing masters? I was really sad to be separated from them. Experiences in wartime, sharing good and bad, leave deep marks in one's heart and soul. I missed them all but especially my most trusted friend, Hinko Špendl.

My first day at work was not too bad. The four of us were allowed to work together. We were building a new defense line. The location, even in the eyes of a non-expert, was ideal for such purposes. From the work area we were able to see far down into the valley, with clear a view of the road switching back and forth up the mountain, appearing out of the woods or from around the ridges. Right behind us were the high points on this ridge, a comfortable retreat path just in case. The officer and his helpers gave separate work assignments to each group for the morning and afternoon shift. The work had to be done during the assigned time, otherwise we had to stay longer, missing lunch or dinner. This was the simplest way to control sabotage. In truth, the assignments were not unreasonable and not beyond our abilities. We were not allowed to leave the place of work even if we finished ahead of time. Our place during the work hours was firm and set. The officer in charge came from time to time to evaluate the progress or to correct the direction and the depth of the ditches. A few armed guards circled around at a leisurely pace but did not act as supervisors. Even though the work day was long, it was, as far as difficulty was concerned, a step above shoveling coal for the hospital in Graz.

One morning the Unteroffizier in charge of supplies and food took the Croatian and me with him to bring food supplies from a storage depot some distance away. When no truck came by, he decided we would walk part of the way. At one point we spotted a dead horse at the side of the road, half deteriorated. The Unteroffizier looked the horse over and declared that we were about twelve hours too late; otherwise we would have had a few pieces of meat in our meals that evening. It became clear to me right away why pieces of meat had been floating in last evening's soup, a rarity in those days. My stomach all of a sudden convulsed, because that half-gone, rotted horse was on my mind. However, there were actually no consequences of that exceptional meal the night before. After all, it was this Unteroffizier's job to feed quite a number of people in that mountain pass station, and he did it as best he could.

After walking for a while, we finally got a ride to the next checkpoint; I believe the place was called Waldenstein. It was several sharp and steep turns down on the road toward Wolfsberg. The three of us had to climb up a steep hill to an abandoned little castle overlooking the road. A huge storage facility was there with, as much as I could observe, all kinds of provisions but no military supplies. The Croatian and I had to carry heavy sacks of flour, one at the time, down to the road. Fortunately, the job was done after four trips up and down that very steep path between the road and the castle. Many of the German guards staffing that post saw us carrying and then loading these supplies on the first available empty truck going in the right direction. In the afternoon the two of us were again digging the ditches.

In the evenings, after the meal but before darkness, we were permitted to take walks on a short part of the road visible from our residence and from the main guard station. This was a pleasant diversion from digging and from sitting on the straw waiting for night to come. Surprisingly, very few took advantage of this opportunity. On one of these walks, two of the soldiers told the Croatian and me that their unit was from the Austrian Tyrol; I do not remember their home city or town anymore. Another evening I had to carry a few supplies to the unit headquarters further down in the village. After the delivery, I noticed one of the soldiers trying to get a few sounds out of a good-looking accordion. I stood there for a while, realizing that the man had never had an accordion in his hands. He asked me if I wished to try. I certainly did, not the left-hand part, but the piano keys. The lady of the house came out of her kitchen to see who was playing, and she could not hold back her tears. The accordion belonged to her son, who was somewhere on the Russian front. Before I left, she told me that I would be welcome at any time.

The four of us on the team did not want to be punished with longer hours for not completing the assignments on time. Therefore, we agreed among ourselves to complete our assignments as soon as quickly as possible and take a longer break. We, of course, had to rest next to the completed ditches while waiting for the command to quit. Some of the Hungarians preferred to stand around, leaning on their shovels, so at the end of the shifts they had to hurry to finish their job so as not to miss a meal. They did miss meals a few times, but that did not convince them to change their tactics.

One late morning on a nice sunny and warm day, when the four of us dozed off next to a completed ditch, I was awakened to see a pair of beautifully shined mountain boots right next to my face. In a split second I was standing at attention, right next to the commanding general and in the midst of a large group of high-ranking and highly decorated German officers. These officers were accompanied by a large detachment of heavily armed and fierce-looking SS troops. My three companions were already standing.

At that moment, the commanding general called the lieutenant who gave us our assignments in the morning and asked a few questions, questions I did not fully understand even though I was standing right next to the general. A deadly silence followed and lasted an eternity.

The young lieutenant turned around and jumped into the ditch, measured the corners, depth, length, and width of the ditch in question under the scrutiny of the commanding general and his entire entourage. The general stood there motionless, almost at attention, as did all others. Not a word was uttered. I could not control myself; my legs were shaking from fear and anticipation. Strangely, however, I did hear the leaves murmuring and a few birds singing seemingly completely undisturbed; all the rest around was a deadly, deadly silence. . . . The lieutenant finally climbed out of the ditch, posted himself in front of the general and reported, with a firm and clear voice, two words, "Alles gemacht."[3]

The general and the three of his closest associate officers then discussed some changes, gave instructions, and then left without looking at or saying anything to us. I could not stop trembling, and neither could the other three. The troops followed the general down the hill and went to their cars and trucks. When the entire entourage left the Packerhöhe, I felt my heart start beating again.

Soon after that the lieutenant returned. He did not yell at us, he just said, "Sie haben Glück gehabt."[4] Never in my life had I thought that I would embrace an officer in a German uniform, but on that day I did, we all did, thanking him for saving our lives. We also apologized for causing him such a serious problem. Our Hungarian co-workers, who were watching this happening from their respective places, came over to shake our hands just to show that they were much concerned about our fate. Nothing else was said later in the evening about the whole incident. We felt, however, that it touched the entire company, including the troops and those in command.[5] It will be a puzzle to me forever why not a single person had a presence of mind to come over and to wake us up when they saw such a large group of German soldiers approaching our work stations.

Only a day after that incident, when we were returning from work after the second shift, I spotted Hinko and his sister Joža at the control station talking to the commanding officer. I could not believe my eyes. Why did they return? What are they doing here? What happened to the other two in our group? As it turned out, they came back to get me out of the latest imprisonment, counting on the "fiancé" relationship. The commander asked to see Joža's and my non-existent engagement rings and refused to release me even though Joža pleaded very convincingly. After failing to obtain my release, Hinko and Joža asked the commander if they could join his team of prison workers, insisting that we were a family. Since there were no women prisoners at this defense-building station, only men, the commander, upon urging of his two assistants, told Joža that she had won. I received my I.D., took my bundle, and said goodbye to my co-workers. The next truck, stopped by the officers, took the three of us away from the Packerhöhe.

Sitting on the truck and riding away from the construction site on the top of the mountain range where I had come so close to execution, I felt very relieved and happy. The three of us were together again with considerably better chances as a group to get around obstacles and danger points. I learned from Hinko how shocked the four of them were when they left Packerhöhe without me. After some consultation near the city of Wolfsberg, they decided that Očka and Francka would continue on their own since they knew what direction to take. Hinko and Joža, however, decided to stay somewhere in the area and wait for me. In their opinion, the whole front was going to collapse in a few days anyway, and everybody on the mountain heights would retreat down the mountain road. Without any difficulty they found temporary day-to-day employment and shelter at one of the farms near the road. At this time during the war, local men were either in the military or working for the war effort away from their homes. Hinko cut wood and did other chores; Joža helped in the kitchen and with children. When the war did not end as quickly as they hoped, they secured a ride back up to the mountain pass with the firm intention of joining the prison labor force in order to stay with me. Joža spoke perfect German, a big help in difficult situations. On the way to Packerhöhe, however, Joža told Hinko that it was worth trying again to get me out of this imprisonment.

My initial good fortune, thanks to Joža, was not without a dark spot on that day either. When we arrived at the next control point at Waldenstein, where a few days before I carried and loaded bales of flour on the trucks under the watchful eyes of the guards and the Unteroffizier, the guard at the control point first looked at Joža's, then Hinko's, ID and returned both with a thank you. The moment he looked at my ID, he ordered me to step down. Why me again? What a shock.[6] Both Joža and Hinko stepped off the truck as well even though the guard tried to tell them that they could go. I claimed that I was released by the commanding officer at Packerhöhe; it did not help. Even the driver of the truck tried to help, telling the guard that he was ordered to take us to Wolfsberg. Nothing helped. Since Hinko and Joža refused to leave, the guard took Hinko and me to a house and locked us in the cellar. Joža demanded to see the commanding officer of this post. She was free; women were not detained. Hinko and I sat in the cellar for about two hours; it was getting dark. Finally Joža returned with one of the guards. We were released. Apparently, it took a lot of persuasion and her insistence that they telephone Packerhöhe to confirm that I was released. Fortunately, the commander at Packerhöhe outranked the one at this control station and that helped.

It was already pitch dark and the curfew was fast approaching. We were not allowed to stay overnight in this village. We must have angered the German military at this post considerably since they chased us out of their protected territory with comments to get away from this control station as fast as possible and never to return. We found ourselves on the road in the darkness of the night, worried that a German night patrol would show up. Every few minutes we stopped and listened for footsteps. There was no vehicle traffic at night on the road. After approximately one hour of walking, we noticed the prefabs of a small prison camp on the right side of the road. Fortunately, it was abandoned; nobody was there. We entered one of the barracks and had a fairly peaceful sleep until the early daylight hours.

CHAPTER THIRTEEN

Almost Home

May 1945

❦

The news about President Roosevelt's death on 12 April 1945 spread with exceptional speed. What will be new President Harry Truman's directives and policies? These question was on everybody's lips.

A memorable event was the first face-to-face meeting between American and Soviet soldiers on 23 April 1945 at Torgau on the Elbe River.

The first conference of the United Nations took place in San Francisco on 25 April 1945. Many hopes were raised on this day that, from this point on, the world would be better prepared to handle disputes between nations or governments.

On 30 April 1945, the initiator, the cause, the individual responsible for millions of deaths, indescribable tragedies, and the person who developed, sanctioned, and ordered acts and policies of catastrophic consequences, Adolf Hitler, committed suicide—ne in manu hostium veniret.

It may be an injustice to the people of Wolfsberg to claim that passing through or around their city was an exceptionally tough task in those days. Experience had taught us that the closer we came to home territory, in this case the lands inhabited by the Slovenes, the tougher it became to avoid detention or arrest by the local authorities. Everybody realized that the end of the war on the European continent was very close at the end of April 1945. This crippled state of affairs was the reason that we were able to get over so many hurdles without negative consequences. A year or two before we never could have crossed over these obstacles. The attitude toward prisoners and forced laborers of all nationalities had also changed. Unfortunately, there were still fanatics in the military and among civilians, and we feared these fanatics the most. One never knew who would take the "law" in his own hands in the name of some higher authority.

Until we arrived near the city of Wolfsberg, the three of us, Hinko, Joža, and I, successfully avoided control points. I do not recall where we boarded a train going south. The train was only half full; at this stage of the war the people avoided trains unless absolutely necessary. The low-flying planes, coming all of a sudden out of nowhere—no sirens were able to announce them in time—attacked locomotives and often the rest of the train as well. During such attacks the train usually stopped, and everybody tried to reach either nearby woods, if there were any, or to look for cover in the ditches next to the tracks. The logical rule was get as far away from the train as fast as possible.

We found empty seats on one side of a passenger compartment, hoping that no other passengers would join us. An unavoidable problem, always present, was the language. The moment you were asked a question by a fellow passenger, you gave away your foreign identity and that usually had negative consequences. On that day, just as the train started moving, a young, tall, thin, and blond SS man entered and sat down on the opposite side of the compartment. He had on his chest many decorations, including the Iron Cross. If I recall correctly, he had the rank of Leutnant (lieutenant).

Hinko looked at me and, by eye contact, we decided to keep silent. Such silence was really a strange behavior; therefore, Hinko and Joža exchanged a few words in German. The man, however, did not pay the slightest attention to us; he sat there in deep thought, so it seemed, looking at the country passing by. Encouraged by the situation, we started whispering among ourselves in our native Slovene language. One or two stations later, when Joža just left her seat, a German police Hauptmann (captain) entered our compartment and demanded to see our IDs. He did not want to hear any explanations about our release from the forced labor camp of Auschwitz and started yelling at us, saying, "Who did we think we were, trying to fool him?" It looked as if he would use his authority to arrest us. At that moment, however, the SS man came over and with a commanding voice told the Hauptmann to leave us alone. To this command, he added something like, "Don't you have enough as yet?" With his height of almost a head over the rest of us and his sudden appearance on our behalf, he made an impressive figure. The Hauptmann, in great anger, threw our IDs on the floor, turned around, and left. Hinko tried to thank the officer for his help, but he only gave a trace of a smile, sat down in his corner, and continued looking out the window.

When this SS officer left the train at one of the next stations, we tried to guess why we received this unexpected help from a person belonging to the always-feared Waffen SS. Our guess went in three directions. First, the man really had had enough of the war and that he was aware of his error in joining and fighting as a member of the SS. Second, there were certain animosities among various factions of military and police forces, and here an opportunity presented itself to show disapproval and displeasure. Third, that the man had heard us speaking Slovene, and maybe, just maybe, he still remembered this language from his childhood, before speaking Slovene in public was forbidden soon after the Anschluss of Austria in 1938, and he wanted to help us for that reason. Whatever the reason, we probably avoided another arrest and all the consequences.

When we arrived in Dravograd, my pre-war home, no transportation by railroad was scheduled for a day or two in the westerly direction toward Klagenfurt/Celovec. The reasons were not clear, but we assumed that the tracks were damaged either by the low-flying planes or by the partisan forces in the area. Hinko and Joža insisted that I return with them to Maribor, located in the opposite, easterly, direction. Since I did not know if staying anywhere in Dravograd would be safe for me, I accepted their offer in some embarrassment. In a short time we arrived in Maribor. Several inspectors walked through the train on the way there, but not a single one asked for our identification or for the reason we were on this train.

To reach Špendl's residence in Maribor, we had to cross the Drava River from the right to the left bank. Not an easy task since the bridge was always guarded. Joža inquired whether, at certain times during the day, there were fewer controls. One person suggested that we try the narrow pedestrian bridge not too far away; lately that bridge seldom had guards stationed there. There was no visible pedestrian traffic on the bridge from a distance. There were no guards visible at either end. We decided to try.

The Drava River is strong, wide, and fast at this location. Maybe not as fast as in Dravograd, where I once swam across and back and barely made it, but those waters were still impassable without proper equipment. During wartime any attempt to cross in a boat without proper permission from the police would have ended in disaster. The narrowness of the pedestrian bridge forced us to walk in a single file: Joža first, Hinko next, I was last. When we were in the middle of the bridge, we noticed three men in black uniforms approaching the bridge. There was no longer a chance to turn around; that would have been too suspicious. Joža said to keep our mouths shut unless we were addressed directly. The three Gestapo men made themselves comfortable by placing themselves side by side on the bridge's protective guard rail. When we came closer, Joža recognized one of them: She just recently sold some equipment for his wife in the hardware store where she was employed. She greeted this man by his last name and asked if the equipment successfully reached his home in Germany. While this man talked to Joža, Hinko and I walked by, saying only "Guten Tag" (good day). A short distance away we stopped and waited for Joža, who exchanged a few more pleasantries with the three men. Even though the three men were apparently not on duty, without Joža we would have never crossed the bridge on that day.

It was clear that hiding at the Špendl's residence for a longer period of time would not work. Joža, her mother, and her sister Nada did everything for us. Joža went even that far that she purchased a few pieces of classical piano music for me to play on their upright piano. Having two young men in the house was certainly a rarity in those days; therefore, we had to look for another solution. A friend of the Špendl's family, a German widow, owned a small house not too far away from Špendl's. The house had been almost totally destroyed during an air attack, so she was living with relatives in the city. She offered us the use of a basement room in the bombed house, a room still accessible and furnished. Even though this house was only a block from the Gestapo headquarters in Maribor, we accepted her offer with gratitude. The basement had a separate entrance at the rear of the house; thus, coming or going was at least partially hidden from the main street.

I remember very distinctly the day President Roosevelt died (12 April 1945). We heard the news on the radio, the Voice of America, or the BBC from London, I cannot remember. We, of course, did not understand English but were able to figure out what was going on even before the translation came over the air. The radio we used for listening to foreign broadcasts was sealed to prevent access to everything except local broadcasts, but with minor adjustments a bypass was not difficult to achieve. The determined voice of Roosevelt's successor, President Truman, would forever ring in my ears even though I did not understand a word of his first speech to the nation. The local German press did not lack information either; the reportage was shaped by the office of the propaganda minister, Goebbels.

Hinko and I apparently did not learn to hide very well. We felt claustrophobic in our hiding place with no daylight. We took too many chances out in the open even though we remembered what happened the last time we were too daring.

It was Joža's and Hinko's idea to go to a movie theater one afternoon. I was very much against it, but Hinko thought that we should go with his two sisters at least once to something different and pleasant. I received strict instructions from them not to talk in the theater in my broken German, much less in my native tongue. Standing in the lobby of the movie theater and waiting for the doors to open, among a crowd of tightly squeezed moviegoers, was a torture in itself. We formed a circle and the two sisters exchanged some empty talk in German among themselves so as not to draw attention to our group. This whole thing was a depressing experience for me. We were in Maribor, but not a word in our own language was heard. And that was not the case only in the lobby of the movie theater; on the streets, in the stores, everything was German. Our language was forced into the privacy of homes, behind the walls. When Adolf Hitler visited Maribor after the defeat of Yugoslavia on 26 April 1941 and gave the order, "To make this land German again," the city of April 1945 was exactly what he had in mind.[1] Even the nice romantic movie about a world somewhere far away or not really existing anywhere anymore did not remove these somber impressions from my mind. One must admit, however, that there was a distinct difference between the situation in Maribor and that of Ljubljana, where, under the Italian occupation, the Slovene language was still in daily use everywhere.

The Eastern Front was coming closer and closer. My wish to return home was strong, and we all thought about how to achieve this goal in a practical and sensible way. Hinko even wanted to go with me if we could find a good solution or a working possibility. I was totally against Hinko's leaving his family; this would simply be too much of a sacrifice even for a best friend.

Then my cousin, Franz Legat, from Eisenkappel/ Železna kapla, who served in the German military as a communication *Unteroffizier* at the Police Headquarters in Maribor, thought that he found a possible solution. When I was at his home one evening, after he picked me up fully dressed in his uniform for security purposes, he mentioned a German military transport of wounded soldiers scheduled in two days for transfer to Klagenfurt/Celovec. He thought that he might be able to arrange my travel, since he thought that he knew the person in charge of the transport. I would thus be able to reach our relatives in Eisenkappel/ Železna kapla, a town near my mother's birthplace. There I would found someone to help me to cross over the border from Annexed Austria to Yugoslavia and finally to my home in Ljubljana. This plan was full of "ifs," but it was the only one we were able to come up with. Hinko and the Špendl family had many reservations; they understood, however, that my return would mean a lot to my family.

The day of departure finally came. Cousin Franz came over on his bicycle and brought his wife's bicycle with him. He was in his uniform with all the insignia, dressed to perfection. We had to cross the main bridge, always heavily guarded. Franz instructed me to ride on his left side and as close to him as possible. There was considerable traffic when we approached the bridge, and many people, pedestrians and bicyclists, were being checked. Franz told me not to slow down unless he called me. Franz rode his bicycle as close to the guards as practical and safe, gave an efficient salute, and we continued riding without giving the guards a chance to stop us. The power of his uniform and his decisive action worked as planned.

At the entrance to the railroad station, we successfully passed through heavily guarded control points without being stopped, probably because Franz was talking to me in German. The next thing on Franz's plan was to put me in the men's restrooms, in one of the inner enclosures where would be hard to see me. "Stay there and don't move," were his instructions. It took a while before he returned. He then took me to the transport leader, who assigned me a corner in the corridor on one of the railroad cars. I had a slip in my hand, probably identifying me as a member of this transport. Cousin Franz tried to assure me that everything would go smoothly, that the man in charge would keep his promise, whatever that was.

While the train was being prepared for departure, I noticed that most of the passengers were soldiers with minor injuries, most of them in good enough shape to climb up on the train; some with assistance. There were only a few stretcher cases. The train did not have any Red Cross insignia. There were no military escort people on the train, just the transport leader and two or three helpers. When the train left the station, Franz was still standing there with his two bicycles, waving to me.

The train went slowly with several stops at various stations. Nobody entered the train; occasionally, however, I saw the train leader talking at various stops to officials there. When we arrived in Dravograd, it was announced that the train would stop there between three to four hours, and a whistle would announce the departure thirty minutes ahead of time. All those in good enough shape were permitted to disembark and spend that time at the station building or in the nearby restaurant. I found myself in a peculiar situation since many people were now walking back and forth through the railroad cars. As a civilian I felt out of place or, to be more correct, in slight danger. Therefore, I left my corner on the train and climbed up the embankment behind the railroad station. Up in the woods, overseeing the activities at the station, I consumed part of the presents the good people in Maribor gave me for my trip. I felt very sorry for myself that in my own town, even though I lived there only a few years, I had to hide from everybody like a lost dog. I did not want to be recognized by the wrong people in the town, but even talking to friends would probably not have been a good idea. When the signal at the station finally sounded after what I felt were very long hours, I went back to the station and took the same corner assigned to me in Maribor. It was already getting dark when we departed, and passed through the towns of Gustajn/Ravne[2] and Prevalje, where I was born and enjoyed my happy childhood.

A complete silence, such as embraced our train, gives you the feeling you are approaching the last few hours before the final blow of fate. As on the train from Poland to Czechoslovakia in January 1945, the wounded soldiers on this train did not have anything to say to one another. One felt that they lost their ability to retain any positive thoughts. It seemed that they were wounded twice, first physically and then in their hearts and souls. Maybe their concerns were far away; what they would find at home; if that was their destination.

It was pitch dark when the train stopped again and the order came, "Alle aussteigen" (everybody off the train). I wondered why. Then I saw through the darkness that there was no bridge ahead over the Drava River. What was left of the bridge was in the river, visible here and there in rushing waters. Nearby was an emergency pedestrian bridge, and the Germans were preparing to get everybody across the river via that bridge. Commands were flying as to how to organize that most efficiently. At first I thought that it was my obligation to help since these were wounded soldiers, but I soon decided against it. Instead, I walked across the temporary bridge before anybody else, and on the other side I disappeared into the darkness on the only road I was able to find. Even though I was not completely sure of my direction, I assumed that I was walking in the direction of Klagenfurt/Celovec in southern Carinthia.

I still had a general sense of this area from a few trips with my family before the war; unfortunately, especially during the night, my memory did not help much. In addition, I was very afraid of meeting anybody, German patrols or partisans. I was aware that partisans were occasionally active in these territories, but to what extent, I did not have the slightest idea. The fact was, if you were ever stopped by any armed people, their first reaction was suspicion. Walking at night, during curfew hours, was even more suspicious and dangerous. I tried to make as much noise as possible with my hiking boots to give the impression that I was not trying to hide. I also soon became very tired from a day of nerve-wracking actions. I decided, therefore, to doze off at the side of the road for a while. Apparently, I fell asleep right away. Raindrops woke me up. I got up and to my great surprise noticed a small railroad station building only some three hundred yards away. I went there for shelter.

I must have looked exhausted. A man without a right arm, who was devouring a large sandwich with something appealing between the slices, came over and asked if I were hungry. He still had a little of his sandwich left and offered it to me. I was impressed with his generosity and also surprised that he talked to me in Slovene. He said that he had a feeling that I was a Slovene although he could not give me any reasons for his correct guess. Probably all the German police or control officers had the same "feelings" when they looked at me. The man had lost his arm during an air attack on the Klagenfurt/Celovec railroad station. His train had just arrived when the bombs started falling; it was too late to escape. Since I still had enough food, I thanked him most sincerely for his generous offer. He was headed in the same direction as I and he promised to help me. Two hours later we boarded a train.

When the train stopped at the Klagenfurt/Celovec railroad station, even before the train came to a full stop, my new acquaintance's personality changed suddenly and completely. Without saying anything to me, he jumped off the train and ran at unbelievable speed over the railroad tracks away from the station and disappeared into nowhere before I was able to get off the train. It became clear to me that the loss of his right arm had done a lot of damage to this individual both physically and mentally. I never caught up with him; he was gone.

I hoped to go via Villach/Beljak, still in Austria, or Germany at that time, to Jesenice in German-occupied Yugoslavia. I walked on the less-used south side of the Wörther See west toward Villach/Beljak, a frequent target for air attacks. At first I was tempted to take the northern route, where a cousin of mine lived in a small but beautiful town that Johannes Brahms had frequently visited during the summer months: Porchach/Poreče. But such visitors as I did not bring good news and good fortune to relatives. Therefore, I decided on the southern route. Even though I walked almost all day, I was stopped only once. However, on that occasion a police officer confiscated my Auschwitz ID *(Ausweis),* saying that I would not need that anymore. In spite of my protests, he refused to return it and took it into the police station.

The next morning, after I hid next to the road and then at a small railroad station outside Villach/Beljak, the train for Jesenice arrived. At Jesenice police officers were stationed almost at every arriving railroad car and inspected the passengers. The train stopped there; it was the final station. I was grabbed even before I stepped on the ground. This time my Auschwitz story worked very well, especially the part about inquiring there about my release. Why I then went to the air raid shelter behind and north of the station, I do not recall. I was probably looking for people who would know more about how to get to my hometown, Ljubljana. It was a nice, sunny day; the sun warmed me up after the night's ordeal as soon as I made myself comfortable outside the entrance to the air raid shelter, where many other people were resting.

Some sixth sense told me that sitting at the entrance of the air raid shelter on a such bright and beautiful day was not a good idea. I got up, walked inside, and turned to the right down a side corridor. I had only taken a few steps when with tremendous thunder bombs fell right on the entrance of the shelter. Apparently, a bomber squadron appeared all of a sudden over the south mountain ridges and attacked the railroad station and the city, including the shelter I was in. The light went off; the people were screaming in real fear of being buried alive. I was just a few feet from the collapsed entrance corridor and wanted to move further away. I did not get far before bumping into other people who thought that escape was possible in my direction. It would be hard to forget the tremendous panic in the dark shelter, especially the high-pitched screams of women in all possible languages.

We then heard a rough, real German command voice yell that everybody should sit down immediately, or the armed personnel in the shelter would start shooting everybody moving around or causing panic. In a split second there was silence.

In a much calmer voice the same person then announced that the damage was not that great and that he thought it would take only a few hours to get us out. Cigarette lighters helped a little at first to evaluate the situation and count the people in the shelter, but they were soon extinguished on command to conserve the fresh air in the tunnels. This air shelter was allegedly huge, with many corridors in different directions. How many people were caught inside I did not know. Following orders, I was sitting on a wet board and listening to two women nearby sobbing constantly and whispering to each other that we will never get out, that we were doomed.

Our ordeal lasted a long time, from about nine in the morning until four in the afternoon, before the rescue team broke through and led us out in an orderly fashion. How pleasant it was to see the daylight again. When I asked one of the rescuers if people had been killed or wounded at the entrance, people with whom I had probably exchanged a few words before I decided to enter the shelter, I received the rude answer that these things were none of my concern.

I left this dangerous place at a fast pace.

There were other former prisoners on the way home walking in the direction of the city of Kranj. Nobody, however, knew anything about how and where to cross the border between the German and the former Italian zones. This border was said to be almost impossible to cross successfully without proper permission papers. Now I badly needed Hinko and Joža; they would have found a way, I thought.

It was already toward the evening when I left Kranj and headed toward Viševek, my father's birthplace. I was sure that my uncle Silvester, father's youngest brother, would gave me a comfortable place and protection of a sort for a few days. After I inquired in the back of one restaurant whether it was safe to march at this time of the evening toward Viševek, I received a positive reply. The woman even offered me something to eat in the restaurant. However, when I saw three German uniforms sitting at one of the tables, enjoying their food and drink, I thought I better not.

Uncle Silvester could not believe it when I suddenly stepped into his modest farm kitchen, built in the previous century. He kept embracing me, something not usually done among our peasants. The first thing, before he even asked from where I came, I had to drink a shot of homemade brandy. After that I forgot about tiredness, about hunger, about past difficult and dangerous days. I just kept talking, talking, and talking. . . .

My presence in the village did not go unnoticed for too long. There were no young men at home. Still, I had two restful days with my relatives. My uncle tried to explain what had happened the last four years. In general, the people in the village held together even though there was no lack of differences of opinion as to who would or should get the final control of the land at the end of the war.

On the second day I received a summon to report to the Home Defense station in Tupaliče, the nearby village. My uncle did not have any experience in these matters and felt that I would be able to explain to the authorities there why I arrived and from where and that would suffice for getting a temporary residency permit. I was hesitant about going but did not have much choice; either I would report or they would come for me.

Reluctantly, I went to the Home Defense station. I hoped that this time I would not have any difficulties in explaining my situation. In my own language it would be much easier than trying to do the same in German as I had numerous times before. Only one person was in the office when I arrived, and when I mentioned my name, he told me that they knew who I was and that I had arrived only a few days ago. Immediately after that, he lectured me on the duties of every young man in these difficult times. My attempts to describe my life and experiences of the past year were rudely interrupted as soon as I opened my mouth. Apparently, speaking the native language did not help at all; on the contrary it was to my disadvantage. I was told to wait until the commander returned; after that I would begin my training.

Crushed by yet another misfortune, I was sitting in a corner of an adjacent room, thinking how to get out of this unexpected difficulty. I had come all the way from Poland and overcame tremendous barriers on the way. Now right here, only a few kilometers from my home in Ljubljana, I was about to be drafted into the military.

Half an hour later, I heard a motorcycle. A young Home Defense lieutenant (poročnik) entered. After a few instructions to the sergeant, he inquired about that person sitting in the other room. Hearing my name, he immediately came over and introduced himself as Francka's brother. He thanked me most sincerely for helping his sister reach home from as far away as Auschwitz. On my part I was most glad to hear that both Francka and Očka arrived home safely. The lieutenant was really delighted to see me and inquired about Hinko, the real savior of all of us, and his sister Joža.

As for my wish to get home as soon as possible and because he knew that I had been a student at the Bishop's Gymnasium at Šentvid, he suggested that I go to Šenčur, where I would find commander X. R. As a former student at that school, he might be able and willing to help me cross the border between the German and Italian zones. Regarding the sergeant's point that I should have been drafted, the lieutenant said such an action would make no sense at that point. Most grateful to Francka's brother, I left the Home Defense station before the station's commander came back; I did not want to take any more chances.

I arrived at Šenčur on a borrowed bicycle the next day. The Home Defense controls were very tight around this town. Use of the commander's name got me through several controls. At the command post, I was refused entry. The commander, however, heard my plea through an open window of his office and invited me in.[3]

He did not ask many questions about my past but fully understood my wish to go home. At the moment, he told me, the situation was very tense and uncertain, but as soon as things improved, there would be no problem getting me across the border. He even promised to send a messenger to Viševek when the time would be right. When we parted, he added that he would be delighted to do something for another student from Bishop's Gymnasium.

The end of the war, the official end, was one thing; the territorial last battles and everything associated with them were another. The enormous and cataclysmic retreat from Auschwitz and the one from Hungary of a slightly different nature did not prepare me for the events that took place during the beginning days of May 1945. The other two disasters were in foreign lands; retreat was a last hope to save oneself from an unknown but probably even more intolerable life. In both previous situations, however, I had somewhere to go; I had a home, while the majority of others did not. In that minor detail, I was different; I was just an insignificant part of those unfortunate masses, but I saw a bright little light in the remote but still-reachable distance. No, something of such tremendous cataclysmic consequences could not happen here, here in our own land. But it did! It happened at the beginning of May 1945.

It was obvious that the tremendous assembly of military power advancing from the East could not be stopped even with combined efforts of all opponents of the Communist takeover. Why did these opposing forces not attempt a last stand? Were they ideologically too far apart or did military realities make it impossible? I did not immediately realize how much change had taken place in a little less than a year while I was absent from home territory. When it became clear that the Liberation Front would be victorious militarily and politically, it seemed fashionable to join just to be on the winning side. One had to admit that the list of individual names, groups, and organizations that joined OF in the last year of the war was remarkable.

First it was a rumor. Soon, however, the word came that all those opposing Tito's forces would retreat for the time being across the border to Carinthia in Southern Austria. That was the only exit still open out of the former Yugoslav territory in the direction of the Western Allied forces. The southern route to Trieste/Trst was already closed because of Tito's major thrust toward that city and beyond.

Confused and concerned, I walked to Kranj to see what was going on. The announced retreat was in full swing already. During the first day the majority of refugees consisted of Home Defense units and their followers. Wagons were overloaded with their possessions. It was most depressing to see small children sitting on these wagons, not understanding why their parents had left their comfortable homes. I tried to find out more about the situation from a few individuals who were willing to talk; however, the answers varied. The majority thought that this retreat was only temporary; that the Allied forces would enter Slovenia in a few days and help establish a democratic government. The retreating forces and refugees would then be able to return. After all, the British and the Americans were practically at the door.

Almost by accident I found my brother Ciril among these thousands of people. He was not any better informed than the rest of the people I talked to. He wanted me to join his unit, thinking that I would be better protected than going on my own. However, I was not convinced that joining anything at that stage of the war would be sensible. In a way I liked my freedom even though that freedom did not rest on any firm ground. Undecided about what to do, I returned to my uncle's place in Viševek.

The next day my mother came to Viševek with my sister Marija. My mother thought that Marija would be safer in the country than in the big city during the first days of the takeover. She herself was determined to return to Ljubljana as soon as possible to join my father. A few people were allegedly urging my father to leave Ljubljana. He, however, said that in his life he had been a refugee twice[4] and had no intention of leaving his home for the third time. As a lawyer he firmly believed in law, and therefore he had nothing to fear from the new authorities.

Mother and I went to Kranj hoping to find Ciril there. While walking through the city, we heard a few rifle shots fired at the retreating troops, allegedly from one of the city residences. The Home Defense soldiers immediately cleared the city streets in anticipation of a partisan attack. Mother and I suddenly faced a Home Defense soldier pointing a weapon at us. It was a tense moment. I was holding mother's hand; she was shaking. We were then allowed to step into the vestibule of the nearby house to wait there until the emergency was over.

Mother was in tears when she said goodbye to Ciril. He had tried to convince her that everything would turn out well. Mother, however, could not stop crying, even a long time after we left the city.

We were holding hands and walking in the direction of Ljubljana. From time to time we stopped and tried to decide about my future. Should I return to Ljubljana and continue my studies, especially my music, which I missed so much? Would it be safe for me to return? I was not a member or a sympathizer of the Communist-controlled Liberation Front. This fact was not unknown, especially after my arrest by the Gestapo in June 1944. Thoughts of the events of 1943, the massacres after the defeat at Grčarice and Turjak, kept crossing my mind as well. On the opposite side of the road, walking in the other direction, were thousands of people. There must have been a good reason for so many people to leave everything behind, including their homes and their land. Among them I recognized a few from my high school days. Several asked where I was going. One of them, Silvo Marinčič, my friend from Bishop's Gymnasium in Šentvid, whom I last saw at the end of the school year 1939/40, even used the famous book title, slightly embellished, of Henryck Sienkievicz, *Quo vadis, Methodius,* to get my attention and also to give me some friendly advice. Mother and I faced an incredible and heartbreaking dilemma.

Approximately ten kilometers south of Kranj, after another brief stop, I told my mother I had decided to turn back. In a few days or weeks the things would settle down, and then it would be time to come home. Mother kept embracing me but did not try to persuade me otherwise. I could not say anything to her when she left me standing there and neither could she. Gradually she disappeared behind the first turn on the road; she was the only person walking in that direction. I almost came home, almost.

CHAPTER FOURTEEN

Viktring/Vetrinj:
Cruel and Brutal Deception

May 1945

Kdo solze naše posuši? Kdo tisoč mrtvih obudi?
Kdaj ti spomini oblede in želje v nas zaspe?
—(Pavle Borštnik, Pozdravljena zemlja)

Who'll dry the tears we have shed? Who'll wake the thousands of our dead?
When will our bitter mem'ries fade, Our yearnings be allayed?
—(Translation by Tom M. S. Priestly)

On 2 May 1945, the German Army in Italy surrendered. Their military units tried to reach their home territories in Austria and Germany as fast as possible and by any means. The retreat of thousands was underway.

Among those looking to find safety in Switzerland was Benito Mussolini. He was recognized at Lake Como by the Italian partisans and executed in April 1945.

The German Army in the West surrendered unconditionally on 7 May. Officially, 8 May 1945 is recorded as the end of the war in Europe.

Hostilities and many other tragic events, however, continued for a few months, causing repercussions that will be remembered for a long time, together with the immeasurable catastrophe of World War II.

Part I

After the last sight of my mother vanished, I turned around. For a little while I stood still, struggling with myself. Dark thoughts kept entering my mind; my heart was racing. There was nobody to seek advice from, if any kind of advice was possible. Those walking on the opposite side of the road had made their decisions, or somebody had made the decisions for them. They were so many, and more and more were coming. Where would this mass of people go? North, across the border, was the immediate answer.

There was no good reason for me to hesitate much longer. The chances of a safe return to Ljubljana were diminishing with every minute. In my mother's company I certainly would have had a better chance than going on my own. Sooner or later I would be stopped by this or that group or by an individual who had the power. I had no idea where the battle lines were at that moment, maybe very close, maybe still far away. But who would want to take the risk? A more positive thought crossed my mind; I should walk north with the others close to Ciril's group. I hastened my formerly slow and heavy steps.

Kranj was packed with people. However, those who had arrived a few hours before were now gone, including Ciril's group. Renewed determination and previous experiences with similar long marches helped me to regain my physical strength. Encouraging thoughts, however, did not seem to increase. I walked on the left side of the road; it was more open and the progress faster. In Tržič, the last town before the road became progressively steeper, a few people suddenly showed up with pairs of new boots, shoes, and other leather products. Apparently, somebody had broken into a leather factory to equip himself. In order to partially justify his action, he told others in the retreating column about the factory, and many followed his example. I heard that the place was emptied in a few minutes.

This exodus was fast becoming a conglomeration of people of all sorts. Military units and individual military personnel were in the majority. At one point a panic report reached us that a kilometer behind us two tanks had been placed across the road to slow down the partisans, who allegedly were already in the vicinity. Those wagons behind that point were stuck, because there was no way to remove the heavy tanks or go around them. An hour later the situation was resolved when the crew of another tank pushed the first two off the road.

I had a bad experience on one steep stretch. A German officer with a pistol in his hand ordered me off the road. I hesitated for a second, because the drop on that side of the road was very steep. However, I realized immediately that he was serious, and I slid down a few yards into the ravine. I was still at their mercy, apparently. The right of way on that steep road up to the mountain pass or toward the roughly completed tunnel became more and more crucial for all concerned. The organized military units proceeded with less difficulty, but civilians were often pushed aside. The German military, used to getting their way and still well-armed, held the upper hand. I was very pleased, therefore, to witness an incident involving a high-ranking German officer sitting in a motorcycle sidecar driven by a well-armed soldier and the Home Defense lieutenant, I. K., whom I knew from my high school days in Ljubljana. (He was two or three years ahead of me.) The German officer's driver was forcing his way through the mass of people by blowing the motorcycle's horn. People were stepping to the side and making space for the two to pass. Lieutenant I. K., however, probably had enough of this kind of superiority. He stepped in front of the motorcycle and ordered his men to point their weapons at the two. In broken German he told the officer and his chauffeur to get out and off their vehicle and walk with everybody else. The two had no choice. In a few seconds the empty three-wheeled motorcycle was rolling down the hill and ended with a loud crash on a large rock in the middle of a puddle.

Walking toward us on the way home were a few concentration camp prisoners, easily recognized as such by their striped attire. This brought back memories of Auschwitz, where I first saw these strange uniforms. The former prisoners were tight-lipped; they would not even reveal the name of the camp they were returning from. One did ask me, apparently very puzzled at the sight of the people in the column, why and where so many people were going. I hope that I gave him a correct or at least a satisfactory answer.

Not too long before we reached the tunnel, the word came that it was closed. Because of the extremely large and increasing mass of people, the road toward the tunnel was packed with people and vehicles. There was no traffic in the other direction. The German military now posted heavily armed guards at the entrance to the tunnel, thus preventing anybody but German units from entering. For all others the only option was the tough climb over the Ljubelj/Loibl mountain pass (elevation: 4,487 ft). I did remember that road from the pre-war years when we once crossed the pass in a car, something not to be forgotten because of those scary, steep switchbacks, almost impossible to handle. This time, everybody not willing or unable to handle that dangerous passage was directed off the road to the former concentration camp there or out on the open land to any available space. Thus, in one still-not-fully occupied hut, I found my neighbor, a lawyer, and his daughter with a few others, and they invited me to share their primitive accommodations. One of the persons in this group was a Home Defense soldier who had lost his eyesight in a mine explosion. A young lady, a friend of my neighbor's daughter, helped him and cared for him on this difficult retreat.

Actually, we were now trapped, blocked on all sides. Though the German armed units were in the minority, at least at the time I was on the road—the majority were Slovene people and the Slovene Home Defense units—it seemed that the Germans were still in control. Who negotiated and where the right of way through the tunnel was not known, but it was apparent that the negotiators gave in, on a temporary basis we were told, to the German demands for exclusive rights. The area in front of the tunnel was filling up fast; not much space was left along the sides of the road. We were told repeatedly to keep calm and that the partisan advance units were still some distance away, that there was no immediate danger of entrapment. However, I began considering the rough march over the pass on the next day.

In the mid-afternoon a colleague of mine, I. Z., whom I knew from the Classical Gymnasium and from the Academy of Music in Ljubljana, came rushing to our hut and told me that he had seen my sister and one of her friends down on the road. I never expected anything like that. It was a shock. That was the only time in my life that I was not happy to see my sister. She and her friend, Ružica Dučkič, a Catholic girl from Kosovo, were looking for temporary overnight accommodations, when I. Z. spotted them. A Home Defense soldier offered to help them push Marija's bicycle up the steep road if they would let him put his backpack on it. The three traveled together. In the camp area before the tunnel this soldier had to return to his unit, and he was looking for someone to help the two young girls. I thanked him for his generous help. He gave me his and his unit's name just in case we would need further help. Then I took Marija and her friend to our hut.

Her story was simple. A few young women, the neighbors in Viševek, had been told that it would be advisable to leave their homes for a few days or weeks until things settled down. Under the influence of this hysteria, Marija decided to join them. Our Uncle Silvester in Viševek did not know what to do and he let her go.[1] She packed a few things and took a bicycle for easier travel. Somewhere on the road she met her friend from school, Ružica, and they formed a team. Where and when she separated from the other women from Viševek, I do not recall.

Her presence made my situation much more difficult since I became her guardian and I was no longer alone; however, we both thought that together we would survive with less trauma. There were quite a few broken-up families among the departed, which further confirmed the fact that this exodus was considered a temporary event.

The huts of the former concentration camp were still in satisfactory condition. We settled ourselves as best we could with whatever we brought along. Our neighbor from Ljubljana acted as an informal leader of our group. Thus, we formed a functional group, even though the division of labor did not always please everybody. In general, we worked together well. My colleague, I. Z., had the best connections to the higher Slovene civilian representatives. His job was to seek information, or to be more correct, to find out how serious and precarious our situation was. We soon realized that those often-mentioned connections with the Western Allies had no basis in fact. Early in the morning on the second day at Ljubelj/Loibl, I saw a Serbian officer examining with his binoculars the tops of mountain ridges all around us. Nothing was moving on those heights, fortunately for us, he said. It would not take many properly armed people occupying those heights for this entire mass of people to be trapped for good, he added. The tension among us grew with every minute; we saw that we were already trapped.

Mid-morning of that second day, a large group of Serbian Chetniks appeared at the entrance to the Ljubelj/Loibl tunnel. They were well-armed, mostly mature men, many with beards in the old Chetnik tradition. When the traffic controllers on the road tried to direct them to an area by the road, they ignored instructions and continued toward the tunnel. From our hut we saw that they went right toward the entrance, a few on their horses, most walking. Then came a touchy confrontation with the German armed detachment at the entrance. The Chetniks demanded passage: they were ready to use their weapons to get their way. Fortunately, negotiations followed, not a bloody confrontation. The Germans had to agree to the Serbian Chetniks' 50/50 proposition. Thus, half of the tunnel on the one side was still reserved for the Germans, but the other half became available for all those masses already assembled in the area and for those still farther back on the road. The guards remained at the entrance to the tunnel to keep control and to prevent a panic rush through to the only way out. When our turn came, we approached the tunnel in an orderly manner, keeping together. Prior to that we had received some information as to what to expect.

There were no lights in the tunnel; the roadway was in a rudimentary state. There were water puddles of all possible sizes, and the rounded ceiling was cracking and dripping gradually or in most uncomfortable sudden spurts. The left lane of the tunnel was reserved for all of us, the right lane for the Germans. After a few steps into the tunnel, we were in the dark. Here and there a cigarette lighter or a flashlight helped a little. We tried to keep together, each person holding to the person in front of him or her. I was walking with a bicycle on my right as protection from the traffic in the other lane. Marija was holding the seat of the bicycle and the back of my pack so that we did not get separated in the darkness. Ružica tied herself to Marija. The German side had more vehicles of all kinds. The most dangerous were the horses, scared and hard to control. Twice I thought they would trample us or kill us with their hoofs. Their handlers had a very hard time. A few times we heard screams or desperate calls when people got separated, but in general all you heard were movements of people, animals, vehicles, and here and there some swearing. The tunnel had no end, it seemed. That nightmare march went on and on. Occasionally I called to Marija behind me; she rarely heard me for all that *timor and tremor* dominating the interior of that horrible place. I do not recall how long it took us to get through the tunnel—a very long time. Finally, we heard way ahead of us happy voices announcing the approach of much-desired daylight. The memory of passing through the Ljubelj/Loibl tunnel that day in early May 1945 still haunts me every time I drive through any tunnel anywhere. While ours was a horrifying experience, my thoughts also went to those concentration camp prisoners who had to work in and dig at this place under terrifying conditions.

The light of the day brought much relief. We were in Austria, out of reach of the Yugoslav or Slovene Partisan forces, or so we thought. The road was still steep and there were many switchbacks, but the worst was over. Where to go from here was now the question, but there were no answers. The flood of people, civilians and military, animals, and vehicles took care of these uncertainties; they pushed us on and on.

Soon the news came that the Carinthian Slovene partisans were denying everybody access to the bridge over the Drava River, near the town of Ferlach/Borovlje, the last major obstacle to open land. A strong detachment of the Slovene Home Defense units attacked these partisans, who suffered heavy losses in this battle. Although I, like everybody else, felt more secure now that the road to the Drava River was open, I was worried about my cousin and his friends from Bad Vellach/Bela by Eisenkappe/ Železna kapla, who had deserted from the German Army and joined the Carinthian partisans. I was worried they might be among those participating in this battle to prevent the retreating columns from crossing. In the middle of the afternoon, the bridge itself came into view.

We stretched our necks to see what was going on the other side of the river. Only one tank was visible, and at a slight elevation beyond the bridge we saw a few British soldiers, who were taking a break, it seemed. It was difficult to see much else because everybody was now pressing to get over the bridge as soon as possible. The river current was dangerously fast at that point, and one had to wonder how long this bridge would take all this weight and stomping of feet.

With a certain relief I finally stepped on the bridge. I felt that I was entering a new world, the one I had been dreaming about for a long time. On the other side, a few yards from the bridge, a single British soldier of unknown rank stood on duty. I could not see much of what was going on in front of me, except that all weapons were taken and thrown on a pile next to the road. When I came close to the soldier, he had just removed a wristwatch from the man in front of me. The man tried to resist, but two other British soldiers were immediately ready to step in. The confiscated wristwatch then flew through the air toward the soldiers sitting on a slight elevation behind him, who caught it with loud laughs. When my turn came, I noticed that this soldier had both arms full of wristwatches, a nice collection of all possible sizes and makes. He checked both my wrists; I possessed no watch at that time. He evaluated the weight of my pack, said something, and waved me ahead. I could not but think back to the day I was captured in the mountains of Slovenia by the Italian "M" division, and a lieutenant ordered one of his soldiers to return my wristwatch he had confiscated a few seconds before. I realized, of course, that the British soldier at the bridge could not possibly have known I was a supporter of the Allied side, especially since I was crossing the bridge in the company of all kinds of civilians and armed units, including the Germans. Nevertheless, that first encounter with a British person left a bad feeling in my heart, despite the fact that this soldier probably had made his way to this Drava bridge from as far away as North Africa, from Alexandria in Egypt to Tobruk, to Sicily, across Italy, and then into the Southern Carinthia, so those wristwatches were a minor compensation for many hardships. Still, the dark thoughts remained. Where would we find comfort and peace?

One of the commanders of the British forces at the Drava bridge, as I learned many years later, was Captain Nigel Nicolson, who crossed with his Welsh Guards into Austria from Northern Italy on 8 May 1945 and arrived in Southern Carinthia on 12 May. A detachment of Welsh Guards was assigned to accept the people coming from the Ljubelj/Loibl tunnel and crossed the Drava at Ferlach/Borovlje. To explain to the reader the different interpretations of the events that took place during the crucial days of May and June 1945, I wish to quote from his book, where he describes his recollections of the situation and events of those days. Nigel Nicolson writes:

> *Carinthia . . . into which soldiers of several nationalities and thousands of refugee civilians had flooded to escape captivity or oppression by the Russians or Tito's partisans. . . .*
>   *Our duty was to settle them in camps apart from each other, disarm them, compose their political differences as far as we could, before any thought could be given to their repatriation. They looked to us for security.*[2]

We were now under British control, protection, and supervision. Our understanding was, that by submitting to their control, we received political asylum. As Nicolson pointed out:

> *There was no need for refugees to request, or for us to grant, asylum. Our actions were sufficient proof of it.*[3]

Thus, I finally reached the goal which I had pursued all the way from Auschwitz in occupied Poland: I reached the Allied side, although I never expected that it would happen under such unusual and strange circumstances.

The British placed guards at various spots on the road to control the traffic; the guards were very few. South of Klagenfurt/Celovec, near the town of Viktring/Vetrinj, we were directed off the road to open fields. The British selected an old monastery complex as a temporary shelter for civilians.[4] The military had to take care of themselves the best they could in the adjacent fields. The military units were placed in different sections according to their affiliations; for example, the German prisoners were in one area, the Slovene Home Defense units in another, and so on. These units remained under their own commands.

Our shelter in the storage building, although very crowded, provided sufficient protection from the elements. The rest was up to us. The British provided
supplies for our modest meals. These were not British military meals; we received
what was usually distributed in the German labor camps. It was not much but
better than nothing; for the time being we had protection and some food.[5] The
British organization of camp sections by nationalities or other logical divisions
helped to keep groups together. This way the Home Defense units, Slovene Chetniks, and civilian refugees from Slovenia formed one section of the camp. The
British provided guards around the camp, not to keep the people in but to prevent
Tito's partisans from entering. No incidents of that nature happened. Those
standing on guard had to stand there many hours. We were sorry that, because of
the language barrier, no conversations were possible. This lack of communication
made us think that the British soldiers were unfriendly.

It was clear that the camp was a temporary arrangement and that relocations
would be necessary. If my memory is correct, the German prisoners of war were
moved somewhere else first. I observed that they were treated with more respect by
the British than any other nationality on those fields. Maybe it was only my jeal-
ous imagining since I considered myself an ally of the western democracies, and
they, the Germans, were their enemies. The Germans, however, well-disciplined as
always, knew their rights as prisoners of war and expected a release from the
prison camps sooner or later. For them everything was over. Our situation was different. We were at the mercy of whoever would decide our future. We listened to
the radio for daily news and decisions by the Allies. My colleague I. Z. and I put
out a primitive information sheet of the latest developments as reported by various Allied broadcasts. The reports of the increasing friction between Field Marshal Alexander and Marshal Tito raised hopes for Allied intervention in Yugoslavia or at least in Slovenia, a hope fast diminishing after the American and English
forces stopped their advances in Trieste/Trst and in the surrounding territories.
Day by day, however, the main reason for our retreat to Carinthia, a speedy return
to Slovenia with Allied help, seemed less and less likely.

In those most uncertain times, the Slovenes in the Viktring/Vetrinj camp had
shown their ability to be positive, to organize their lives as best they could, to provide a school for their children, and to keep their living quarters neat and clean.
Most of all, the church at Vetrinj was always full of people praying for help. The
military officers kept their units fit and thus tried to prevent discouragement.

A few of the refugees, who were captured by the Carinthian partisans south of
the bridge over the Drava River near Ferlach/Borovlje before the Home Defense
troops secured open passage, escaped, and eventually came to the Viktring/Vetrinj
camp, with fear still clearly showing on their faces. Among them was my school
friend from the Classical Gymnasium in Ljubljana, L. Š., who gave me a detailed
description of what had happened and the treatment he was subjected to during

his hours of capture. Since there was no census of who was in the camp, a few late-comers did not present problems.

We considered the arrival of Special British Personnel a good sign, an indication that the news of our existence reached higher-ups or at least people of influence. Among those I would put in the first place was John Corsellis, who was very visible and showed a sincere concern for our well-being almost from the start of the Viktring/Vetrinj refugee camp. Mr. Corsellis was a member of the Friends' Ambulance Unit, a classification that did not mean anything to me at the time, except that he tried to help whenever he could. One of our medical students, J. J., was often seen with Mr. Corsellis circling around the camp, but no essential new information was produced as a result of this friendship. The information about our status and our future was scarce and mostly rooted in rumors.[6] A couple of British Red Cross nurses also brought a ray of hope. The reactions of some women in the camp to the nurses' offer of help were very positive. If there was any direct communication between the camp people and the Red Cross representatives, I did not have an opportunity to observe it.

Part II

First, there were only rumors. In a camp like Viktring/Vetrinj and in such uncertain times as May 1945, the rumors were plentiful. It was not easy to separate possibilities from the impossible. It did appear, however, that the British authorities either did not have much inkling of how to handle the difficult situations (and there were many), or they did not wish to communicate down the line. Not much came out of the offices of our camp representatives either; they were probably as much in the dark as the rest of us. It became gradually clear, however, that our relationship with the British was not on the level we had dreamed about. Day by day, the situation gradually deteriorated.

Therefore, the news that the troops and civilians of all nations except Germans would be transferred to camps in Italy came as a welcome relief. In a day or two we were to get the transportation schedule and learn what would be expected from us during the relocation.

It was obvious that Viktring/Vetrinj was not a good location for a refugee camp. It was located very close to the demarcation line between the British and the Soviet occupation zones, and at the time the British and Yugoslavs were still disputing occupation rights. In addition, the camp was primitive and without adequate facilities. Therefore, relocation was a must. The Italian camps were allegedly better suited to absorb so many people; the access to supplies was easier, the organization and semi-adequate accommodations were already in place. The climate during the winter months would not be as harsh as in the cold Klagenfurt/Celovec basin. The

German troops, if my memory is correct, had already been moved out of the area to places further north.

The British Klagenfurt/Celovec Command decided to move Serb Volunteer Corps and Chetniks first. The first transport, approximately 2,500 soldiers and some of their followers and families, including a few children, departed the Viktring/Vetrinj camp on 24 May, five days after the British and Yugoslav authorities agreed that the Yugoslav troops would leave Carinthia, a British zone of operation by a previous international agreement.[7] Claims were also circulating that the British wanted to have at these border areas, some still under dispute, clear and open territory without any extra burdens.

To the first Serb transport a small advance detachment of Slovenes was added to prepare the new camps for the rest of the troops and refugees. The transportation schedule of Slovenes was soon announced; the military would be relocated first and then the civilians. The first Slovene transport—approximately 2,500 men and a few civilians—departed on Sunday 27 May at 11:00 A.M. Many people from the civilian camp assembled on the fields to watch them board British military trucks. As I well remember, the British soldiers were fully armed and efficient during the boarding procedure. The Home Defense men were told more than once that their destination was Italy, therefore, those leaving were completely cooperative. Their destination, by some reports, was camps near Palmanova in northern Italy; others claimed that the Slovene Home Defense troops would be added to the Polish 2nd Army under the command of the Polish General Anders, which was part of the British 8th Army. When this first convoy departed, we were pleased that the relocation had finally started. We were convinced that all of us would be together again in a few days. It was up to the Slovene Command to set the order of departure for each day; the British only chose the days and the number of people. Thus on Monday and Tuesday, 28 and 29 May 1945, the same procedure was repeated.[8] The military camp was gradually losing its inhabitants.

But then dark shadows started creeping in regarding the British local command honesty. The British repeatedly assured us that the transports were going to Italy. However, three Serb officers who left on the first transport of 24 May returned to Viktring/Vetrinj camp and told the Slovene authorities that their transport had been handed over to Tito's troops and then taken to Yugoslavia instead of Italy as repeatedly promised by the British officers. I met one of these Serb officers, who told me that the entire group, with a few exceptions, was massacred somewhere near Kamnik in Slovenia. Although these were allegedly eyewitness reports, these officers were not believed. They refused to be taken to the British authorities to give their reports, fearing that the British would arrest them and forced them to return to Yugoslavia. In addition, in their reports they contradicted themselves in a few details. The officers were then threatened by the Slovene Home Defense command with arrest if they kept spreading such news around the camp. Nobody believed that the British would do such a thing, nor did they believe either, that Tito's victorious forces would just massacre these people. The Serbs went into hiding, where and how, I never knew. Rumors said that they escaped to the American zone of Austria. However, bad news started circulating around the camp. The report by the Serb officers was pushed aside as enemy propaganda and an attempt to bring disunity and panic to the camp.

In addition to many and often-repeated assurances by the British that all transports were scheduled for camps in Italy, we also knew that the British handled various groups differently. The Croatian *Ustashi*[9] were never accepted by the British and were forced to return to Yugoslavia, but the Slovene Home Defense, Chetniks, other Croatians, and various Serbian groups were provided temporary shelter and protection by the British at the Viktring/Vetrinj camps.

More and more rumors were circulating around the camp, allegedly also reported by residents of Carinthia. Our trust in British honesty was unshaken, however.

The night before Ciril's departure, he and I spent about half an hour together. He repeated what his superiors had told him. All those rumors about the Home Defense troops being returned to Tito's partisans were just that, rumors. There was nothing to be concerned about. However, that was not a normal conversation for us, who were always very close and had gone through difficult times together in the past. Our feelings were strange, unreal, like a nightmare, but neither of us revealed those feelings, even though I know we both felt them.

30 May 1945. Several minutes before 11:00 A.M., I went to see Ciril before his scheduled departure, supposedly to a new camp near Palmanova in northern Italy. Ciril was already in formation. I approached him and suggested that he leave the column so that the three of us, Marija included, would stay together and depart with a later civilian transport. Ciril hesitated for a moment. Those around him heard my plea and chimed in, saying that my words implied panic and that there was no reason for any fear. Ciril and I then shook hands and he rejoined the column. A few minutes later, he and his friends boarded a British army truck and departed, guarded by British soldiers. It was exactly 11:00 A.M. when I was standing on that field and waving to my brother, not knowing that it was for the last time.

At 3:00 P.M. that same day, four hours, only four hours later, my colleague, I. Z., came back to our place at the temporary shelter. He was pale, shaken up, and whispered that the British were in fact delivering the Home Defense troops and their followers to Tito's forces for transportation to Yugoslavia. This transfer was done in the most treacherous, cruel, and brutal manner. The handover was done at two places: Rosenbach/Podrožca and Bleiburg/Pliberk. The news was brought back to the camp's Slovene authorities by the Slovene medical doctor,

Janez Janež, who gave a complete description of what was happening and was willing to repeat the same in front of the British authorities.

An indescribable sorrow and agony came over those still in the camp after the full truth of the British betrayal became known. Half dazed, I walked around the camp and heard desperate cries, prayers, sobbing, and laments at every step. There was no hope left.

The British order for the last transport of the Home Defense troops, however, stood firm for the next day, 31 May. At this point, the troops were told what was happening and where the other troops had been taken. Now it was up to individuals to decide what to do; the officers released them from their obligations. Some soldiers abandoned their units, especially those who had families in the civilian camp. The next morning I went to the field where many were waiting for the British trucks, and I could not believe that so many were still willing to follow. The words we heard were, "Where the others have gone, we should go, no matter what happens." Again, at 11:00 A.M. this last group departed. We stood there with heavy hearts, feeling totally defeated and facing a most uncertain future.

Fortunately, I did not witness any harsh treatment of the Home Defenders and their followers by the British. However, many rumors were heard in the camp about that. Therefore, it came as no surprise to read years later in Nicolai Tolstoy's book, *The Minister and the Massacres*, about two eye-witness accounts by Ara Delianich and Nina Lencek.[10]

The handover of unsuspecting victims at Rosenbach/Podrožca and Bleiburg/Pliberk was described in detail by many who were fortunate to escape before it was too late. I heard several accounts from my school friends and also from others, some soon after their return to camp, some much later, either directly or through written accounts. The victims were not always believed, even though so many accounts of these happenings could not be ignored. We have, however, the report of the British officer, Nigel Nicolson, who "was present on most of these occasions, as a witness and reporter, not in command, but . . . a party to the accepted lie." Nicolson writes:

> *They were ferried [the Home Defense men and other Yugoslavs] by road from Viktring to two rural stations, Maria Elend and Rosenbach, where they descended from the trucks and clambered aboard a train of old cattle-wagons. For the officers, women and children, two battered carriages were attached at the rear. . . .*
>
> *Our guardsmen slid together the doors of the cattle-trucks when they were full, and padlocked them. They also locked the carriage doors. When all was secure, they drew back from the train, and their places were immediately taken by Tito's partisans who had been hiding in the bushes and station buildings. The wagons were old and through cracks the Jugs [Yugoslavs] cold see exactly what was happening. They began hammering on the inside of the wagon walls, shouting imprecations, not at the partisans, but at us, who had betrayed them, lied to them and sent at least the men among them to certain death. This scene was repeated day after day, twice a day. It was the most horrible experience of my life.*[11]

Hearing reports about forced turnovers from those very few who returned left me with a very slight hope that Ciril's group might have been taken to Bleiburg/Pliberk railroad station near the village of Moos bei Bleiburg/Blato pri Pliberku, where my relatives have a farm. There he would immediately recognize the situation and, if at all possible, try to escape. Apparently, that was not the case. I told Marija very little, but she knew what was happening. I tortured myself about those crucial four hours. Why did this message not get to us sooner? Why did we not believe the first returnees, the Serb Chetnik officers? Why did four hours make so much difference in the lives of so many?

Walking around the camp alone, not really seeing anybody because of such strong inner pain, I just kept thinking about Ciril's and my difficult situations of the past, situations when a person cannot even say a word because one's torments are too great. During the days and hours when torture and death threaten and when any hope for help is gone, the emotional strain and trauma affect you more than any physical suffering. Your life flashes back and forth in your mind and in your heart, questioning this or that step or action, occasionally even bringing up happy moments of the past. Your thoughts keep turning to dear persons to whom you would like to say at least one more kind word or two. Your unrealistic thoughts are trying to dredge up hopes that suddenly and unexpectedly something will take you out of this oppressive nightmare. Each turning of the key of your prison cell, each visit from the guards, each summon to another questioning escalates that inner pain and fear. How long can you take that terrible burden on your mind and in your heart, going from despair to hope and then back again? How long can you stand all this pressure before you lose your sanity or sink into complete depression? There is, however, one consolation left: prayer. This is the only sure, although not earthly, help.

When the British soldiers locked the railroad freight cars and the attached passenger wagon, so cynically reserved for the officers, women, and children, and handed over the Home Defense soldiers to Tito's partisans, that cruel and brutal deception instilled in all of them the conviction that there was no place on earth to seek protection and asylum. This was the end, the very end, the Götterdämmerung.[12] Those who escaped did so primarily to go back and warn their families and others what was happening. Among those who escaped were three of my high school colleagues, M. H., I. L., and M. R.

We just could not understand. We could not believe that officers of an Army, which since the beginning of the Second World War fought courageously against overwhelming odds on all fronts around the world, on land, at sea, and in the air, did not have the courage to tell the truth, to tell that an agreement or decision from much higher up demanded such action. No, they chose, for some inexplicable reason or maybe just for efficiency, to use deception, duplicity, and lies to get the job done. The German troops, their enemies, had certain rights, according to international laws. These other groups—were they considered a lower class or an expendable group of people?—apparently had no rights of any kind, at least not in the eyes of the British Klagenfurt/Celovec military command or their immediate superiors, in spite of the fact that only a week or two before they were—we were—allowed to pass over the Drava River bridge and were provided protection and sanctuary by the British Forces.

However, to hear about the handover from the other side, I have to quote Nicolson again: ". . . we protested against the inhumanity of what we had been ordered to do. . . . I expressed our common disgust in the last two sentences of the sitrep which I issued on 18 May, . . . 'The whole business,' I wrote, 'is most unsavoury, and British troops have the utmost distaste in carrying out their orders. At the moment it is not known what higher policy lies behind the decision.'"[13]

In the same source we find the statement of Anthony Crosland, "who was on the Intelligence staff of the 6th Armoured:" "It was the most nauseating and cold-blooded act of war I have ever taken part in."[14]

Robin Rose Price, who commanded the Welsh Guards battalion called the action, "an order of most sinister duplicity."[15]

There was also no doubt that the British authorities in Klagenfurt/Celovec knew what would be the fate of those returned to Yugoslavia. The massacre of a large group of Croats, men, women, and children, near Bleiburg/Pliberk was one unmistakable example, and the British were aware of it, as Nicolai Tolstoy writes:

> What then occurred [after the Croatian Commander, general Herenčič, under extreme pressure accepted British and Yugoslav terms to return his troops to Yugoslavia at 4:30 P.M. on 15 May] was a slaughter so terrible that its extent can only be measured through the experiences of those who lived through it. Several survivors tell about the immense crimes committed on the field near Bleiburg/Pliberk.[16]

Nicolson also disclosed his troops' opinion of Tito's partisans when they first encountered them on 7 May in northern Italy: "We were left in no doubt what would be the fate of any enemy who fell into their hands. That was their reputation and our foreboding."[17]

Because the Yugoslavs were by betrayal, lies, and deception returned to Tito's partisans only from the British 5th Corps area in Austria and not from any other territory under British or American control, there will forever remain a suspicion that a deal was made in Klagenfurt/Celovec on 19 May at the meeting between General Keightley and Colonel Ivanovič to hand over to Tito the Yugoslav anti-communists, military and civilian, who were at the time under British protection and control in the Viktring/Vetrinj Camp, and elsewhere in British-occupied Austria, in exchange for the Yugoslav Forces' departure from Southern Carinthia. The Yugoslav Forces left Carinthia the day this agreement was reached. I should add that no record exists to substantiate any such secret exchange agreement at the meeting in Klagenfurt on 19 May.

However, those of us who were in the Viktring/Vetrinj Camp cannot remove from our minds the fact that on 19 May Yugoslav Forces suddenly left Southern Carinthia, and on 24 May, only five days later, everything was already in place, on both sides, for the first handover of the Yugoslav refugees. Is it not a strange coincidence, that a joint operation of some magnitude was set up so speedily and efficiently between the British and Yugoslav Forces, who were only a few days before still in a dispute and struggle with each other regarding the right of occupation of Southern Carinthia? It is hard to accept the claim that there was no connection between the agreement of 19 May and the first handover transport of 24 May. The lack of information as to who gave the orders for the handover and who made the arrangements in such a short time for these "efficient" repatriation operations leads to the conclusion that many agreements, decisions, and acts of World War II and in the immediate post-war times were never reported or recorded. This conclusion may be reached most certainly regarding the actions by the British Klagenfurt/Celovec Command of May and June 1945.

Part III

There were approximately six thousand civilians left in the camp. We were in a panic: What would happen to us? Even though the full truth was in the open, the British did not change their repatriation policy. The order came, first heard via the pipeline, that civilians would be removed from this camp the same way as the soldiers of the previous transports were. I do not remember if the date was set for the day after the last Home Defense units were returned or a day later.[18] The civilian camp, however, was under different command, under Major Paul Barre, a Canadian. When Major Barre heard from the civilian camp official representative, Dr. Valentin Meršol, what had happened to those removed on the previous days, he could not believe it and was visibly shaken, as Dr. Meršol reported later. He immediately agreed to accompany Dr. Meršol to the British Command in Klagenfurt/Celovec to investigate. These meetings with the British authorities, commanding officer's numerous phone calls to higher authorities, and the sudden and unexpected decision not to return any more Yugoslavs against their will to Yugoslavia have been described in several sources.[19]

As a result of the visit by Dr. Meršol to the British command in Klagenfurt/Celovec and especially Major Barre's firm stand on behalf of the civilian refugees under his command, we received the news that civilians would not be returned to Yugoslavia against their will. Whether this was just a postponement or a real reversal of the previous order, we were not sure. On the basis of the past events we could not trust any statement by the British command anymore. During these difficult days something kept coming to my mind again and again: the words a Gestapo man said to me at the end of my interrogation in the basement of the prison building in Ljubljana in June 1944. With a cynical smile on his face he said, that we, meaning our underground organization, did not know the British. Considering the treacherous return of the Yugoslav anti-communists units to Tito's forces, his statement acquired a specific meaning.

On 4 June 1945, the announced visit to the Viktring Camp by the Supreme Commander of the Allied Forces in the Mediterranean, Field Marshal Alexander, took place. The field marshal arrived in the camp late morning, accompanied by Major Barre, two British nurses, and a few British officers. In the middle of the camp, with almost the entire civilian population present, he briefly talked to Dr. Meršol, who tried to explain in a few words who we were and why we were there, and asked again for British protection. I was standing very near and heard this conversation very clearly but did not understand a word because everything was in English. However, we became immediately aware that the field marshal gave his word that no Yugoslavs, military or civilian, would be returned by the British to Yugoslavia against their will. After a brief walk through the camp, Field Marshal Alexander left. Major Barre told Dr. Meršol later that he made a good impression on the field marshal and that the civilians would be saved; for thousands of others this order came too late.

That same evening, when we were standing in line to get our evening soup, Mr. Jeglič, a professor, gave us a few more details of the day's happenings. Those who wished to return to Yugoslavia would have to decide by next morning, and the British would then provide the necessary means for return. Those who decided not to return would have to realize that it might be years (or never) before a return to our homeland would be possible. The International Refugee Organization would eventually take over on a temporary basis the care for the refugees and plead with countries around the world to accept them and offer them a chance for a new life. Mr. Jeglič added that for hardworking and diligent hands, there is plenty of work everywhere.

Even though the fear of a forced return to Tito's Yugoslavia was removed, we now faced the harsh truth of a long absence from home or the reality of no return. Only a few individuals and families decided to return the next day, mostly those who had been forced by one group or another to assist those retreating with their farm horses and vehicles. Around sixty people, with their possessions, returned. Among those returning were the nice people from my father's birthplace in Viševek, including those who a few weeks before had persuaded my sister Marija to leave her uncle's farm in Viševek and to join the refugees. Before departure they came to say goodbye. They were apologetic, but I assured them that I agreed with their decision to return, knowing the situation in the village and the family status of their farms.[20]

My mother's older sister, Klara Lanninscheg, a Swiss citizen, came to Viktring/Vetrinj to take Marija and me to her home in Eisenkappel/Železna kapla for temporary protection. I was glad that Marija welcomed this opportunity to depart. I, however, decided to stay in the camp. The plan was that Marija would eventually be able to return home to Ljubljana.[21]

It was not easy to say goodbye, under the circumstances; however, it was a sound decision. In the next few days the officers of the International Refugee Organization (IRO) registered the entire camp population; we received IRO identification cards.

At this point I wish to diverge from the more or less chronological sequence of these memoirs to give the reader an account of the fate of those, like Ciril, who were returned from Austria to Tito's forces by the British treachery in May and June 1945 after the hostilities of the World War II had ended 8 May.

There was probably not a single individual among the six thousand civilians left in the Viktring/Vetrinj Camp who did not have one or more family members or friends among those who were returned to Yugoslavia by British betrayal and lies. The statistics of those thousands who perished fail to tell the real extent of the tragedy—the tremendous sufferings of the victims and the anguish of thousands and thousands of others related and/or associated with each of the victims. The extent of suffering reached not only those in the Viktring/Vetrinj Camp but extended to the home territory and even to places around the world.

The men and others who were returned with them were gone; we knew where they were taken. However, there was still some hope that there would be at least half-decent treatment of those returned. Day by day we expected to see more returnees, more of those who had the opportunity or courage to risk the last escape. The number, however, was minimal, and their reports were not encouraging at all.

To understand the tremendous tragic consequences of the British betrayal and the final fate of those returned to Tito's forces in May and June 1945, we can consult the report of three men who, by nothing less than a miracle, were able to escape just before their last breath of life and their last will to survive expired. They have described their own and their companions' unbelievable ordeal and suffering. Two of these survivors, Milan Zajec and France Dejak, I know well. The third, France Kozina, I never had the opportunity to meet. Their reports were recorded by the International Red Cross, by British military authorities, and by many other agencies. The latest detailed account of these three men is recorded in a recent book in the Slovene, *Ušli so smrti* (They Escaped Death).[22] A detailed description in English, however, can be found in Tolstoy's monograph, *The Minister and the Massacres,* from which I wish to quote a few key sections.[23]

Milan Zajec and his three brothers were on the same train. After leaving Rosenbach/Podrožca, the train left Austria via a tunnel and briefly stopped at the first station in Yugoslavia, Jesenice, and then proceeded to Kranj. In the city, " . . . the authorities had assembled a large mob, who were permitted to stone and beat the cowering prisoners as they descended and were marched off in columns to the nearby camp."[24]

In the camp, Milan Zajec ". . . saw many terrible beatings which left people half-dead with shirts stiff with blackened blood. Unconscious, they had buckets of water thrown over them to revive them for a further bout."[25]

On 1 June they were then moved first to the Bishop's Gymnasium building near Ljubljana and the same day further south to Kočevje, where they were first taken to a high school building. Milan estimated that his transport consisted of approximately two thousand Home Defense men. From the high school, about two hundred men at the time were then taken to another building where ". . . each man had his hands bound tightly behind his back with wire, and was then strapped arm by arm to a companion. . . . and the trussed prisoners were pushed up an improvised log ramp into the back of the vehicle. Six trucks in turn took their loads, twenty or more prisoners to each consignment."[26]

Once on the trucks with partisan guards sitting or standing in the four corners, the victims were beaten continuously at their slightest attempt to look up or to adjust their kneeling position. The guards kept asking if any of the prisoners recognize the surroundings. Nobody answered. The prisoners started to pray, suspecting the worst. When they were leaving Kočevje, the place where they were wired together, two by two, they could not help but notice piles of Home Defense uniforms, many stained with blood. Milan Zajec was familiar with the area as were several others who served in that region during the war. To confuse the victims as to where they were, the trucks made repeated diversion turns before heading into the forest.

After a ride of an undetermined duration, which Milan Zajec thought had lasted a long time, the trucks came to a stop. The ride, because of the rough road, caused excruciating pain to hands and arms tied tightly by wire. The prisoners were now without any mercy pushed off the trucks if they were not able to get off in a hurry by themselves. On the ground their shoelaces were cut and shoes removed. At this point Milan and his co-prisoners were witnesses to an act of unbelievable bestiality:

Close beside them was a young prisoner from a previous consignment. Naked, with his hands tied behind his back, he was covered from head to foot with gashes and stab-wounds. More slashes were being inflicted even at that moment by a fanatical Partisan. From a bare three paces' distance, Zajec saw to his horror that both the boy's eyes had already been gouged out, and blood was seeping from the hollow sockets. The Partisan, ignoring everything else around him, relentlessly sawed away with his knife at what was left of the victim's flesh.[27]

The prisoners were driven in a column away from the road and repeatedly ordered to kneel down and get up to inflict more pain to their tied hands and arms. At the same time the partisans used their knives and sticks to beat the prisoners again and again. Further down the path they were halted, untied, and ordered to strip naked. Naked, they were driven forward between triple ranks of partisans, receiving more blows and knife wounds. They were running down on an incline when the column was again stopped.

Milan glimpsed for the first time what his enemies had planned for them. Before them gaped the black entrance to a huge underground pit, about the size of a small house. It was all happening so quickly he scarcely had time to register that fact.

> Just in front of Zajec a man fell, shot dead, by the edge of the chasm. Two Partisans started forward and began rolling the body over the side into the pit. Another shrieked out a command to Zajec to halt, but ignoring it, he rushed on and sprang over the body in his way. Bullets flew around him, but he plunged unscathed down into the darkness. He landed on an untold seething mass of naked bodies. All about him he could hear people crying, moaning, praying. . . . It was a scene of unimaginable horror.[28]

France Dejak's ordeal varied only slightly from that of Milan Zajec. His transport also left Rosenbach/Podrožca after the British locked them in the railroad cattlecars. They were taken to Jesenice and to a camp near Kranj, where he was kept for four days; there all officers and NCOs were separated from the men and taken elsewhere. He stayed at Bishop's Gymnasium for about a week with his transport, most likely to wait until the executions of those who had arrived before them were completed. The Home Defense men were packed in the Gymnasium's chapel so tightly that there was no place to move, to sit down or to lie down. Here he witnessed ". . . continual ferocious beatings—with rifle butts, sticks and belts—with which their gaolers paid off old scores."[29]

On 8 June they were taken by train to Kočevje. This transport, according to Dejak, consisted of approximately eight hundred Home Defense men. Many to whom he spoke "were confident that nothing too dreadful was likely to happen to them. A trial before a People's Court, six months perhaps in prison—it was hard to believe that worse was in prospect."[30]

In Kočevje, however, they were taken immediately to the former "Home of the Blind." There they were taken in small groups to a special room where they were wired, hands in the back and then by the arms to the next man. Trucks took them the same route as Zajec described to the place of execution in the forest.

> Their shoelaces were cut and their shoes removed. . . . Then they were marched barefoot for about ten minutes towards the pit. It was the morning of Saturday, 9 June, ... The men were halted, untied, and compelled to strip down their clothes. . . . Again they were marched swiftly another couple of hundred yards . . . to the mouth of the pit. Throughout their short march the prisoners were subjected to ferocious beatings, many being battered

to death and left where they fell. Afterwards they saw these corpses hurled into the pit. At the edge of the precipice a guard halted Dejak . . . to check whether he had any gold teeth. . . . He possessed no such prize, and the Partisan raised and cocked his gun. Dejak did not wait for the shot but hurled himself over the edge of the pit. . . . The Communist's gun went off as Dejak leaped, and Dejak felt a bullet tear through the side of his leg. He fell heavily on the mass of bodies. . . . [31]

France Kozina also went through the camp at Kranj and then to the former Bishop's Gymnasium. During a strip search there he was severely beaten by an interrogator. On 8 June, like France Dejak, he was taken by train to Kočevje. All the way brutal beatings continued. In Kočevje, they were wired as the others before them had been and pushed onto the trucks.

> "No one said anything," Frank Kozina recalls. "We started praying. Before we prayed in whisper, but now we prayed aloud. We knew the people we were dealing with, what they were capable of, and we knew we were finished."[32]

When off the truck, he saw his executioners equipped with all kinds of instruments for maiming and killing. At the edge of the pit, he recognized one executioner who ordered him to kneel down. The gun went off, but the bullet only slightly damaged his face. He slid down into the cave on top of an unbelievable number of naked men either death and dying.

Once in this mass grave of horror, among hundreds of dead or dying, Milan Zajec pulled himself to the side of the cave and was thus slightly protected from the bomb explosions and machine gunfire from above and also from falling bodies. Dead or wounded were falling onto the cave every hour. He was fully aware that somewhere among those already in the cave were his three brothers. Zajec estimated that on his first day in the cave about eighty men were still alive but dying every minute. After four days in the cave, while the deadly massacre continued, Milan and a few others who were still alive, realized that they were near death and were losing hope that an escape was possible from this place of horror. All the time while they were in the Communists' hands, they received very little nourishment, usually only soup once a day or something similar, and after four days in the cave they were becoming weaker by the hour.

On 4 June one of the victims tried in desperation to scale the steep rock on the side of the cave. With a tremendous effort he reached the upper edge, and those below still alive now hoped that escape was possible. A minute or two later, however, his body fell back on the top of the heap, stabbed to death. Soon after that unsuccessful escape attempt, the partisans dynamited the edge of the cave to make sure that no one would try that again. The opening at the top was thus enlarged and those below covered with earth and debris of all kinds. Zajec and a few still alive clung to the side of the cave and avoided this renewed attack.

On Zajec' fifth day in the mass grave, when killings above were still going on

and bodies kept falling into the pit, bodies began to decay and the stench was unbearable. The fifth night, Milan realized that his death was close and that he had
to try to escape that night or die. During the second dynamiting of the cave, a tree
slid down into the cave but the trunk was still hooked on the edge. Milan decided
to try.

> He clambered over the shifting sea of death and dying, and began to scramble slowly and
> painfully up the fallen tree. . . . As he emerged into the fresh air of the forest he could not
> for a while really believe that he was no longer in the pit. . . . pausing only to suck up dew
> from the long grass, he stumbled on till daybreak.[33]

France Dejak escaped the same way that Zajec did. His escape, however, took
place a few days later, during the night of 9 June.

France Kozina escaped with two other men, Karel Turk and Janko Svete, a
day later than Dejak, again with the help of the fallen tree.

After days, weeks, and years of hiding and surviving with the help received
from relatives and friends, the three of them, Zajec, Dejak and Kozina, successfully crossed the borders to Austria and Italy and were able to tell their unbelievable story to the International Red Cross representatives, other agencies, and their
families and friends.

The other half of the Home Defense men, those who were returned by the
British by way of Bleiburg/Pliberk railroad station in the same treacherous way to
Tito's forces, went a entirely different route. They were taken southwest through
Prevalje, Dravograd, Slovenj Gradec, Mislinje to their place of execution near
Celje, at a place called Teharje. From the mass graves at Teharje, there were no escapes. Here as well not all of those executed were dead at the time when they were
thrown into the mass graves. Along the way from Bleiburg/Pliberk to Teharje, several men were able to escape and came, after long and difficult hikes, mostly at
night, back to the civilian refuge camps in Austria. From the camp in Teharje only
eleven men were fortunate enough to escape one night, among them the author of
a recent book, *Teharje: Krvave arene,* in which he describes the dreadful conditions and merciless treatment of the Home Defense men in this camp.[34]

Thus, in June 1945, before any international forums started functioning and
regulating the treatments of military and civilian surrendered personnel, the new
communist authorities in Yugoslavia and Slovenia decided to eliminate, without
trials or proof of guilt, by a most inhuman treatment, all those over eighteen years
of age who were members of anti-communist forces of any kind. Close to twelve
thousand Home Defense men, Chetniks, and many civilian followers were massacred. With this action to eliminate any potential opposition and a refusal to be
bound by any set of international rules in handling POWs, the goal of the Communist Party in Slovenia became very clear—the establishment of a Soviet-style
dictatorship under Tito. More than that, these post-war massacres by Tito's forces

nullified the efforts and sacrifices of many thousands who fought with best intentions sincerely and courageously in the ranks of the National Liberation Army against the occupation forces.

In the Viktring/Vetrinj Camp we, of course, did not know anything of these executions at the time; we were still hoping that the men would somehow return or that we would eventually have access to them. Rumors circulated that they had been taken south to Serbia to work in the prison camps there. After we were not able to discover any traces of them and even the rumors had no sources to feed on, we came to believe that they had been transported to the camps in the Soviet Union.

The first news I received from home after 8 May 1945 via the Carinthian connection, was of two entirely different sorts. When the regular train travel between Maribor and Ljubljana started functioning, Joža, Hinko's sister, came to our home in Ljubljana and inquired if I had returned after leaving their house in Maribor at the end of April 1945. According to my mother, Joža was very disappointed in not finding me at home.

Soon after the liberation of Ljubljana, my co-prisoner from Auschwitz and from the Graz hospital, Jože, came to our house dressed in a brand-new uniform with the rank of captain in OZNA, Tito's secret police, and asked for me. He would not tell my family anything more, except that we were together in Auschwitz; neither would he say if he came to help me or to arrest me.

At the end of May, Dore Matul, my co-prisoner from the Gestapo jail in Ljubljana during the summer of 1944, came to our house to inform my parents that he saw me among those being handed over by the British to Tito's partisans. Dore Matul was a railroad official, probably working at the Kranj railroad station when he thought he saw me among the returned Home Defense men. Dore was, of course, mistaken; it was Ciril he saw. He suggested to my parents that they seek any help possible to save me. Nothing could have been done in those days and under those circumstances. Dore, who had been arrested by the Home Defense men and then turned over to the Gestapo, tried to keep his part of the promise that we would help each other after the war, depending on which side would be in power.

It was through the information related to me years later by France Dejak that I have learned a little about Ciril's fate after he was taken away from the Viktring/Vetrinj Camp. France Dejak told a friend of mine that he was with Ciril in the chapel of Bishop's Gymnasium and that Ciril wished to stay with those who came there with Dejak's group. Having spent four years as a student in Bishop's Gymnasium only a few years before, he must have suffered even more at being a prisoner in the chapel where he attended daily mass as a student. Dejak did not know much more, except that he last saw Ciril, wired to another man, when they were loaded on the trucks to the place of execution. Thus, I can assume that his murder took place on Saturday, 9 June 1945. He was 22 years old. I hope that his last days were merciful to him and that he found some strength in his faith. An encouraging message, that someone saw my brother in Italy after his successful escape from the partisans' hands, aroused a false hope that I carried in my heart for two or three years. I hoped that he would appear and surprise me one day. This hope was now dead.

Approximately 25 years later, a young well-dressed man knocked on the door of our house in Ljubljana. When my mother opened the door, he explained to her that he came to inquire about her older son, Ciril. My mother started crying and through her tears told the man he should ask about Ciril's whereabouts among those people who sent him to inquire. The man was visibly taken by surprise by her answer, apologized, and left.

Milan Zajec, France Dejak, and France Kozina are the only survivors, the only people who shared the last days with those murdered and thrown—some dead, others still alive—into the mass graves of the Kočevski Rog. Without their reports the secrecy enforced by the Communist authorities and their continuous denials of these mass murders would have continued. However, the information about these murders eventually came out, first outside Yugoslavia as a result of the reports provided by the three survivors, and during the 1980s internally, largely due to courageous inquiries about the truth by a younger generation, for example, the writer Spomenka Hribar.[35]

Under the pressure of the 1989/1990 changes and the collapse of Communism, the new authorities, consisting mostly in the 1990s of the old cadres, eventually confirmed that these murders and many others took place. However, all attempts and efforts to document this tragedy, to identify the people who gave the orders, who was involved, who were the executioners, are still resisted and blocked every step of the way.

Mass executions on such a large scale are not done by one person or two. Many people were involved in accepting the prisoners from the British, transporting them from the north to the south of Slovenia and then to their graves. One has to ask the fundamental question, a question that burdens the military on all sides: what orders should a soldier obey? There is still no clear answer to that. However, the cruel, bestial treatment the Home Defense men and many others had to endure before they were executed finds no justification in any code of justice anywhere. It is also hard to believe that in the small Slovene nation one would find so many people who would be able, willing, and possess so a complete disregard for another human being as to execute acts of such unbelievable sadism. In addition to the tremendous sorrow for thousands murdered in May and June 1945, it also hurts immensely that such acts occurred after World War II in Europe was already over, in May and June 1945 and that they took place in the land called Slovenia.

CHAPTER FIFTEEN

From Uncertainty to New Beginning

June 1945–June 1950

The fate of thousands of refugees who found themselves in the Western-occupied zones at the end of the war in Europe was entrusted to the care of the United Nations Relief and Rehabilitation Administration (UNRRA, 1943) though refugees remained administratively under the control of the military.

These refugees had to clarify their status. Two options were offered: first, to immediately return to their home country as soon as arrangements could be made; second, to apply for Displaced Persons (DP) status. The second group was then provided with temporary basic accommodations in the Displaced Persons camps.

The Potsdam Conference, attended by the heads of the victorious countries and their staff, started on 16 July 1945 and ended with the Potsdam Declaration on 26 July. The discussions centered on the treatment of Germany after the war, politically and economically. An appeal to Japan to surrender was also issued at the end of the conference. While this conference was in session, it was easy to detect that there were noticeable differences between the United States of America and Britain on the one side and the Soviets on the other among many topics, even on such details as how each side understood and interpreted the word "democracy."

The atomic bomb was dropped on Hiroshima by a single U.S. Air Force plane on 6 August 1945 and a second on Nagasaki three days later. Japan unconditionally surrendered on 14 August; World War II ended on 15 August 1945.

We became Displaced Persons, or DPs for short, after we were accepted by the United Nations Relief and Rehabilitation Administration (UNRRA). The designation of Displaced Persons gave us an official status; the term itself, however, soon received in the minds of many a negative connotation. Reasons for this were numerous, but the most crucial one was the fact that we were so many. Those residing in the refugee camps, like Viktring/Vetrinj, remained under the British military administration. The occupation forces kept control of this huge number of people.

In the Viktring/Vetrinj Camp we heard in the middle of summer 1945 that the camp would be abandoned and the people transferred to other locations in British-occupied Austria. Consequently, the Slovene civilian refugees were transferred to two new camps, near Lienz in the Austrian Tyrol and in Spittal an der Drau in the Austrian Carinthia. The accommodations there consisted of standard prefabs or barracks as we referred to them. In spite of the assurances from top British administrators, we were still very suspicious about their intentions regarding the relocation destinations. This time, however, those who were transferred first, immediately notified other people in Viktring/Vetrinj, that they, in fact, had reached the place mentioned to them before departure.

Why just a small group of refugees, myself included, was transferred to a tent camp near the city of St. Veit an der Glan north of the Klagenfurt/Celovec was a puzzle to us. Our group consisted of a few families, single men and women, and a small detachment of Serb Chetniks (approximately thirty men) under the command of a lieutenant. A soft-spoken British Army captain was in command of the camp with a dozen soldiers in assistance. The captain favored self-administration and acted accordingly. One sergeant who was setting up the tents the first two days used in his much-too-frequent expressions of anger a word we did not understand; we started repeating this word until informed about its real meaning. However, everything else went smoothly.

My colleague, pianist Ivan Zupančič, and I were assigned to a tent where one side was already occupied by a young family, husband and wife, a teenage daughter and a younger son. Two other single men were also bivouacking on our side of this large tent. We all felt uneasy about this unusual arrangement. It took a special effort by Ivan and I to get permission to move to a small two-person tent, our own domicile.

The provisions in this camp were slightly better than at Viktring/Vetrinj, but we were still hungry most of the time. A few families still had some meager supplemental reserves, but we did not. Those few who tried to beg at nearby farms were mostly unsuccessful. However, some extra fresh supplies kept appearing in some tents. The sources were not difficult to trace—nearby farm fields. Ivan and I did not want to participate in these improper activities. However, when a young Serb civilian offered his expert help, we both closed one eye (or both) and readily accepted supplements in exchange for a few cigarettes. No wonder that the farmers hated us; they had to stay up at night and guard their fields. Our Serb supplier had no problems. He only yelled at the farmer once—in Serbian, of course—and the farmer from then on let him pick up modest amounts from his field, while all other nightly visitors were successfully chased away. The Slovene camp authorities finally persuaded everybody to stop these nightly activities in order to maintain good relations with the neighbors. Nightly deliveries to our tent then stopped; nevertheless, Ivan and I regretted our double standard.

The Serb Chetniks detachment provided some evening entertainment by singing and dancing to their folk tunes. These celebrations were well received by camp people and by a few British soldiers who came and observed from a distance. When a month or so later an order came that the Chetniks were to be transferred to other Chetnik units in Italy, we were sorry to see them go. The fear of trickery was still on everybody's mind. Before their departure, the Chetniks' lieutenant received from Slovenes in the camp the exact description of the route to Italy just in case. Since there were no armed British soldiers in charge of their transport, we were beginning to feel more confident and less suspicious. The lieutenant promised to get word back to us. A month later he made the rough trip back to our camp from Italy and then returned. Only then were we finally convinced that the treacherous British repatriation of Yugoslavs had in fact stopped.

The camp at St. Veit an der Glan had only three or four large barracks located near the entrance: all other accommodations were under tents. One day, to Ivan's and my surprise, the British brought to the largest barrack a beautiful Steinway concert grand piano. At first we thought the captain might be a pianist. After a day or two when no music came from that barrack, we asked via our interpreter for permission to enter and to use this beautiful instrument. We told the captain that we were former piano students in Ljubljana. Permission to play the piano was granted on a limited daily basis. That Steinway was a beauty in every respect though it needed a good tuning. Ivan, who was an excellent pianist with good chances for professional success, and I then tried to retrieve from our memories those pieces of music we memorized as students at the Academy of Music in Ljubljana. In addition, we had in our possession a few printed compositions. However, nobody ever came to the barrack to listen to our practice sessions.

Therefore, we were very much surprised when we received an invitation (or a command) from the captain to come one evening to the large hall and to play for the soldiers. We did not want to go, but orders were orders. Would the soldiers be willing to listen to the classical music we had in our repertory? I knew a few popular tunes from the times in Auschwitz and Graz but certainly no tunes from the British territories.

With our interpreter, who was also invited, we found the British soldiers already sitting at the tables, drinking and eating. The captain told us to play our repertory, any pieces we wished. The soldiers politely applauded after every composition. Ivan and I took turns. During a short intermission we received some refreshments and drinks. Not used to that kind of liquid stuff, we just tasted it, but the soldiers filled our glasses again and again to the rim. My popular piano pieces became all of a sudden much more lively with notes added just to make a better impression. But when the piano keys started to move left and right, I realized that the contents of my glass were working on my system. Our host, a young soldier, kept offering toast after toast for the two pianists. In desperation, I emptied my glass a few times into a nearby flower pot—secretly of course—in order to accept another offer of the excellent stuff from the British reserves. Ivan and I kept repeating our repertory over and over, how, I would really not wish to know. Not a single British soldier touched the piano.

Exactly at midnight the captain stopped the party. In less than a second, all gaiety stopped. In complete silence the room was cleaned up to the last detail; bottles were put in boxes, glasses collected and food as well. Everybody seemed to know what to do. The captain thanked us for our participation. Leaving the barrack, Ivan and I had a difficult time walking straight; the alcohol was working. We noticed no such signs on any member of the British group.

In the camp we had very little to do, mostly just keep the place in good order. After the tents were set up, we were able to make some improvements in the interiors; however, we had only limited materials and tools. The center of activity, the kitchen, functioned very well thanks to a few women who enjoyed that extra responsibility. The British crew maintained their distance but nevertheless kept a watchful eye over the camp. They proved that during a fire. The speed of their arrival with fire extinguishers prevented a major disaster; we had no means or skills to deal with such an emergency.

The day of required disinfecting of the entire camp population brought the British and us for the first time in a more direct contact, physically, and to a point, socially as well. On that day the soldiers arrived equipped with hand-held pumps filled with disinfecting powder; I believe it was referred to as DDT. Everybody in the camp, man, woman, and child, with exception of very small children, was required to get three puffs on the three most sensitive areas of the body. That stuff burned and itched like hell as soon as it touched the skin. It was difficult to take this treatment without pain and discomfort. A few women shrieked and laughed loudly at the same time, providing all present with a few moments of entertainment. Most of us, however, clenched our teeth until the sharp itching subsided. Soldiers were visibly delighted in these duties; their positive and friendly attitude made the entire procedure more tolerable.

The roads, paths, and streets around the camp and in the city were, because of the lack of proper security personnel, still open to all, and a person was rarely stopped and asked for identification. This situation enabled us to explore the area in the vicinity of St. Veit. We stayed out of the city itself to avoid any difficulties with the local authorities, who did not like seeing camp people visiting their community.

One late evening we heard loud voices and strange noises coming out of the barrack where the piano was located. As the night progressed, this disturbance became louder and louder. Apparently, the British were having a party. Whether the participants were soldiers stationed in our camp or others from the outside, we did not know. Obviously, the captain in command was not in the camp. After midnight, Ivan and I, who tried to observe these celebrations from a safe distance, heard repeated unmusical pounding on the piano keyboard. Here and there a few sound combinations made some sense but not many. Later during the night the soldiers began singing and dancing; a few decided to demonstrate their dancing abilities on the top of the beautiful Steinway. When the party finally ended in the first daylight hours, we did not dare to investigate what happened in the hall during the night. Finally, mid-morning, when the soldiers were nowhere to be seen, we entered the hall and found the piano without legs lying on its belly on the floor with many signs of rough treatment on its case. What was the captain's reaction to this, we never knew. The place was cleaned up later that same day and locked; the piano, however, remained resting on the hall's floor, legless, of course.

A day later a good-looking and well-dressed woman came to the camp headquarters and visited the captain. With her was a girl, seven or eight years old. Rumor had it that she was the wife of a high Nazi official, who was either hiding or in prison and that the Steinway had been confiscated from their home. She must have been shocked when she saw what happened. That same afternoon a local piano-moving company arrived and took the piano away. Needless to say, Ivan and I were very sad.

In the middle of August the news came that we would soon be relocated to a more permanent location. "Start packing" was the order. There was not much to pack. After my many experiences of moving from prison to prison during the war and from camp to camp later, my reaction to the news of transfer to another place was not positive. After you adjust to one place and become aware of your surroundings and your possibilities for a tolerable life and/or survival, you are not in favor of starting to adjust to yet another set of circumstances. Of course, these were different times; the war was over. I realized as well that a tent would not offer sufficient protection during the fast-approaching cold months.

The move itself went smoothly. One drawback was our new man in charge, X. W., an English-speaking Slovene former Yugoslav army officer. He gave one the impression that he was angry at himself around the clock, and maybe for this reason he treated us as army recruits. We avoided him as much as possible. Our new residence was near the town of Kellerberg in the Drava River valley, northwest of Villach/Beljak. The Kellerberg Camp, as it became known, consisted of new prefabs, new barracks. Except for the structures and beds, the interiors were bare at first. However, the new arrivals soon took care of many needed improvements; thus accommodations became quite comfortable under the circumstances. Single people had their own barracks (separate for men and women), and families enjoyed life in much-desired separate locations.

Those of us from the Camp St. Veit and der Glan were the first to arrive. Later, other individuals and families came from all areas under the British administration of Austria, including those who either escaped or were expelled from Yugoslavia. This was the camp for all who became displaced persons for one reason or another.

The camp was multinational. Slovenes were the largest group, followed by the folks from the Baltic countries and from other Eastern and Southeastern countries of Europe. Since it was possible to take care of the camp's daily needs with only a small portion of the camp population, the Slovene contingent organized educational courses and sport activities to keep people of all ages involved. Ivan and I became piano teachers. Our students consisted mostly of young ladies eager to discover the secrets of piano playing. The instrument we used did not compare by any measure of imagination to the instrument we had been privileged to use for a short time at the St. Veit an der Glan camp. In addition to our jobs Ivan and I attended German and English language courses offered by camp volunteers. Lack of books or language texts made the progress difficult. Then an unexpected and highly positive message came, a message of far-reaching consequences, though it applied only to a select group of individuals.

It happened toward the end of summer 1945. The British authorities offered to transfer university students and those who already completed high school (gymnasium), to a student displaced-persons camp in Graz in the Austrian province of Steiermark, providing the students with an opportunity to take classes at the university and other educational institutions of higher learning in the city. This decision applied to all student displaced persons in the British refugee camps in Austria.[1] Who exactly deserved the credit for this decision would be difficult to verify without the access to the appropriate documents. It was probably a mutual effort by both the British and the refugee representatives. The roles of the Karl Franzens Universität, the Technische Hochschule, and other institutions of higher learning in Graz was were also influential.

In a very short time we had to decide whether to go or not. As far as I remember, the response, at least in Camp Kellerberg, was a hundred percent. Our student group in Kellerberg was small. Even though we came from different regions of Slovenia, we soon found several common denominators for discussions during the short trips into the neighboring hills and fields. The British set a ten-kilometer maximum radius for walks outside the camps, thus considerably restricting our excursion possibilities. There was a good reason for that: Thousands of refugees were in Austria at that time, mostly from Eastern and Southeastern Europe, from the Soviet Union or from the Soviet-occupied or dependent states, waiting for resettlement decisions. The Western occupation forces sought to put the occupied states on their own feet as soon as possible. In this process we, the refugees, were not a minor obstacle.

The Slovene refugee community in Kellerberg, as before at St. Veit an der Glan, formed a close and cordial relationship in a short time. Those of us who had no family or any other connections with the camp people were pleased to feel that we belonged. We students wished to express our appreciation to the camp's Slovene community before our departure and also to those who had the administration of the camp on their shoulders. The evening before our departure we prepared a piano and violin concert in the dining hall. Ivan Zupančič and I, with the important assistance of the violinist, Mr. Kalister, a former member of the Yugoslav Royal Navy orchestra, performed works by Beethoven, Rebikov, Tschaikovsky, Schumann, Novak, Mozart, Drdla, Bortkiewitch, and Schubert. Matej Resman, a law student, thanked the camp administration and the camp community in the name of departing students for everything they did for us. The concert and the farewell evening were a success and proof that the people at the concert and in the camp wished us success in our forthcoming academic endeavors.

The personal belongings that we carried to the train the next morning under misty rain were not much to talk about: old and worn-out clothes, a book or two, and a few pieces of piano music were all I had, packed in my most reliable rucksack, a veteran of many, mostly involuntary, journeys. The camp administration provided us with modest food supplies for the trip. In Klagenfurt/Celovec we had to wait several hours for students arriving from other camps. Soon an impressive number of students from all possible European countries assembled there, ready to depart for Graz. Among the assembled students were also several slightly older individuals, who did not waste any time impressing us beginners with their pre-war attendance at several universities from Moscow, Paris, and London to Rome and Madrid, and about their exciting experiences there. We were puzzled, and wondered how that kind of life was possible without a lot of money in one's pocket.

After arrival in Graz, we were first stationed in an empty and deteriorated high-school building, the Keplerschule. Today nobody wishes to remember this place of misery; it was cold, dark, dim and unpleasant. The food amounted to much less than in Kellerberg and in other refugee camps. Thus, the hunger and the living conditions during the months of November and December 1945 almost completely deflated our spirits and hopes of success. We tried to supplement our meals in a nearby restaurant. The only thing they had to offer was an aspic of questionable ingredients and nutritional value. You had to close your eyes while eating it. Even portions of the aspic were small and not always available.

At the Karl Franzens Universität in Graz they greeted us cordially. Although many of us had difficulties with the German language, helpfulness and patience were notable characteristics of the university officials and employees. The program of study was structured in advance, and there were not many options in the selection of courses. I decided to enroll in the Law School.

We enjoyed good relationships with Austrian students. Before you spoke to another student, you were expected to greet him as "Herr Kollege" and shake hands. That was an old and established tradition and protocol among students. For women students—there were not many in the Law School—the greeting would have been "Fräulein Kollegin." Less pleasant were our encounters with the Student Association, the Studentenschaft, where a few of its student employees attempted to Germanize our first names, a practice reminiscent of the German, Italian, and Hungarian occupation authorities.

After the Christmas/New Year recess of 1945/46, we moved to the "promised land." On the northern end of the city, near the radio station, on a small hill under an appealing vineyard, stood a small barrack camp, our new home, that was during the war reputedly a residence for Hitlerjugend, who received their training and indoctrination in the city. We referred to it as Hochsteingasse 37, although the official name was Studentenlager Hochsteingasse. This was definitely a considerable improvement over the Keplerschule. A British officer, Miss Margaret Jaboor, was appointed camp commander and administrator. Miss Jaboor decided to assign us to rooms in the barracks not by nationalities but by the field of study, as practiced by the British residential colleges. The objectives were clear: more opportunities for professional discussions and faster progress in our studies. One barrack housed women students, where, because of their small numbers, assignments by the field of study were not practical. At the very beginning there were only a few women in the camp; gradually, however, their number increased. We adjusted without difficulties to the new residential arrangements and accepted them as a complement to our academic endeavors and a step toward a better understanding of each other's ethnic characteristics.

Slovene Jože Jančar, a medical student, became the first student representative in the camp. He was one of the few English-speaking students and also the leader of the Slovene contingent, the largest national group. The next largest were Ukrainians, then Poles, students from the Baltic States, Hungarians, Albanians, Russians, and Serbs. Later arrivals were primarily Volksdeutsche from Yugoslavia. The Slovene additions in the first two years came from the Slovene Refugee High School in Spittal and der Drau, a school that received official recognition in Austria primarily through the efforts of the former director of the humanistic gymnasium in Ljubljana, Marko Bajuk.

During the first semester we were required to pass an oral colloquium in each selected subject of study in groups of three students at a time. I must say that all professors were most understanding of our difficulties with the language and made sure that we understood their questions. Even though I did pass all tests, the marks were on the lower end of the passing scale. Several students at the advanced levels, however, received recognition for their work during the first semester and thus demonstrated to the British authorities that the experiment—offering students an opportunity—promised to be a success. The financial support for the camp came from the United Nations Relief and Rehabilitation Administration (UNRRA).

Gradually, our meals improved in quantity and quality. The Marshall Plan, which saved Europe from starvation and many other catastrophic possibilities, no doubt had a lot to do with better care for the displaced persons in the refugee camps, ours included.

Because we were under British military control and in the British occupation zone of Austria, we occasionally received surprise visits from the British Military Police. We called them "red caps," because of their very visible headgear. Protocol demanded that they stop in the administration office first. The news about their arrival spread around the camp immediately; nothing positive was to be expected from their visit. Nobody knew at the time what kind of information was in their hands and from whom they received their data. The origin of possible accusations, however, was not difficult to guess. As far as I recall, a few individuals whom the British Military Police were looking for had sufficient time to escape and hide, since the "red caps" took their time walking from the administration office to this or that barrack. In a year, even these visits declined in frequency and eventually stopped.

The Studentenlager in Graz was a miniature sample of refugee camps in Austria. Therefore, high-ranking officers, officials, and reporters often visited us. In the summer of 1946 a group of Allied Forces correspondents came to the camp and carefully examined camp facilities and a few individual barracks as well. They asked our camp commander, Miss Jaboor, to select a few individuals for personal interviews; I was one of those selected. The interview lasted almost a half-hour. The correspondents asked many questions, reaching back to the times before the war until the present, about reasons for this or that action or decision. The interview was very cordial; the correspondents seemed to enjoy doing their job. The entire time they hastily jotted their notes into their small notepads, in shorthand, it seemed to me. At the end of the interview, the American correspondent, a young, well-dressed woman, asked if I would be willing to return to my country of origin if the Four Powers would guarantee my peaceful integration into the home society. That question sounded strange to me, and I responded to that effect and I received, in return, a few friendly laughs.

The British general Fitzroy Maclean, while on the way to Belgrade to a visit with Marshal Tito, also stopped in our student camp. In his short speech he was neither diplomatic or encouraging. His opinion about our chances in the future were less than positive. With permission of the British authorities, a representative of the Yugoslav government, a Slovene, came to the camp. He offered, on behalf of his government, a safe return for all of us to Yugoslavia. During the question-

and-answer period, the first question asked was, "Where are the twelve thousand returned by the British from Viktring/Vetrinj camp to Yugoslavia and, as far as we knew, disappeared from the earth?" The representative either did not know the answer or was not allowed to cover that topic; he left the camp immediately.

The winter of 1945/46 was extremely cold and tough. Allocations of wood to heat each room were small. During the nights we often shivered. We noticed occasionally that the students in the technical room lived in a warmer climate. Noticing this obvious discrepancy, we in our so-called "jurists" room debated for a time the Latin saying, *verba docent, exempla trahunt* [Words teach, but examples draw attention]. After it got colder and colder, we decided on *exempla trahunt*. During a snowstorm a tree behind our barrack disappeared without a trace: in our room, however, we enjoyed a few warm and pleasant days and nights. Miss Jaboor soon discovered these illegal activities and took action. For one month the two rooms proven guilty were not allocated any firewood: the technical people were punished because of their illegal initiative and the "jurists" because of all people we should have known better.

In spite of minor transgressions, our relationship with the camp commander, Miss Jaboor, was on the highest level. We had no doubts she did everything in her power for us and more. She truly deserved our gratitude and thanks for her care of the camp and for every individual who found a new home, even though only a temporary home, at Studentenlager Hochsteingasse. After the tragic experiences with a few key British commanders in Klagenfurt/Celovec, we recognized in Miss Jaboor a representative of the British Empire of entirely different qualifications and attitudes—a caring and altruistic officer. In addition, we appreciated the opportunity for studies at the institutions of higher learning in the lovely city of Graz.

Furthermore, we soon became aware that in the camp's multinational society we each represented our own nationality. Therefore, we used our extra energies, skills, and abilities to do so as well as possible.

Individual national groups attempted to present, occasionally with outside help, the key characteristics and culture of their nation. The main goal was to reach the members of other nationalities, the British authorities, and the Austrian guests. A shining example was the Ukrainian evening, centered around their poet, writer, and painter, Taras Grigorievich Shevchenko (1814–1861). His poetry was presented, in addition to the Ukrainian originals, in translations into many languages. Stane Šusteršič, a law student, formerly enrolled in the Drama Academy in Ljubljana, participated at this evening on behalf of the Slovene students by reciting one of Shevchenko's poems in a Slovene translation. No less successful was the cultural evening presented by the Croats. Several Croats in the camp were highly educated and advanced in their professions.

Slovene evenings (there were several) were carefully prepared and well presented. Two of these deserve a special mention, since on these occasions the direction of the Slovene chorus in the camp was entrusted once to Franc Cigan and once to Silvo Mihelič. These two excellent *regens chori* trained and conducted the outstanding choral groups in Spittal an der Drau and Lienz camps, respectively. The emphasis at the Slovene evenings were on the choral performances of the Slovene folk and art songs. The Slovenes were the only group that had a mixed chorus.

Twice during our stay at Hochsteingasse 37, the Doberšek sisters' trio visited the camp for a concert of selections from their rich repertory. The Slovene men's quartet, consisting of Žižek, first tenor; Marjan Pograjc, second tenor: Rado Škofic, first bass; and Lojze Rigler, second bass (after Rigler's departure Jože Lekan took the second bass part) also enjoyed great success with its inaugural concert during the first visit of the Dobersek sisters. I helped these men with rehearsals for their concerts. In addition to the art and folk songs, the quartet successfully performed songs of a contemporary popular nature, favorites of many audiences.

Very active in the camp was also the men's chorus *Sraka,* consisting of twelve singers. This choral ensemble sang at Mass each Sunday at the nearby Carmelite church, where we rehearsed. The group was under the direction of the former organ student at the music school in Ljubljana, Aleš Šimenc, at the time attending the Konservatorium in Graz. After the evening rehearsals, on the way to the camp, we stopped under the windows of a girls' boarding school and sang one or two songs for them. The girls were very pleased, waving from their windows; the same, however, could not be said about their superiors.

Almost by accident we learned that a pastor of a poor parish on the southern end of the city was one of the two Austrian priests who during the war came voluntarily to Slovenia to serve the people after the native Slovene priests in German-occupied Slovene territory had been expelled to Serbia or to other regions of occupied Southern Yugoslavia. With our choral group we thanked him for his help to our people during those difficult, tragic years.

Public festivities, group entertainment, and dances were not permitted under the British administration during the first two years of occupation. This rule did not apply to the Studentenlager Hochsteingasse. The student representatives of all nationalities therefore agreed on three entertainment festivities per year: at the beginning of the academic year, on the last Saturday before Lent, and at the conclusion of the spring semester. The entertainment part of these evenings was in the hands of the most talented and inventive Bruno Dirigel, a Croat.

Together with musical numbers offered by the camp violinist, H. Speer, baritone Dr. M. Kabalin, and pianists I. Zupančič, myself, and a woman from Romania whose name I cannot recall, and the short sketches that Bruno wrote and prepared based on contemporary issues attracted the most attention at the entertainment. Many of these sketches touched not always favorably on the British occupation administration and on British post-war policies as well as on the Austrian attitudes and characteristics of the time. Each time Bruno had to defend himself the next day in the office, since with these sketches he often embarrassed Miss Jaboor in front of her superiors, who enjoyed coming to these affairs in substantial numbers. Never, however, were any sketches directed at Miss Jaboor herself. On the contrary, at one of these evenings Bruno gave her the honorary title, "Unsere Mutter," and the entire audience agreed with a tumultuous standing ovation.

These evenings and the following dances attracted many university students living in the city. Thus, we can say that these dances helped us to know each other better and opened the doors for social interactions. We had our own campus dance band, the Baby Kapelle, consisting of four musicians: Henry Perles, piano accordion; Dušan Šurman, clarinet; Ivan Vrančič, piano; and Alexander Gjud, percussion.

During the second academic year I transferred from Law School to the Landeskonservatorium in Graz to study music history, theory, and composition. In the music composition class, taught by the extraordinary professor Valdemar Bloch, there were several of us from the Studentenlager: Dr. Mladen Kabalin, Dr. Franc Cigan, Rudi Knez, Aleš Šimenc, and Miodrag Savernik. A few of the compositions I wrote under the inspired direction of Valdemar Bloch helped me later when I applied for admission to another music institute.

The year 1948 brought the first chances for resettlement. Representatives of many countries, almost exclusively from overseas, came to the camp and explained what possibilities existed and under what conditions they would accept newcomers. The most attractive offer was from Canada. After one year of obligatory contractual work, you would be free to start on your own. Canada was accepting only young and single individuals of both sexes, no families. There were also strict health requirements. The first transport to Canada left Studentenlager toward the end of Summer 1948. Among those departing were several Slovenes. Needless to say that this first departure and separation caused many heartbreaks. Ties and promises of staying together or in touch at such long distances often came to an end after periods of long separation. The second major group departed for Argentina, mostly families. Argentina did not pose restrictions. The United States also accepted families, but a one-year private sponsorship was required. A few colleges and universities in the United States offered scholarships to a select few. These scholarships were granted exclusively to students at the entry level or first-year students. Among the lucky ones in the Studentenlager Hochsteingasse, the Slovene women received the largest number of scholarships.

The beginning of emigration brought other changes as well. It was clear that the support from UNNRA would sooner or later decrease or stop. Those still in the camp would have to provide their own means of support. Additional help for Slovene students came, on a temporary basis, from the League of Slovene Catholic Americans, theoretically in the form of a loan, although individuals did not have to sign any contracts. Father Bernard Ambrožič, pastor at St. Cyril Church in

New York City, kept records of the amounts spent for the Slovene students in Hochsteingasse. I believe that most students, after establishing themselves in the new countries, returned to the League the amount provided during the year(s) of urgent need. For the students in the Hochsteingasse, the worry about finding the necessary financial support presented an additional pressure to start looking for opportunities in any new land.

During the years of uncertainty and hopeful expectations, three key events played a crucial role in my life. First, the arrival in the Viktring/Vetrinj camp of Field Marshal Alexander and his words of promise and assurance that no Yugoslavs would be returned to Yugoslavia against their will. This decision most likely saved my life and the lives of many thousands of others and spared me from the often-considered alternative of going into hiding and waiting months or years for better and safer times; second, the decision of the British occupation administration in Austria to provide the displaced university students an opportunity for continuation of studies during the long waiting period before resettlement; third, at the very end of the year 1949, I received, to my great astonishment, an unexpected letter from the U.S. consul in Salzburg, Austria, telling me that I had a sponsor in the United States of America and that the Consulate would start preparing for my immigration.

Never, never in my life had I any dreams of going to the United States. This letter came as a gift from heaven. *Alea iacta est,* exclaimed Julius Caesar before he crossed Rubicon.[2] I exclaimed the same words as Julius Caesar did a thousand years before, in great exuberance, jumping for joy, except that in this case I was not the one who caused the die to be cast. Far away, in New York City, a generous person, Mr. Karl Klezin, signed my affidavit papers and initiated the process for my entry into the United States of America.[3]

Each one of these three key events had profound consequences for me during the immediate tragic, uncertain, confusing, and sometimes tormenting years after the war. Old goals, old dreams, old hopes were gone, gone forever. We had to search our hearts and souls to decide in which direction to go from here and where to aim our efforts, hopes, and risks. Thus, the Interludium in Hochsteingasse, starting in late September 1945 and stretching over the following few years, was not only a time well spent for academic work but offered all of us a significant measure of positiveness and confidence for regaining a constructive outlook on life and on the future.[4]

Epilogue

Tempora mutantur
et nos mutamur in illis
—*[Times change and we change with them]*

My status, my disposition, my goals, my outlook naturally changed when I received an affidavit for entry into the United States. How much of my educational accomplishments would I be able to transfer to the New World? Though the day of departure was not expected to be announced for a while, I nevertheless started to conclude my studies and other activities in Europe. At the Landeskonservatorium in Graz the administration agreed to allow me to take my final examinations a few weeks ahead of time in case I had to depart before the end of the 1950 spring semester. The faculty outlined for me very clearly all final requirements. Two persons on the faculty who had colleagues in the United States gave me a few pointers. I knew that I would dearly miss at least two of my professors, Valdemar Bloch, music composition mentor, and Erich Rabensteiner, my piano instructor and an excellent interpreter of Chopin.

During the spring break, I traveled for the last time to Carinthia to visit relatives on my mother's side in Eisenkappel/Železna kapla and to Moos bei Bleiburg/Blato pri Pliberku to relatives on my father's side. I had spent many summer months at both places, the last few years more or less as their guest, even though on the farm at Blato I did try to be helpful by working in the fields. Had I decided to stay in Austria I would have certainly received temporary help from these relatives, but I never asked. I realized that my goals were different from those I would be able to pursue in Southern Carinthia after completion of studies in Graz. The opportunity for immigration to the United States was too great to consider any other alternatives.

Equally difficult as saying goodbye to my more-than-concerned relatives, who had helped me many times during my refugee years, was leaving behind that beautiful land I learned to appreciate so much. My friend and hiking colleague, Lojze Gregorin, came up with the idea that before departure overseas, we criss-cross Southern Carinthia on foot to gain a lasting impression of this land. It was a memorable trip, almost equal to our hikes in the Austrian Alps each summer, which had culminated two years before with the ascent of the highest mountain in Austria, the Grossglockner (12,470 ft.) in the Hohe Tauern between Carinthia and Tyrol.

On the evening before departure, we took some time in my barrack room to reminisce about our good and bad times in the refugee camp Hochsteingasse, realizing that for most of us the time of "togetherness" had come to an end. Thus the evening, planned as a happy celebration, had an abundance of sad overtones as well.

I was not alone when I boarded the train the next morning for a trip to Salzburg, the assembly point for emigration from Austria. Anton Kompare, an engineering graduate and his wife, both residents of the Studentenlager Hochsteingasse, traveled to the United States at the same time. We had a fairly happy journey to the refugee assembly camp in Salzburg. There we went through the necessary paperwork procedures and were briefly greeted by the United States consul. On the day before departure the final visit with the consul took place. Mr. and Mrs. Kompare came from the consul's office with smiles on their faces after being confirmed for immigration to the United States of America. Then came my turn. When I entered, the consul was standing, looking at some papers on his desk. Then he turned toward me and asked me when was the last time I visited Salzburg. I was taken by surprise because this was my first visit to Salzburg and I said so. The consul told me—with apologies—that he had to send me back to the transit camp for an uncertain duration. He gave me no reason for this decision and no opportunity to explain myself. With heavy heart I embraced my friends and waved to them as they were taken to an area reserved for those departing the next morning.

This new uncertainty was a puzzle to me. Back in the camp I had to do manual work. I was most resentful when forced to load heavy wooden cases belonging to the Hungarian nobility and high-ranking officers, while the camp work leaders, also refugees, collected substantial tips for this work. A refusal meant a report of insubordination to the American authorities and a risk of not being admitted to the United States. This unpleasant situation lasted more than one month. Although I tried to reach the office of the consulate several times to clear up any discrepancies, nobody was willing to talk. At the OSS[1] office in Salzburg, a friendly officer in charge looked in a black binder, found a page, and said that he was sorry for not being able to offer me any clarification or assistance.

After more than a month in the transit camp in Salzburg, an order came one afternoon to report immediately to the American consulate. After I arrived with a lot of fear in my heart, the consul invited me into his office. He was very friendly and apologized for the long delay. He shook my hand and that was it; no explanation, nothing else. Two days later I was on the train to Bremenhaven, a seaport city in Northern Germany.

While at the Bremenhaven transit camp, we listened for the first time, with great emotion, to the U.S. national anthem, during the raising and lowering of the flag at the beginning and end of each day.

The embarkation two days later, 12 July 1950, on the *General M. L. Hersey* was organized most efficiently.[2] The embarkation process was run by Polish troops under American command. The routine they set up for getting so many people on the ship in such a short time was probably based on the American experience with troop movements during the war years.

The stormy Atlantic shows its full force as soon as you get to the open sea. The twelve-day trip on the *General M. L. Hersey* was not exactly pleasant. Except for a few, myself included, everyone on the ship was seasick almost the entire journey. We, the fortunate ones, had to do a lot of not-so-pleasant cleaning to keep the ship in a good and healthy state. On the morning of the arrival in the Canadian port of Halifax, the sea was calm and smooth as a glass; the sun was shining, and all those sick passengers were suddenly back to normal. Half of the passengers, the "New Canadians," left the ship. We, the remaining passengers continued sailing south and toward the evening we arrived at the port of Boston. Before arriving in Boston, the man in charge of our transport informed us that the ship will not anchor in New York harbor but in Boston and that we would continue to New York City by train.

The train left Boston after midnight. I was sitting at the window, unable to sleep, looking at the dim lights slightly illuminating the nearby areas. They seemed to be everywhere, many of them in clusters, others in single but organized rows. The night itself was very dark, no stars or moonlight. My mind wandered back and forth from the past years to the uncertain future. At this point my future was still as dark as the night: but the lights piercing the darkness were encouraging signs for my future, for my New Beginning.

On the ship, when the sea waves and ship's movements provided steady, murmuring background, there was ample time and solitude to think about the ten years just passed. These years changed everything and destroyed with one blow all our youthful hopes and expectations. The goals and dreams were gone; but we still had our lives, a treasure lost forever to many thousands of others. The war left a horrible statistic: fifty million victims.

The goals forced on the free world by the totalitarian regimes of Germany, Italy, and Japan were reached in Europe on 8 May 1945, in the Pacific on 2 September 1945. The world was now at peace. In the West, life gradually returned to normal.

The Potsdam Conference (17 July–2 August 1945), however, showed the first signs of a polarization of two different systems touching almost every aspect of life. Two opposing blocks started forming, with tensions and mistrust between them rising day by day. The "Iron Curtain Speech" by Winston Churchill in 1946 on a visit to the United States, only confirmed the fact that a dividing line from the Baltics in the north to Trieste in the south now separated the former allies. East of this line were now several Central and East European States. Between the two world wars these states had been independent, if not always democratic. Now they became the pawns of the "Big Three" decisions and agreements on the post-war settlements and peace on earth.

The first clear opposition by the West to the communist aggression took place in Greece (1944–1950) and later in Korea (June 1950–July 1953). The West demonstrated it was determined to oppose any attempts by the other side to bring additional territories under its sphere of influence and control.

To avoid the crisis after World War II, when people in Europe were starving, the United States devised the Marshall Plan. In Western Europe the benefits were felt almost immediately. The Marshall Plan did not only prevent post-war starvation in Europe, it also indirectly aided the efforts to establish and maintain democratic forms of government in Western Europe.

Among the deepest wounds that are still bleeding were the enforced repatriations and/or deceptions after the conclusion of the hostilities that were authorized and enforced at least to a degree by representatives of the Western alliance. Because these wounds would never heal, efforts are made from time to time to cover them up forever. As one who witnessed some of these events and who lost a brother and many friends in this process, I will feel these wounds forever.

Nobody could believe the rumors during the war, and it is still extremely hard to comprehend that entire nations and races were indeed targeted for annihilation. Documentation came to light after the war which confirmed the unthinkable, that such plans were set and organized and were systematically carried out. With documented proofs of all kinds of atrocities, eyewitness accounts, access to an abundance of photos confirming starvation, persecution, and executions of millions of all races, it is an unthinkable reality that such terrible acts are still taking place in our time, more than fifty-five years after the end of World War II.

Notes

⟡

Introduction

1. The initial paragraph is taken from my first, very brief account of my war years, published in the *Slovene Studies: Journal of the Society for Slovene Studies,* Volume 16, number 2, 1994, pp. 31–47, and in Slovene translation by Henrik Ciglič in *Nova Revija: Mesečnik za kulturo,* "Iz mojih izkušenj v vojnih letih 1941–1945," Letnik XV, Maj 1996, pp. 134–143.

Chapter One

1. A brief summary in English about Mežiška dolina and its socioeconomic history during the 19th and 20th centuries, with a series of photographs can be found on pp. 179 ff, in Jakob Medved, *Mežiska dolina: socialnogeografski razvoj zadnjih 100 let* (Ljubljana: Mladinska knjiga, 1967). For a more contemporary description of progress and development of this region, summaries in English and German on various topics are included in *Jugovzhodna Koroška,* ed. Jakob Medved (Ljubljana: Geografsko društvo Slovenije, et al., 1970), 23–25; 55–59; 71–73; 84–86; and 103–105, by chapter authors Svetozar Ilešič, Ivan Gams, Jakob Medved, Marjan Žagar, and Milan Natek.

2. From its inception in 1918 until 1929, the new state was known as the Kingdom of Serbs, Croats, and Slovenes.

3. Franc Sušnik *In kaj so ljudje ko lesovi: Koroški zapisi* (Maribor: Založba obzorja, 1968), 5.

4. Many works have been written regarding the causes and consequences of the Carinthian plebiscite of 1920. Different points of view are presented in three key works on the subject: *Koroški plebiscit: Razprave in članki,* ed. Janko Pleterski, Lojze Ude and Tone Zorn (Ljubljana: Slovenska Matica, 1970); Claudia Kromer, *Die Vereiningten Staaten von Amerika und die Frage Kärnten 1918–1920,* Aus Forschung und Kunst, 7 (Klagenfurt; Bonn: Geschichtsverein für Kärnten; Habelt in Komm., 1970); Thomas Mack Barker, *The Slovene Minority of Carinthia,* East European monographs, 169 (Boulder, CO: East European Monographs, 1984).

5. During World War I, my father served in the Austrian/Hungarian army as an officer, first in Galicia and after 1916 on the Italian front, where he commanded a section of the Austrian defense line in the mountains of the Wishberggruppe. He described some of his experiences in his article, Jan Milač, "Aus meinem Tagebuch," in *Der Krieg in der Wischberggruppe: Berichte einstiger Mitkämpfer,* ed. Norbert Nau (Graz: Leykam Verlag, 1937), 26–33. Readers may wish

to consult also Gustav Renker, "Fünf Männer bauen einen Weg: Ein Alpenroman," *Delhagen & Klasings Monatshefte* 48. Jahrg., no. 8. Heft (April 1934): 113–300, and Heinz von Lichem, *Der Tiroler Hochgebirgskrieg, 1915–1918 im Luftbild: die altösterreichische Luftwaffe* (Innsbruck: Steiger, 1985). In his book, Lichem mentions that Erwin Rommel was in command on this front of a German Army detachment.

6. The Gross family owned a resort and a hotel (Bad Vellach) next to the Skalar's property. During the pre-auction negotiations among neighbors, Gross agreed not to push the price over a certain limit to enable several Skalar relatives to repossess this property. However, during the auction he negated this agreement and made the final bid. Gross later became an active and feared member of the Nazi Party. After World War II, according to local reports, he never appeared in public or left his house until he died. His widow, my mother's youthful friend until this auction, by her will, left this property to a branch of the Evangelical Church.

7. The scout organization was at this initial stage for boys only. Our friends from the opposite sex, however, helped in the production of the home-made tents.

8. On 6 January 1929, King Alexander I dissolved the parliament, abolished the constitution, and assumed dictatorial powers.

9. I should add that our instructor, a teacher in the elementary school and post-World War I refugee from the Slovene lands assigned to Italy, Boris Stres, often used his free time, in addition to his duties, to guide and supervise our extracurricular winter and summer sport activities.

10. In reference to Antonin Dvořak's composition, "Als die Alte Mutter" (Songs My Mother Taught Me), op. 55, no.4.

11. The year when this *Tabor* took place may have been a year or two later.

12. The last such ceremony took place in 1414 when Ernest Železni/Ernest der Eiserne was installed as the duke of the Caranthanian region.

13. The original is preserved in a Museum in Klagenfurt/Celovec, Austria. In 1941, after the Nazis occupied this part of Yugoslavia, one of their first acts was the destruction of this symbol of Slovene history.

14. On one occasion, a year or two after the plebiscite, Uncle Lojze, on the way home from Bleiburg/Pliberk to his farm in Moos bei Bleiburg/Blato pri Pliberku, was brutally beaten by several men, who were waiting for him hidden in the darkness behind a wayside shrine (znamenje na polju). He was left unconscious by the side of the road. "They left me here to die," he told me years later, pointing out the location. Fortunately, a neighbor coming down the road found him just in time.

15. For information about the events in Austria in 1934, two sources may be useful. Gottfried-Karl Kindermann, *Hitler's Defeat in Austria 1933–1934: Europe's First Containment of Nazi Expansionism*, trans. Sonia Brough and David Taylor (Boulder, Colorado: Westview Press, 1984); and Wissenschaftliche Kommission der Theodor-Körner-Stiftungsfonds und der Leopold-Kunschak-Preises zur Erforschung der österreichischen Geschichte der Jahre 1927 bis 1938, *Das Jahr 1934: 25. Juli. Protokoll des Symposiums in Wien am 8. Oktober 1974*, Veröffentlichungen, Band 3 (München: R. Oldenbourg Verlag, 1975).

16. My father was the chief administrative officer of the okraj (county) Dravograd. Between the two World Wars, Slovenia was divided into twenty-four counties; Dravograd was number twenty-four.

17. The German government requested from the Yugoslav authorities for these Putschists a temporary asylum. Eventually they were all assembled and interned at some facilities near Varaždin, Croatia, and later transported by German ships to Germany. Rumors circulated that, while in internment, they were very well provided for by the Third Reich. Interesting information about Yugoslav-German diplomatic exchanges, the tense political situation, and Austrian

Nazis' departure from Varaždin is to be found in Ludwig Jedlicka, "Der aussenpolitische Hintergrund der Ereignisse vom Frühsommer 1934 bis Oktober 1934," in *Das Jahr 1934: 25. Juli* (München: R. Oldenbourg Verlag, 1975), 46–57.

18. I attended with my mother Hans Legat's funeral in Eisenkappel/ Železna Kapla, Austria. It was a state military funeral attended not only by high-ranking Austrian military and government officials but, to the best of my recollections, two Italian officers were also present.

19. One source in German, a group of symposium papers, may be consulted as a useful summary of events that preceded this Anschluss and the changes Nazis initiated in occupied Austria immediately after March 1938: Wolfgang Etschmann, *Die Kämpfe in Österreich im Juli 1934*, Militärische Schriftenreihe, 50 (Wien: Heeresgeschichtliches Museum/Militärwissenschaftliches Institut, 1984).

20. This description of the river is now no longer true. Some time in the past a dam at that location completely changed the environment and, of course, the flow of the Drava River in Dravograd.

21. Nowadays TV reproductions of parts of Hitler's speeches don't seem threatening: they seem something to be easily ignored or something unrealistic, even funny. In those times the threat sounded very real and very frightening.

22. The events leading to the Anschluss, the Nazi terror immediately after, and increased persecution of real and possible opponents after the *Volksabstimmung* (elections) of 10 April 1938 are described in detail in conference papers. Slovenski znanstveni institut. *Der 'Anschluss' und die Minderheiten in Österreich / Anšlus in manjšine v Avstriji*. Disertacije in razprave / Dissertations und Abhandlungen. Ed. Avguštin Malle and Valentin Sima (Klagenfurt/Celovec: Drava, 1989).

23. The funeral of Vinko Poljanec was attended by Slovenes from both sides of the border, including many priests from the diocese of Maribor. The German authorities did not prevent attendance. However, on the return trip from Carinthia, the border controls held up the train for two hours in order to search those returning. The Gestapo agents not only searched but harassed, especially clergy, on this occasion. My mother was one of those attending the funeral and returning on this train.

24. During the month of September 1938 the eyes of Europe and probably of the world were focused on meetings in Munich, where England and France attempted to reach some agreement with Hitler regarding Sudetenland. The last and deciding meeting took place on the 29 of September. British Prime Minister Chamberlain, returning to England, happily waved an agreement with Hitler, believing that it brought "peace in our time."

25. I cannot say if this was an authorized translation or a paraphrased edition.

26. The Russo-Finnish War, 1939–1940, as this war is referred to, is described in some detail in Martin Gilbert, *The Second World War: A Complete History* (New York: Henry Holt and Company, 1989), pages 31–32, 34, 36, 38–39, 40–42, 47, 49.

27. The Allied forces, British, French, and Polish, which were helping Norwegians in the northern region, were eventually evacuated. For a brief account of the Norwegian campaign, see entries in Peter Young, Editor, *The World Almanac of World War II: The Complete and Comprehensive Documentary of World War II*, First Revised Edition (New York, Bison Book Corporation, 1981), interspersed on pages 50–61.

28. For a summary report about the evacuations at Dunkirk, consult Gilbert, ibid., 75–84.

29. The text of "The Tripartite Pact Between Germany, Italy, and Japan," signed at Berlin, September 27, 1940, in English translation is included in the Appendix III of Neil Balfour and Sally Mackay, *Paul of Yugoslavia: Britain's Maligned Friend* (London: Hamish Hamilton, 1980), 314–315.

30. Italians attacked Greece on the 28 October 1940 from their strongholds in Albania. Peter Young, *The World Almanac of World War II*, 80.

31. Ibid., 87.

32. A treaty of friendship, however, was signed between Hungary and Yugoslavia on 12 December 1940. Ibid., 84.

33. In Tone Ferenc, *Nacistična raznadovalna politika v Sloveniji v letih 1941–1945* (Maribor: Založba Obzorja, 1968}, p. 141, a monograph about the Nazis' tactics in occupied Slovenia, is a photograph depicting a young German reporting to Hitler in Maribor about the fifth column activities in the Slovene Styria months, maybe years, before the German attack. This was in no way an isolated case.

34. It is now known that the Germans gave Yugoslavia an ultimatum of five days to decide whether to join or not.

35. The text of this agreement and of the Three Notes explaining this agreement is included in Appendix III of Neil Balfour and Sally Mackay, *Paul of Yugoslavia. Britain's Maligned Friend* (London: Hamish Hamilton, 1980), 313–314. It is interesting to note that parts of these Notes were classified by the German Governments as secret, not to be made public without German consent.

36. Again, it was just a rumor, but among those who were marked was apparently also my father as the chief executive of the county of Dravograd and the head of the Maribor police force. My father dismissed these rumors as nonsense.

37. It turned out later, that the father of this talented student was one of the Nazi sympathizers and fifth columnists in Ljubljana. After the defeat of Yugoslavia, this person assumed a responsible post in the German occupation administration in Celje.

38. In Chapter 5, "The Tripartite Pact and the Conquest," in Frank C. Littlefield, *Germany and Yugoslavia 1933–1941: The German Conquest of Yugoslavia* (Boulder: East European Monographs, 1988), 87–130, the author provides a detailed account of developments regarding Yugoslavia from the later part of 1939 to April 1941.

Chapter Two

1. A *Putsch* by officers of the Yugoslav air force on 27 March 1941, and subsequent demonstrations against the treaty in many parts of the country, especially in Belgrade and Ljubljana, enraged Hitler. Many historians are of the opinion that this side action into Yugoslavia delayed Germany's attack on the Soviet Union for a month or two, thus moving the timing of that attack back—closer to the winter and all its consequences.

2. After World War I, when the new state of Yugoslavia came into being, the German minority in Slovenia and probably the rest of Yugoslavia did have grievances and unresolved disputes with Yugoslav and Slovene governments regarding their rights and status. With Hitler's rise to power, many members of the German minority became involved in illegal pro-Nazi propaganda and spying activities. For a brief overview of the grievances of the German minority between the two world wars, consult Helga H. Harriman, *Slovenia under Nazi Occupation, 1941–1945*, Studia Slovenica XI (New York-Washington: Studia Slovenica, 1977), 20–26.

3. After the 1938 *Anschluss,* Austria ceased to exist as an independent state until the end of the Second World War. For this in-between period, Yugoslavia had common borders with Germany, borders identical to the present Slovenia/Austria demarcation line.

4. Information about my family's retreat from Dravograd was provided to me at various times by my parents, Marija, and a few other individuals who were in Dravograd at the time of the attack.

5. Terzić states "Thus, units of the 51 corpus attacked on the front of the Dravska divizija in the direction of Radgona-Ptuj and Šentilj–Maribor and a little later also on the front Sv. Duh-Dravograd . . . on this first day then, the German troops occupied Radgona, Murska Sobota and Radence, on the front Sv. Duh-Dravograd, they broke through to the left side of the Drava

River. During the day of 6 April until 9:00 P.M. units of the German 2 army occupied mountain passes at Podkoren and Ljubelj, Jezersko, Sv. Duh." Velimir Terzić, *Slom kraljevine Jugoslavije 1941: Uzroci i posledice poraza* (Ljubljana-Beograd: Partizanska knjiga, 1982), vol. 2, 300 and 300b.

6. "On the sector of the 7 army, German troops were engaged in heavy fighting with the units of the 6th, 7th, and 8th Garrison regiment. While they had some success in the direction of Ptuj and Maribor, they were pushed back on the sector Dravograd-Slovenj Gradec by the soldiers of the 6 regiment and one battalion of the Dravska *divizija* which defended the right bank of the Drava River." Terzić, vol. 2, 316.

7. The information about the 6 April German air attack on Belgrade, the casualties, destruction, and consequences, is accessible through many sources, including *The New York Times*, Apr. 7 1:4–8. Other references, from different times, give more details: Svetislav-Sveta Petrovich, *Free Yugoslavia Calling*, trans. and ed., Joseph Ciszek Peters (New York: The Greystone Press, 1941), 259–261, which gives Edward Angly's eyewitness report of the attack and devastation in the *New York Herald Tribune* and that of the American Minister in Belgrade, Arthur Bliss-Lane; Frank C. Littlefield, *Germany and Yugoslavia 1933–1941: The German Conquest of Yugoslavia*, East European Monographs, No. CCXLIV (Boulder, Colorado: 1988), 129; and Terzić, Ibid., vol. 2, 289–230, who provides many detailed statistics.

8. Two days later, at night at a railroad station, I saw a few men breaking into a railroad freight car and starting to remove large sacks of white flour. When they saw me, they offered one sack to me in return for help with loading their booty on a small wagon stationed several yards away. In this case, I decided against it, realizing that these sacks belong to someone, somewhere. Actually, I felt relieved, when railroad officials arrived and prevented further removal of the goods.

9. According to Terzić, the first such uprising started north of Bjelovar in Croatia, where some Croatian members of an army regiment disarmed and/or killed some officers and soldiers of the Serb ethnic group and refused to proceed toward the front. These kinds of uprisings, initiated and organized by the *Ustashi*, a fascist Croatian anti-Yugoslav underground organization, spread then to other areas, where units were predominantly Croatian, thus causing a mortal blow to the Yugoslav defense efforts in both Croatia and Slovenia, and for all practical reasons opening the area to German and Italian troops. Terzić, vol. 2, 333.

10. The changing and critical situation in northern Croatia after the events in Bjelovar, forced the Yugoslav army command to order a retreat in Slovenia in two stages to reach a new defense line south of the rivers Sava and Kolpa. As a result, Germans then advanced from the areas of Dravograd and Maribor, where units of the Yugoslav Army successfully held the line, toward Celje (occupied 11 April), Zidani Most, and Brežice. This retreat was ordered for the night of 8 and 9 April, a day after the Bjelovar uprising. Terzić, vol. 2, 337, 341–342, 352, 358, 366, 368, and 375.

11. *Pfaffen* is a derogatory expression in German for priests.

12. There is still a dispute regarding the participation of the Communist Party on this National Council. While members of the assembled political parties claim that communists were invited but declined, the Communist Party insists that it offered to join but was rejected on the grounds of not being recognized as a legitimate political party in Yugoslavia. More about this dispute from different points of view may be found in Bogdan C. Novak, *Trieste, 1941–1954: The Ethnic, Political, and Ideological Struggle* (Chicago, London: The University of Chicago Press, 1970), 50; Zveza slovenskih protikomunističnih borcev, *Vetrinjska tragedija* (Cleveland: Ameriška Domovina, 1960), 8–9; Velimir Terzič, *Slom Kraljevine Jugoslavije 1941*, vol. 2, 376.

13. More information about this proclamation is in Novak, *Trieste, 1941–1954*, 49–50; Metod Mikuž, *Pregled zgodovine narodno-osvobodilne borbe v Sloveniji* (Ljubljana: 1960), vol. 1; and Terzić, *Slom Kraljevine Jugoslavije 1941*, 376. Terzić offers an additional note about a National

Council's request via Dr. Natlačen to two Yugoslav generals, Pandurović and Lavadinović, in command of Yugoslav troops in Slovenia, a request to place all Yugoslav troops on Slovenian soil under the authority of the Council, which both of them categorically declined.

Chapter Three

1. For information on how and when agreements were made regarding the partition of Slovenia, see: Peter Rehder (HG.), *Das Neue OstEuropa von A–Z* (München: Droemer Knaur, 1992), 295; Ahmet Đongalić, Žarko Atanacković, and Dušan Plenča, trans. Lovett S. Edwards, *Yugoslavia and the Second World War* (Belgrade: Međunarodna štampa, 1967), 33–34; Ciril Žebot, *Neminljiva Slovenia* (Celovec: Mohorjeva, 1988), 204.
2. How the court proceeding later turned out I do not know. To the best of my information there were some reparations.
3. Mr. Čebin's son and I were school friends at Bishop's Gymnasium at Šentvid near Ljubljana. However, neither Mr. Čebin nor my father knew that at the time of their conversation. Mr. Čebin just said that he will do anything to help people who were forced to leave their homes.
4. It should not be forgotten that the people of these regions offered assistance and support to the best of their abilities to Slovene victims of the war in April 1941 and the years after.
5. To prevent these demonstrations, trains were subsequently scheduled to run after curfew.
6. This person was former sergeant *(narednik)* Rajko Kotnik, a key member of the first Slovene defense force under Lieutenant Malgaj in Carinthia 1918–1920, who is mentioned in Prežihov Voranc's novel *Požganica*. Kotnik was first imprisoned in Klagenfurt/Celovec and later executed (beheaded) in a prison yard in Graz. This information was confirmed by Rajko Kotnik's relatives in an e-mail message in May 1997.
7. His name in the underground organization was Bratko.
8. Dušan's appeal for joining an underground effort, in this case the Yugoslav army resistance group, although the first, was certainly not the only one I was invited to join. Knowing and trusting the liaison person(s), under the difficult circumstances, was for me the deciding factor.
9. If my memory is correct, this underground literature carried the title *Svoboda ali smrt* (Freedom or Death). The content included some news from the fronts but mostly short articles to encourage resistance participation and some true (or not so true) reports about Mihailović Chetniks' successes against the enemy forces in Serbia. About Mihailović, see *Time: The Weekly Newsmagazine*, vol. xxxix, 25 May 1942, 22–23 and cover page.
10. Many years later, while reading detailed accounts of the history of World War II in Ljubljana, I found out that only a few houses away from our home, on the same street, the Communist-led *Proti-imperialistična fronta* (Anti-Imperialist Front), renamed after the German attack on the Soviet Union on 22 June 1941 *Osvobodilna fronta* (Liberation Front), held some of its initial meetings. Mestna konferenca SDZL, *Ljubljana v ilegali II: Država v državi*, ed. Vladimir Krivic et al. (Ljubljana: Državna založba Slovenije, 1961), 69 and 388.
11. The Non-Aggression Pact between Germany and Soviet Union, signed in Moscow on 24 August 1939, was a great and unexpected shock for everybody.
12. The words of my gymnasium professor, Franz Trdan, that the outcome of any war never brings desired results for either side all of a sudden made a lot of sense and had a new meaning.
13. The exact date when this happened is listed in *Ljubljana v ilegali III: Mesto v žici* (Ljubljana: 1967). The time of the day is listed as 9:30 A.M. The same source reports the execution of Dr. Lambert Ehrlich, a Catholic priest, who was one of the Yugoslav representatives at the Paris Peace Conference in 1919–1920 as an expert on the Carinthian question. Executed together with Ehrlich at 8:00 A.M. was his companion, the student Rojc.

14. How much was known at the time about this organization and its members would be difficult to clarify, because information varied considerably depending on the person explaining or commenting. For a brief discussion of this organization, the reader may consult Leopoldina Plut-Pregelj and Carole Rogel, *Historical Dictionary of Slovenia,* European Historical Dictionaries, No. 13 (Lanham, Md., and London: The Scarecrow Press, Inc., 1996), 242.

15. Ibid., p. 242.

16. T. R. survived the war, and resettled in Argentina, where he joined the Argentine Merchant Marine. He passed away several years ago.

Chapter Four

1. We learned only later that a large city block was cordoned off, an encirclement referred to by the Italian term *razzia.*

2. The debate is still going on as to who guided or advised the officer in making his decisions. Both the communist and the anti-communist sides claim that opposition informers were giving signals to the officer from the nearby covered truck, telling him who to release and who to arrest. I do not believe that anything of that nature took place. As became clear later, all points of view were present among us who lost freedom on that day. The officer probably decided to eliminate people who would be most likely to offer resistance to the occupation forces.

3. In his account, "Bežigrajski študentje v Kočevskem Rogu, poletje 1942," Peter Klopčič remembers that we received a piece of bread Sunday the 28th while in Italian captivity. Peter Klopčič, *Ameriška Domovina* (Cleveland, OH, April 18, 1996), 17–20.

4. I am using the word "partisan" as a general term for those members and units of the resistance movement in Slovenia and the rest of Yugoslavia, which was under the control of the Front of Liberation *(Osvobodilna fronta [OF]),* even though the term itself has a much broader meaning.

5. Rumors circulated later that a few prisoners were wounded and that two were killed during the initial partisan attack. I was not aware of any casualties unless those who were hit stayed behind. It was dark, great confusion; everything happened in a split second. Klopčič, however, reports that a few prisoners were wounded in the attack. Klopčič, "Bežigrajski študentje," ibid., 17, col. 1. Another source, which I cannot identify anymore, had the number as follows: two Italian soldiers killed, one wounded; three prisoners killed, seven wounded; one partisan killed, one wounded.

6. That camp was in the vicinity of Vinji vrh at an abandoned sawmill.

7. Privately, a few partisans who participated in the attack, told us that according to their information a train carrying gasoline was scheduled for that time. Instead, Italians added a special prisoner transport for that night, the first of that nature. The partisans were very surprised when all of a sudden they heard screams.

8. In his book, *Druga grupa odredov in štajerski partizani 1941–1942* (Ljubljana: Knjižnica NOV in POS 2, 1972), 318–321, Ivan Ferlež provides some details about the attack on the train at Verd. He also states that about forty of those rescued from the train were released on their own request and that they all returned home. The number is definitely not correct; I recall only ten or twelve, since I was present when they were led away under heavy guard. Their fate, on the other hand, is at least implied if not confirmed by Edvard Kocbek. Kocbek refers to a letter from a friend whose brother-in-law was liquidated by the partisans. This person was one of those rescued from the train at Verd. He, according to Kocbek, refused to join either the partisan army or the labor battalion and remained with those who opted for release. Edvard Kocbek, *Tovarišija* (Ljubljana: Državna založba Slovenije, 1949), 292, 308–309.

9. Even though I am not certain that our intended destination was the mountain region of

Pohorje, many years after the war I searched through the book by France Filipič, *Pohorski bataljon* (Ljubljana: Državna založba Slovenije, 1968), to trace our acquaintance's path after we separated. Pohorski bataljon, possibly a successor to the unit he belonged to, was surrounded by a strong German force on 8th January 1943 and annihilated to the last person near the village of Osankarica, Pohorje. Only one wounded partisan was captured. He was later executed as a hostage. The name of our acquaintance is not listed among those who perished (*Pohorski bataljon*, 600–652). I did hear rumors that he survived the war. In July 1995, while visiting Dravograd, a person in town told me that this was the case and also gave me the name of the individual. He died ten or fifteen years after the war.

10. Only after the war, seeing his photographs in various publications, I fully realized that it was Edvard Kocbek, writer, poet, editor, and politician, who played a leading role among those in command when we were incorporated into the partisan movement in June of 1942. Edvard Kocbek, a key figure of the Slovene Christian Socialists, joined the communist-led Liberation Front in the initial stages of its existence. For more information about Kocbek, the reader should consult, *Historical Dictionary of Slovenia,* by Leopoldina Plut-Pregelj and Carole Rogel, European Historical Dictionaries, No. 13 (Lanham, Md., and London: The Scarecrow Press, Inc., 1996), 141–142.

11. According to a note in the article, "Odlomki iz spominov na leto 1942" by Vladimir Krivic, political commissar of the Krim Battalion, Fric Novak was later condemned to death by the partisans themselves. Krivic, *Ljubljana v ilegali III: Mesto v žici* (Ljubljana, 1967), 352.

12. I saw M. K. only once more, a month later, when his unit passed by our location. He looked very tired but determined. We waved to each other but were not permitted to talk.

13. One of the other two troika members name really surprised me. I have never mentioned to this individual to this day that he was named in this incident.

14. I knew Polak-Stjenka from track and field competitions in Ljubljana.

15. I often think back, hoping that one day I will find out, who made the crucial decision to redirect us to the Polhograjski Dolomiti instead of toward the forever-unknown destination or fate.

16. Božidar Jakac and Miran Jarc, *Odmevi rdeče zemlje [Echoes of Red Earth]* (Ljubljana: Jugoslovanska knjigarna, 1932). For Ciril and me, this was the first literary/artistic impression of America, that mysterious land so far away. Božidar Jakac's paintings of the land and Miran Jarc's poetic descriptions made a deep impressions on us.

17. Miran Jarc did not survive the Italian offensive in August 1942. Exhausted from long day and night marches trying to avoid capture, he was killed by Italian forces somewhere near Kamenjak or Novi breg. Dušan Moravec, "Miran Jarc," *Ljubljana v ilegali, III: Mesto v žici* (Ljubljana: 1967), 218–220.

18. The song was part of the partisan repertoire, introduced to us by the partisan leadership because of its communist content and especially because of the words: "Viva Stalin, a basso Re!"

19. If the promise of relocation to Germany proper was really made, I was unable to verify. That was what we were told, when we were asking why there were so many empty houses and an almost empty town. These Germans were settled in Kočevje territory in the 12th and 13th centuries and established their own communities and culture there. Now, after many centuries, they were relocated to German-occupied Slovene territories near the border with Croatia. After the end of the war in 1945, these Germans had to abandon their newly acquired homes and properties. For information regarding German migration to Kočevje territory, consult Milko Kos, *Zgodovina Slovencev* (Ljubljana: Slovenska Matica, 1955), 201–202.

20. Dr. Plajh, like poet Miran Jarc, did not survive the war. According to a statement in Vladimir Krivic, "Odlomki iz spominov na leto 1942," *Ljubljana v ilegali, III: Mesto v žici*, 368, Avgust Plajh was killed during the partisan attack on the Yugoslav armed forces (Chetnics) at Grčarice

in September 1943. However, the names of those killed in Grčarice during the battle are known and so are the names of those who were condemned to death and executed by the partisans after the Kočevje Trials. With exception of nine who escaped, all the others of the Yugoslav armed forces, who surrendered to the partisans and were guaranteed their lives as condition of surrender, were secretly executed at various places near Kočevje during October and November 1943. Among these victims was also Dr. Avgust Plajh. For more detail about Plajh and the fate of the Yugoslav armed forces in Grčarice, consult Pavle Borštnik, *Pozabljena zgodba slovenske nacionalne ilegale* (Ljubljana: Mladinska knjiga, 1988), 53–56.

21. Dr. Lambert Ehrlich was killed by an assassin on 26 May 1942 at 8:00 A.M. while leaving his church after morning mass. With him was a university student, Rojc, who was also killed in the attack. Dr. Ehrlich was condemned to death and executed by members of the VOS, an arm of the Slovene communist-led Liberation Front.

22. According to geographical maps, there are two villages, upper and lower, with the name Topla reber. During my stay at Topla reber, I was not aware of this. The reference to our location was always only Topla reber.

23. A year and a half later, I noticed in one of the newspapers a photograph of our Topla reber commissar. The newspaper reported that he had been captured in Bosnia as a partisan courier.

Chapter Five

1. I am often asked, how is it possible that I remember the exact time of my capture at Topla reber. When the soldier returned my watch, the time was 9:00 A.M.

2. According to a source which I can no longer identify (pp. 307, 316—I have photocopies, however, title pages are missing), four battalions of unit "M" participated in the big Italian August offensive in and around Kočevski rog. Each battalion had approximately 700 men. We were in the hands of one of these four battalions.

3. From several post-war reports, I can deduce that we, the members of the Pioneer detachment, almost the entire group, were among the first captured during the Italian August 1942 offensive. This happened because Topla reber was in the primary direction of the initial Italian attack and because of the insufficient knowledge of the terrain by the partisan leader. Peter Klopčič describes in some detail what happened to the main body of the Labor battalion and its efforts to avoid capture, in his article, "Bežigrajski študentje v Kočevskem Rogu, poletje 1942," *Ameriška domovina* (Cleveland, OH, April 18, 1996), 18–20. Thus, the report in the same unknown source (p. 317), that members of the Labor battalion, including members of the Pioneer detachment, voluntarily crossed over into the Italian captivity, is not based on facts.

4. For years, however, I was convinced that this person was the poet Miran Jarc, because the photograph in the commanding officer's hands resembled Jarc in several ways. Years later I found out that this was not the case.

5. Dr. Erat told us a year or two later that he established his office in Novo mesto in 1942, after escaping from the German zone. One night, during curfew, two civilians came to his home and forced him to take his medical bag and accompany them by secret passage into the nearby partisan territory. There he found a seriously wounded partisan in great need of help. Dr. Erat did what he could. He had to promise that he would be back the next day. The partisans also put pressure on him to join them since they needed the medical help urgently. How his nightly trips to the partisan territory came to the attention of the Italian authority, he did not know. However, according to him, the Italians were well-informed.

6. We heard rumors occasionally, while we were with the partisans, that former Yugoslav officers

intended to organize themselves to eliminate the communist-led partisans from the Italian zone. We considered these rumors empty propaganda.

7. The Island of Rab is located off the coast of Croatia, in the area of Mali Kvarner. It measures a total of 36 sq. miles and had in 1961 approximately 8370 inhabitants. *Webster's New Geographical Dictionary* (Springfield, MA: G. & C. Merriam Company, 1977), 995.

Chapter Six

1. The official name of the camp was, Campo Concentramento de Internati Civili di Guerra (Concentration Camp for Civilian Prisoners of War). Some prisoners interpreted this designation of civilian prisoners of war as an attempt by the Italian authorities to circumvent the Geneva Convention regarding prisoners of war.

2. The term "capo" in almost all World War II camps was associated with bad, often cruel, and selfish behavior. This was not the case in Concentration Camp Rab. Our capos were selected by the Italian authorities on the basis of their ability to communicate in Italian. I know of no case where a capo overstepped the rules governing his authority. Our capos were friendly and helpful; they were part of us.

3. Čabar is in Croatia. The region of Čabar, however, is on the border between Slovenia and Croatia. Most likely the prisoners from Čabar in Concentration Camp Rab came from both sides of the border.

4. We estimated that between ten and twelve thousand prisoners were in this camp at the height of concentration camp activities between August and December of 1942. Post-war efforts by several researchers to arrive at some reliable number of prisoners in Concentration Camp Rab differ considerably. A comprehensive study by Božidar Jezernik, *Italijanska koncentracijska taborišča za Slovence med 2. svetovno vojno* (Ljubljana: Društvo za preučevanje zgodovine, literature in antropologije, 1997) lists several of these sources, including statistics. The highest number listed is 9,537 prisoners (p. 34). Even this number is probably not all-inclusive.

5. We went through this procedure every morning and evening.

6. Božidar Jezernik gives 11 September 1942 as the date for this visit. Jezernik, *Italijanska koncentracijska taborišča . . . ,"* p. 305.

7. Two years after the war, when I had a chance to stay and work a few summers on my uncle's farm, he told me that he received the letter and cried. They prepared a package right away. However, the German postal officers in Bleiburg/Pliberk refused to accept it even though my cousin Micka begged at the post office several times.

8. The term *zidaro* was adapted from the Slovene term *zidar* (bricklayer or mason) by the Italians.

9. As far as I recall, the prisoners were not regularly involved with transportation of coffins to the final resting place. Such involvement would reveal the number of daily and weekly deaths to all remaining prisoners in the camp. That work must have been done by outside workers. The day we were assembled to do part of the job must have been an exception. There were no graves where we dropped these coffins; that work must have been done there or nearby on the following days. Thanks to a kind letter and photos I received in 1998 (10/22/98) from Dr. John Spindler of San Diego, California, who visited Concentration Camp Rab area that year and provided me with a map of the Island of Rab, I am almost certain that we carried coffins to the place marked on the map as the Concentration Camp Rab cemetery.

10. The question of how many people died in Concentration Camp Rab and/or as a consequence of being imprisoned there, will never be completely resolved. We who were there and observed daily removal of corpses from the camp, even though done as discreetly as possible,

were convinced that close to 5,000 prisoners, men, women, and children, died there or soon after they were released or were transferred to other camps. According to an unknown source on the electronic mail RokPress of a few years ago, 4,641 people died in a period of one year. However, Božidar Jezernik in his study, *Italijanska koncentracijska taborišča* . . . , writes that the prisoners' cemetery on Rab lists 1,066 names (Jezernik, p. 286). This "official" number is certainly much too low since other statistics and many rumors list or mention much higher numbers (Jezernik, pp. 285–288). An entirely different number was reported also by Bishop Srebrnič in Vatican in August 1943, who gave a figure of over 1,200 deaths but added that the undertakers told him that they buried over 3,500 or even over 4,000 victims (Jezernik, pp. 287–288). Bishop Srebrnič's figures do not take into account those victims who died after they were transferred to other camps, such as Gonars, Treviso, Padova, and Renicci, or those who died after they were released.

11. Božidar Jezernik summarized the real truth about Concentration Camp Rab by saying very correctly that, according to the high mortality rate, this camp belonged among those where, during the Second World War, with the exception of the German extermination camps, the greatest number of victims died in the shortest period of time. Because of so many deaths in the first four months in this camp, the rumors circulated that all those transported to Rab were designated to die there (Jezernik, p. 33). The original text in Slovene reads: "Rabsko taborišče se je po visoki umrljivosti zagotovo povzpelo med tista, kjer je bilo med drugo svetovno vojno razmeroma največ žrtev (z izjemo nemških tovarn smrti) v verjetno najkrajšem časovnem obdobju. V pičlih štirih mesecih je bilo žrtev toliko, da so se daleč naokrog razširile vesti, da so vsi ljudje, poslani na Rab, zapisani neogibni smrti." It is also interesting—or extremely disappointing—to note, that the *Enciklopedija Jugoslavije* (Zagreb: Jugoslovenski Leksikografski Zavod, 1968) has no description of what was happening in Concentration Camp Rab and includes no information about the multitude of deaths in this camp. It only mentions the liberation of the camp after the collapse of the Fascist regime in 1943.

12. The city of Ljubljana was since 23 February 1942 completely encircled with barbed wire. It was difficult to get permission to leave and return. For this reason, most of the messages given to us before departure from the camp were from the prisoners who were, prior to their arrests, residents of Ljubljana.

13. According to the Italian version of the names, a father's first name translated into Italian was added to each name. My name, therefore, was Milač Metod di Giovanni.

14. From an acquaintance (whose name I no longer remember), who remained on Rab until the very end and was there at the time of the liberation of this camp on the 23 September 1943, I learned that the conditions in the camp were much improved after our departure, starting around the middle of January 1943. Most of the sick prisoners were transferred to better facilities, where they received some medical attention. For those remaining in the camp, the food was improved; they were eventually moved to barracks, where they had access to adequate toilet and washing facilities. In my acquaintance's opinion, it was the committee of officers who visited the camp in mid–December that brought to this camp some sense of civility and many crucial and, for many prisoners, life-saving changes.

15. We never found out anything about our release or to whom we would have to say thank you for such crucial assistance. Four possibilities existed: (1) It was the decision and recommendation of the committee of sixteen officers that we and others were released; (2) The Track and Field Club in Ljubljana (SK Planina) where we were members, made many applications to the authorities for the release of its members; (3) The Classical Gymnasium and the Teachers School also tried to get their students back from the concentration camps; and (4) My mother, after a father's co-worker told her that the chief Italian administrator of the Department where

238   Resistance, Imprisonment, and Forced Labor

my father was employed spoke German (he was probably from South Tyrol), went to him and pleaded for our release. The cordial administrator did not promise anything but very willingly took from our mother all the necessary information.

Chapter Seven

1. Concentration Camp Gonars was located near a small town of the same name several miles east of the city of Palmanova in the Italian Province of Friuli-Venezia Giulia.
2. Pavle Borštnik in his book, *Pozabljena zgodba slovenske nacionalne ilegale* (Ljubljana: Mladinska knjiga, 1998), p. 114, fn. 11, gives 16 September 1941 as the date when at the III plenum of the Liberation Front such a declaration was agreed on. This information was more widely known considerably later.
3. *Bela knjiga (The White Book),* published by the Historical Section of the ZDSPB Tabor (n.d.), several years after World War II, lists on pages 21–74 the victims executed in the years 1941–1942 before any anticommunist units were organized in the Italian zone of Slovenia. One of my father's long-time friends, a resident of a small village but with a successful dairy business, was accused of trying to organize an anticommunist unit in his village. One late evening three partisans entered the house and charged him with "illegal and traitorous" activities. Two of the three partisans then left the house and stationed themselves outside, while the third remained apparently on orders to carry out the execution. The accused person's wife was present and begged for mercy. The man in the house kept hesitating even though the two men outside were calling for action. The execution then took place and the three partisans disappeared into the woods. We were told about this execution soon after it happened; the details, however, I heard only several years after the war.
4. Von Paulus capitulated on 31 January 1943 with his entire army. The last Germans in Stalingrad surrendered on 2 February 1943. Of the 280,000 Germans in Stalingrad, 90,000 surrendered; 40,000 were evacuated; the rest were killed or died as a consequence of the extremely harsh winter at the time of battle. Only around 5,000 came back to Germany from the Soviet prison camps, the last in 1955. *The World Almanac of World War II* (New York: Bison Books Corporation, 1981), pp. 198–199.
5. 250,000 Italians and Germans were captured at the end of the North African campaign. Ibid., p. 211.
6. The exact dates, 26 and 29 August, are provided in *Ljubljana v ilegali*, IV (Ljubljana: Mestna konferenca SZDL, 1970), pp. 197–198, and 203.
7. This young soldier was with a detachment of the German Army that arrived in Ljubljana either at the end of August or the beginning of September 1943. We were not able to find out from him if his detachment would be staying in the city or if they were just passing through. He would also not tell us where he was stationed in Ljubljana.
8. Many people took advantage of the situation during the two or three days when blocks were not guarded. Some used this opportunity to try to join this or that clandestine formation in anticipation of new developments. Not all of those departing reached their destinations. The attempts to join were associated with many risks since departures were in most cases only loosely organized and led. Getting into the hands of the "wrong" group or into the hands of occupation forces could have had dangerous consequences. A friend of mine from Dravograd left Ljubljana on his own to join the partisans. After three days of wandering around and meeting some groups in the hills, not knowing exactly what their goals were, he concluded that these uncertainties were not for him and he headed back home. At the city controls, already guarded by Germans, his knowledge of the language helped him to get admitted without the required pass.

9. I am using the term Slovene National Clandestine Resistance Force in my memoirs instead
   of Slovene Chetniks for two reasons: (1) The term Chetniks was in recent years associated
   with many depressing and criminal acts, acts that have absolutely nothing to do with the activities of the Chetniks' resistance efforts in Slovenia during World War II; (2) The other
   term, Plava garda (Blue Guard), in reference to the blue uniforms worn by the pre-war Yugoslav Royal Guards, was used by the partisans to stigmatize this organization with goals of
   pro-centralism and pro-Yugoslavism as the solution for the post-World War II political organization in Yugoslavia.

10. In *Pozabljena zgodba* . . . (Chapter VI, pp. 53–57) Borštnik describes the circumstances leading
    to this disaster, the battle, and the fate of those who were captured at Grčarice. See also chapter
    "Grčarice" in *Svoboda v razvalinah: Grčarice—Turjak—Kočevje*, eds. France Grum and Stane
    Pleško (Cleveland, Ohio: Zgodovinski odsek ZSPB, 1961), pp. 65–76.

11. Ibid., chapter "Turjak," pp. 77–127.

12. Borštnik, *Pozabljena zgodba* . . . , p. 45.

13. "da bom . . . v skupnem boju . . . proti banditom in komunizmu, kakor tudi njegovim za-
    veznikom, svoje dolžnosti vestno izpolnjeval. . . ."

14. The names of my classmates: Mitja Mejak, Ernest Ludviger, Franc Erjavec, Herbert Grün,
    Dušan Šustaršič, Ludvik Golia, Janez Zabukovec, and Vladimir Kobler.

15. Being in a hurry to get home, I did not see if he entered this hotel or walked past. I did recall,
    however, that I once before noticed by accident in his portfolio several professionally pro-
    duced photos of beautiful women, which struck me a little strange, knowing his refugee sta-
    tus. Hotel Miklič was known as one of the main centers where German officials were sta-
    tioned in Ljubljana.

Chapter Eight

1. At this time we were still using the lire.

2. In the pre-war Yugoslavia 28 June was a national holiday, remembering the defeat of the Serb
   Army by the Turks on the Kosovo polje in 1389. Our underground organization wanted to have
   a modest celebration of this holiday in their secret facilities in the middle of Ljubljana at the so-
   called Bata Building; looking back, that was not a very smart, maybe even an irresponsible,
   move. Gestapo agents apparently learned about this celebration and conveniently found many
   adversaries assembled at one location. They were all arrested on the spot. More then that,
   Gestapo agents stationed themselves during the entire day at this location and arrested every
   person that arrived there. Since I never knew about this location, was not invited to the celebration, and therefore never entered that place, Gestapo agents must have found my name
   listed somewhere in that room, or someone under pressure and torture released my name.
   Therefore, my arrest came only early in the morning of the next day.

3. Intelligence Service.

4. I did not understand the reason why the Gestapo man said that to me. The person I named was
   never arrested by the Gestapo and survived the war. Nevertheless, that information confused me
   at the time and placed additional worries into my mind. Did I name the wrong person?

5. The landing of American, British, and Canadian forces in Normandy on 6 June 1944 was probably the reason that the Gestapo decided to deal with our organization during the month of
   June 1944.

6. One of Milojka's brothers was captured at Grčarice and executed by the Slovene Partisans in
   September 1943 at an unknown location near Kočevje. Borštnik, *Pozabljena zgodba*, p. 55. The
   brother who was in a cell in the same prison and on the same floor as Milojka and I perished in

the Baltic Sea after the German ship, taking him and other prisoners to another work place in Germany, was sunk by British planes. Ibid., p. 95.

7. I heard a few months later that this man, chief of the Slovene workers in the prison, was arrested by the Gestapo, severely beaten, and later sent to Dachau for helping prisoners with messages and by all other means possible. He brought me that crucial message in the toilet pot on my second day in prison.

8. Open passenger cars provided a clear view of the entire inside from either end of the car. There were no enclosed coupé facilities on this train.

Chapter Nine

1. The sign in German read, *"Arbeit Macht Frei"* (Work makes you free). What they meant by this was not very clear to us and probably puzzling to every person who entered that place against his or her will.

2. "Everybody get off" (the train).

3. When I saw in recent years Spielberg's motion picture, *Schindler's List*, I was extremely impressed with how faithfully his movie presented the arrival of prisoners in Auschwitz.

4. Even though the official designation was *Lager* II, meaning Camp II, this was actually an open residential facility for all kinds of officers and workers most likely connected with Auschwitz productions. Those coming on business to the I.G. Farbenindustrie and other German camp officials of various middle and lower ranks. often stayed overnight in *Lager* II.

5. People in the striped uniforms were inmates of the Auschwitz concentration camps. Those of us in forced labor camps kept our own clothes.

6. In Auschwitz, we considered every man in black uniform to be a member of the Gestapo. If this applied to everybody dressed like that we were not sure. Because we were most likely still under Gestapo jurisdiction and had to deal with these men from time to time, it was advisable to keep as much distance as possible from the men in the black uniforms.

7. I am very sorry that I don't remember her name or at least how we referred to her in the camp. Working with her was a pleasure. She knew a lot about the situation in the forced labor camps, spoke perfect German, and seemed to know how to work with people on all levels, responsibilities, or ranks. Why she was in Auschwitz and when she arrived she never disclosed. She was definitely very helpful to us in all respects and advised us when problems arose.

8. The ability on our part to understand other Slavic languages in their simplest versions came from the fact that in our high schools the curricula included Serbo-Croatian language in addition to the strong concentration on our own Slovene language. We had the most difficulty with the Polish; it took a little longer to get used to the rapid Polish pronunciation.

9. Until we had that unique opportunity to exchange a few words with the Serbian prisoner from Belgrade, we were of the opinion that our transport was the only one to Auschwitz from Ljubljana and possibly one or two from Zagreb. Except for our office manager and what she told us about the Croatian men who had our jobs before us and a few others, we did not meet other Yugoslavs in the forced labor camps. Therefore, I was surprised when I came across the book by Tomislav Žugić and Miodrag Milić, *Jugosloveni u koncentracionom logoru Aušvic 1941–1945* (Beograd: Institut za savremenu istoriju, 1989) and learned about the thousands of Yugoslavs from all parts of the country who suffered in Auschwitz, many of whom never returned.

10. Alfred Sulik does mention that in parts of Oberschlesien only Soviet, English, and Italian (after the fall of 1943) prisoners of war were imprisoned. However, Sulik does not specifically confirm the English presence in Auschwitz. Alfred Sulik, "Volkstumspolitik und Arbeitseinsatz:

Zwangsarbeiten in der Grossindustrie Oberschlesiens," in Ulrich Herbert (Hg.), *Europa und der "Reichseisatz:" Ausländische Zivilarbeiter, Kriegsgefangene und KZ-Häftlinge in Deutschland 1938–1945* (Essen: Klartext-Verl., 1991), p. 118.

11. According to Tine Golež, who checked this information for me, this service was called *Le service du travail obligatoire* (Le S. T. O.), the obligation for the French to serve in the German industry. The total number of participants in this service was 641,000. This way, the French avoided serving on the German front lines. The reader will find more information about *Le service du travail obligatoire* in Yves Durand, "Vichy und der 'Reichseinsatz,'" in, Herbert, *Europa und der "Reichseinsatz,"* p. 190.

12. Aleksandr I. Solzhenitsyn reveals in *The Gulag Archipelago* (New York: Harper & Row, 1972), p.21, what happened to some of the captured and liberated women in the hands of the Soviet frontline soldiers. See also Solzhenitsyn (Ibid., pp. 238–250) regarding the Soviet treatment of their own prisoners of war after the war.

13. The extensive programs of forced labor the Germans instituted in the occupied Eastern territories is the topic of Rolf-Dieter Müller, "Die Rekrutierung sowjetischer Zwangsarbeiter für die deutsche Kriegswirtschaft," in Herbert, *Europa und der "Reichseinsatz,"* pp. 234–250.

14. Throughout the period of the Nazi regime in Germany, their opponents, those under any kind of suspicion, those capable of organizing resistance, were arrested and put away into concentration camps, first in Germany proper and after the 1938 Annexation of Austria, in that territory as well. After the attack on Poland in September 1939 and on the Soviet Union in June 1941, additional concentration camps were set up in the Eastern occupied territories, further away from populated areas in order to assure as much secrecy as possible for what was going on in these camps.

15. The only concentration camp we came close to on our walks was Monowitz. The others were quite a distance away. Straying that far from our residence camp would in itself raise suspicions and expose a person to interrogations by the Gestapo. Mostly we stayed in the vicinity of Lager III.

16. Martin Gilbert writes in Chapter 33, "The End of Auschwitz," pp. 324–327, of his book *Auschwitz and the Allies* (New York: Holt, Reinhardt and Winston, 1981) about mass killings almost to the very end of Auschwitz, including during the times I was there.

    The last executions are reported in the book, *The Nazi Civilization: Twenty-Three Women Prisoners' Accounts: Auschwitz Camp Administration and SS Enterprises and Workshops*, compiled, transcribed, and edited by Lore Shelley (Lanham, Maryland: University Press of America, Inc., 1992), p. 270, where the reader will find the following information: "Four Jewish women prisoners: Alla Gartner, Roza Robota, Regina Saphirstein, and Esther Wajeblum, who had smuggled gunpowder out of the Union factory for the resistance movement, were hanged in the camp extension in front of the prisoners." Taken from the Appendix B, Synopsis of Major Dates and Events Referred to by Participants. The date of this execution — January 6, 1945.

17. Not until years later did I find out about the enormous number of victims who perished in the gas chambers in the Auschwitz camps and about the planning for these killings at the Nazi Wansee Conference of January 20, 1942, with the agenda, "to discuss the final and complete destruction of as many of Europe's Jews as possible." Martin Gilbert, *The Second World War: A Complete History*, Revised Edition (New York: Henry Holt and Company, 1989), p. 292. Martin Gilbert also offers the following approximate statistics in Chapter 44, "The worst of all camps," on p. 337 of his book *Auschwitz and the Allies*: ". . . a minimum of two million Jews had been killed there [in Auschwitz concentration camps], as had as many as two million Soviet prisoners-of-war, Gypsies, and non-Jews from all over Europe."

18. I am still wondering, if the folks who gave us the information about the true Auschwitz knew much more then they were willing to share with us. Fear of betrayal was always present.

19. "Night of (broken) glass," of November 10, 1938, when Nazi SA groups attacked Jews, their homes, their businesses and synagogues. The radio reports of these acts of terror were brief. It is a possibility that this kind of news was kept to a minimum in Yugoslavia in order not to offend the powerful neighbor in the North.

20. After the April 6, 1941 attack on Yugoslavia, the Nazis removed and expelled from their part of the occupied Slovenia to Serbia, Croatia or Bosnia almost the entire intelligentsia and almost all the priests. Many from these social groups were arrested and immediately sent primarily to Dachau. Among those sent to Dachau was the priest from my town, Prošt Munda. He lost his right hand in an accident while working as prisoner in a stone pit. However, he survived the war.

21. I was not able to establish if the British war planes ever attacked Auschwitz. The reason that I am even mentioning the British as well as American is, that according to my memory, there were more air attacks on Auschwitz than listed in *The Army Air Forces in World War II: Combat Chronology, 1941–1945* (Washington, D.C.: Office of Air Force History, USAF, 1973).

22. That grenade-shaped structure was probably once a guard station or an entrance for the camp.

23. In the records of *Army Air Forces in World War II: Combat Chronology, 1941–194 5* (Washington, D.C.: Office of Air Force History, USAF, 1973), two air attacks (18 and 26 December 1944) are listed and one reconnaissance flight on 14 January 1945. My recollection is that there were more attacks during that period.

24. Although the initial work to establish a concentration camp in and around the town of Oświęcim goes back to the end of the year 1939, the decision by Himmler to build a concentration camp in that Polish territory is dated April 27, 1940. *From the History of KZ-Auschwitz* (New York: Howard Fertig, 1982), pp. 1–2.

25. Martin Gilbert in his book, *Auschwitz and the Allies* (New York: Holt, Rinehart and Winston, 1981), p. 336, lists the following concentration camps where prisoners from Auschwitz were taken: Gross Rosen, Ravensbrück, Sachsenhausen, Nordhausen, Buchenwald, and Bergen-Belsen.

26. Many years after the war, my mother met a person who told her that she was with me in Auschwitz and asked if I survived the war. She added that the Soviets brought all of them back to Slovenia by air soon after the war was over. My attempts to find out what was happening in Auschwitz, in *Lager* III, and to our friends, the women from the Soviet and Polish territories, after the Soviets arrived on 27 January 1945—a full week after our departure—and what were their experiences during the remaining months of the war were not successful.

27. None of us in the groups I associated with while in Auschwitz were aware of the full and terrible truth about Auschwitz and of the extent of killings committed there. Even though pieces of information were circulated in the camps, the Nazi Command was successful in hiding their murderous work even there. Although fairly free to move between the camps in off-duty times, as a rule we avoided coming close to what most considered "dangerous areas." Years after the war, when the whole truth came out from many eyewitness reports, it was difficult for us to understand and accept the fact, that even being so close, much of what went on in that huge territory was not known to those stationed outside the concentration camps. Each individual, even if interested and concerned with more than just his or her survival, had access only to a minuscule part of the whole.

Chapter Ten

1. Many times after the war I thought about that moment on that road in Southern Poland, when a single and apparently insignificant action caused such an important turn in my life. This

event was not the only one that hounded me later in life, but one, because of its insignificance at the time, remained deepest in my mind.

2. A year or two before World War II, Hinko visited Prague as a member of the Yugoslav *Sokol* gymnastic team. During the competition he got hurt. A Czech family took him in for a month or two until he fully recovered. He became sufficiently versed in Czech during his stay in Prague.

3. Only in recent years did I find the information about the Soviet arrival in Auschwitz on Saturday, 27 January 1945. The Soviet account of their arrival, investigation, and photographs taken of the camps and the people they found there, was, however, done a month later and was, therefore, staged. The Soviet military photographer, Alexander Woronzow, interviewed about the Soviet recording sessions, did provide a sequence of the events in connection with preparation of this information. Looking at this Soviet account, done a month after the actual liberation of Auschwitz (Polish people from the vicinity of Auschwitz acted as former prisoners) just added to my curiosity and wishful hopes of finding out more about what happened to my own co-prisoners from the former Lager III, those who decided to stay and wait for the Soviet troops. The Soviet account is available on a videocassette with the title, *Liberation of Auschwitz* (Waltham, Mass.: National Center for Jewish Film, Brandeis Univ. [distributor], 1985).

4. When Germany attacked Yugoslavia in April 1941, Hinko joined many others and escaped in time from the German zone of Slovenia and came to Ljubljana, which was under Italian control.

5. Franz Legat is a native of Eisenkappel/ Železna kapla in Southern Carinthia, where he is now enjoying his retirement. He was present when his older brother, Hans, was mortally wounded by a Nazi supporter during the Nazi *Putsch* in Austria in 1934. His younger brother, Vili, was killed as a German soldier on the Murmansk front in an army truck accident during a night march from the front lines.

6. It was interesting to note that during the chief's long and threatening speech, he no longer referred to "Banditen Gebiet" (bandits territory) as in the past, but referred to these territories as "Partisanen Gebiet."

Chapter Eleven

1. When I returned to Graz as a university student late in 1945, I could not resist visiting the *Betrieb* and especially that Austrian worker. On the day I visited the place with a friend, he recognized me right away and was visibly scared of seeing me walking around with the *Betriebs Leiter*. I thought that scaring him a little was enough punishment for his behavior during the last months of the war.

2. Because of ever-stronger partisan activities in Southern Carinthia and many desertions to the partisans from the German Army, the Slovene soldiers, residents of Southern Carinthia, no longer received permission to visit their homes during their leaves. The city of Graz was one of the areas where meetings with parents and relatives were still possible.

3. The date for Easter Sunday in 1945, if my memory is correct, was April 1.

4. The Austrians credited this decision to the Soviets, probably on the basis that the message came from Moscow. In fact, this information was part of the document, "The Moscow Declaration on Austria," of 30 October 1943, an agreement between the United Kingdom, the Soviet Union and the United States of America. Robert H. Keyserlingk, *Austria in World War II: An Anglo-American Dilemma* (Kingston [Ont.] and Montreal: McGill-Queen's University Press, 1988), Appendix 3, pp. 207–208.

Chapter Twelve

1. The mountain range of Koralpe lies west and south of the city of Köflach.
2. In order to reach the region of Carinthia (Kärnten) in southern Austria, and from there Slovenia, we had to use the mountain road connecting the cities of Köflach (in Styria) and Wolfsberg (in Carinthia). The highest point on this mountain range is 1,169 meters near the Packsattel.
3. Everything is done.
4. You were very lucky.
5. Today a new highway bypasses this village, the house were we slept and the hills where I exposed myself unnecessarily to such a great danger so close to the end of the war. I visited that location twice and for some unknown reason I wish to go there again just to stand on that mountain ridge and look down into the valley.
6. I cannot guess why I was singled out, stopped, or arrested so many times when guards at the control stations looked only at my ID, not even at my face. My typical Slavic name must have made me immediately suspicious.

Chapter Thirteen

1. There exists no documentation that Hitler gave this order, "Machen Sie mir dieses Land deutsch," on 26 April in Maribor. According to Tone Ferenc's research, this order may have been given at the end of March or in early April 1941 to Dr. Uiberreither at the time of his selection as the head of occupied Lower Styria (Štajerska). Tone Ferenc, *Nacistična raznadovalna politika v Sloveniji v letih 1941–1945* (Maribor: Knjižnica NOV in POS 35, 1968), pp. 141–142, fn. 316–317.
2. On the new maps the former Guštajn/Ravne is now Ravne na Koroškem.
3. The commander's younger brother and I were in the same class at Bishop's Gymnasium for four years. The commander was three years our senior.
4. First in 1920 after the Carinthian Plebiscite and, second, after the German attack on Yugoslavia on April 6 1941.

Chapter Fourteen

1. As I found out much later, when our parents heard that she left Viševek, they were shocked and terribly upset. They could not believe that Uncle Silvester would let her go.
2. Nigel Nicolson, *Long Life* (London: Weidenfeld & Nicolson, 1997), p. 116.
3. Ibid., p.119.
4. The group I was with found protection in one of the several empty storage facilities. If this old building belonged to the monastery I was not aware of it. Neither did I know whether anyone was placed in the Viktring/Vetrinj monastery proper.
5. Ibid., p. 117. According to Nicolson the supplies came "from the food dumps, which were ample because Carinthia had been the major German supply base for the Italian campaign."
6. Mr. Corsellis kept his interest and concern for the people he was trying to help in the Viktring/Vetrinj camp in May and June 1945 all his life. More than that, his research on the events of the time, as well as his articles and lectures offer a major step toward possible clarification of what happened, why, and where, and with whom lies the key to thus far still-hidden responsibilities.
7. As Count Nicolai Tolstoy documented, Brigadier Toby Low and Yugoslav Lt. Col. Hočevar met in Klagenfurt/Celovec on 15 May to discuss administrative matters and return of the Croat forces to Yugoslavia. The agreement about the departure of Yugoslav troops from the Austrian

territory, however, was reached between General Keightley and Colonel Ivanovič on 19 May 1945. Nicolai Tolstoy, *The Minister and the Massacres* (London, Melbourne, Auckland, Johannesburg: Century Hutchinson Ltd., 1986), pp. 115 and 139.

8. In the monograph, *Vetrinjska tragedija*, published by Zveza slovenskih protikomunističnih borcev (1960), the authors list which units were selected on specific days for relocation, pp. 40–41.

9. The Croatian group, the *Ustashi*, approximately 200,000 strong, were stopped by the British near Bleiburg/Pliberk and refused sanctuary. They were forced to return to Yugoslavia by much superior British forces. The British tanks and artillery pieces blocked their travel into the Austrian territory. As my uncle told me later, the British tanks and artillery were also stationed on his farm at Moos bei Bleiburg/Blato pri Pliberku, facing east. The tension was high while negotiations were going on in the nearby castle of Graf Thurn between the British authorities and Tito's Army representatives on one side and the representatives of Croatians on the other. My other relatives, who have a farm at Schwabegg/Žvabek, on the way to the bridge at Lavamünd/Labot, observed these Croatians, depressed and demoralized, passing by their farm for two days and two nights almost without interruption.

10. Nicolai Tolstoy, *The Minister and the Massacres*, pp. 170–174.

11. Nicolson, *Long Life*, p. 121.

12. Twilight of the gods; the end of civilization.

13. Nicolson, *Long Life*, p. 122. This statement is taken from Nicolson's report of 18 May, the day before the repatriations began.

14. Ibid., p. 123.

15. Ibid.

16. Tolstoy, pp. 103–107.

17. Nicolson, *Long Life*, p. 118.

18. Later reports revealed that the order given to Major Barre, commander of the civilian camp, directed him to have 2,700 civilians ready 1 June at 5:00 A.M. for return to Yugoslavia; 1,500 to be transported to Rosenbach/Podrožca and 1,200 to the railroad station at Bleiburg/Pliberk. Tolstoy, pp. 191–192.

19. I wish to mention two sources. Nicolai Tolstoy, *The Minister and the Massacres*, a book which for the first time offered detailed documentation in English of many sources about the tragic events and about the sinister duplicity of the British Klagenfurt/Celovec command, sources up to then either not easily accessible or not open for research. In this book much of the documentation, previously available only in Slovene, became accessible in English as well. The second source is an article by John Corsellis, "Uspešen odpor proti prisilnemu vračanju," *Pričevanja: Graški zbornik* (Celovec-Ljubljana-Dunaj: Mohorjeva založba, 1996), pp. 39–61. (English text translated by Uroš Roessmann).

20. As I learned much later, they all came home safely and continued to work on their farms. More than that, even all the Home Defense men from the village were saved—a rare case—and came home. The credit for that has to be given to the local communist representative (called *terenec* and plural *terenci* in Slovene), a school teacher, who always kept to himself. Since he was the only teacher in that small village school, he knew people very well. He allegedly went to Kranj and persuaded the partisan authorities there to release everybody from the village of Viševek, including the Home Defense men, and brought them home.

21. Marija returned home, but not without difficulties. She was taken illegally across the border into Yugoslavia by a few family Carinthian friends, who most likely had good connections with the Yugoslav border authorities. Not known to any of us or to her guides, she had in her possession letters from a refugee to his relatives in Slovenia, and when asked on the Yugoslav side if she had

any messages to deliver, she confirmed that she had several letters in her possession. She was immediately arrested and it took special efforts to get her released from prison. I never liked the person who gave her the letters. Marija, however, when pressured, did not think that there was anything wrong in delivering this mail, since regular postal mail services at the time were practically non-existent.

22. *Ušli so smrti: Poročila treh rešencev iz množičnega groba v Kočevskem Rogu* (Celovec-Ljubljana-Dunaj: Mohorjeva založba, 1998).
23. Tolstoy, op. cit.
24. Ibid., p. 177.
25. Ibid.
26. Ibid., p. 179.
27. Ibid., pp. 179–180.
28. Ibid., pp. 180–181.
29. Ibid., p. 189.
30. Ibid., p. 190.
31. Ibid., p. 191.
32. Ibid., p. 195.
33. Ibid., pp. 184–185.
34. Ivan Korošec, *Teharje: Krvave arene* (Ljubljana: Založba Ilex-Impex, d.o.o., 1994).
35. The questions she raised and comments she made are to be found in Tolstoy's *The Minister and the Massacres*, p. 201, and in Korošec, *Teharje: Krvave arene*, p. 185.

Chapter Fifteen

1. Part of the text that follows is an abbreviated and revised version of the narrative published in Slovene in *Nova zaveza*, with the title "Spomini na študentovsko taborišče v Avstriji" (Ljubljana: *Nova zaveza*, letnik V, številka 4, December 1995), pp. 82–87.
2. *Alea iacta est* (the die is cast) exclaimed Julius Caesar (100 B.C.–44 B.C.) before he led his army south across the Rubicon. No Roman army commander had the right to cross the Rubicon with his army without specific permission from the Roman senate. On that occasion, in the year 49 B.C., Julius Caesar broke that law.
3. As I have learned later, a friend of my mother's, who came to the United States of America only a month or two before, saw my name on a list of those waiting in the displaced persons camps for resettlement and asked Mr. Klezin to take on his shoulders the responsibility for my first year of residency in the United States, one of the required conditions for admission.
4. As far as I know, the *Studentenlager Hochsteingasse* under the British military administration in Graz, Austria, was the only displaced persons camp reserved exclusively for university students in Western-Powers-occupied Europe.

Epilogue

1. Office of Strategic Services.
2. I described the trip across the Atlantic Ocean in more detail in an article in Slovene, "Petje druži nove priseljence: ustanovitev in prva leta Pevskega zbora Korotan" (Choral Singing Unifies New Immigrants: Founding and First Years of the Singing Society Korotan), in *Dve domovini/Two Homelands* (Ljubljana: Institut za slovensko izseljenstvo ZRC SAZU, 1977), pp. 49–70.

Works Consulted

Atlas Slovenije. Ljubljana: Mladinska knjiga; Geodetski zavod SR Slovenije, 1985.

The Army Air Forces in World War II: Combat Chronology, 1941–1945. Washington, D.C.: Office of Air Force History, USAF, 1973.

Balfour, Neil, and Sally Mackay. *Paul of Yugoslavia: Britain's Maligned Friend*. London: Hamish Hamilton, 1980.

Barker, Thomas M. *The Slovene Minority of Carinthia*. East European Monographs, 169. Boulder, Colorado: East European Monographs, 1984.

——. *Social Revolutionaries and Secret Agents: The Carinthian Slovene Partisans and Britain's Special Operations Executive*. East European Monographs, CCLXXVI. Boulder, Colorado: East European Monographs, 1990.

Beloff, Nora. *Tito's Flawed Legacy: Yugoslavia & the West since 1939*. Boulder, Colorado: Westview Press, 1985.

Bethel, Nicholas. *The Last Secret: The Delivery to Stalin of over Two Million Russians by Britain and the United States*. New York: Basic Books, Inc., 1974.

Biber, Dušan. *Nacizem in Nemci v Jugoslaviji*. Ljubljana: Cankarjeva založba, 1966.

Borštnik, Pavle. *Pozabljena zgodba slovenske nacionalne ilegale*. Zbirka Spomini in izpovedi. Ljubljana: Mladinska knjiga, 1998.

Calvocoressi, Peter, and Guy Wint. *Total War: The Story of World War II*. New York: Pantheon Books, 1972.

Carmichael, Cathie, compiler. *Slovenia*. World Bibliographical Series, vol. 186. Oxford, England–Santa Barbara, California–Denver, Colorado: Clio Press, 1996.

Center of Military History, United States Army. *German Antiguerilla Operations in the Balkans (1941–1944)*. Washington, D.C.: U.S. Government Printing Office, 1989: 246–441.

Corsellis, John. "Uspešen odpor proti prisilnemu vračanju." *Pričevanja: Graški zbornik*. Knjižna zbirka: Celovški rokopisi, 2. France Vrbinc, ed., Uroš Roessmann, trans. Celovec–Ljubljana–Dunaj: Mohorjeva založba, 1996.

Czech, Danuta. *Auschwitz Chronicle 1939–1945*. New York: Henry Holt and Company, 1990.

Deroc, M. *British Special Operations Explored: Yugoslavia in Turmoil 1941–1943 and the British Response*. East European Monographs, vol. CCXLII. Boulder, Colorado: East European Monographs, 1988.

Djilas, Milovan. *Wartime*. New York and London: Harcourt Brace Jovanovich, 1977.

Đonlagić, Ahmet, Žarko Atanacković, and Dušan Plenča. *Yugoslavia in the Second World War.* Trans. Lovett S. Edwards. Belgrade: Međunarodna štampa–Interpress, 1967.

Durant, Yves. "Vichy und der Reichseisatz." In Herbert, *Europa und der 'Reichseisatz.'*

Enciklopedija Jugoslavije. Miroslav Krleža, ed. Zagreb: Jugoslovenski leksikografski zavod, 1968, s. v. "Rab."

Etschmann, Wolfgang. *Die Kämpfe in Österreich im Juli 1934.* Volume 50 of Militärische Schriftenjahre. Vienna: Heeresgeschichtliches Museum/Militärwissenschaftliches Institut, 1984.

Eubank, Keith. *The Summit Conferences 1919–1960.* Norman, Oklahoma: The University of Oklahoma Press, 1966.

Ferenc, Tone. *Kapitulacija Italije in narodnoosvobodilna borba v Sloveniji jeseni 1943.* Maribor: Knjižnica NOV in POS 34, 1967.

———. *Nacistična raznadovalna politika v Sloveniji v letih 1941–1945.* Maribor: Založba Obzorja, 1968.

Ferlež, Ivan. *Druga grupa odredov in štajerski partizani 1941–1942.* Ljubljana: Knjižnica NOV in POS 2, 1972.

Filipič, France. *Pohorski bataljon: Poglavje iz zgodovine narodnoosvobodilne borbe v severovzhodni Sloveniji.* Ljubljana: Državna založba Slovenije, 1968.

Foregger, Richard. "The Bombing of Auschwitz." *Aerospace Historian* 34 (June 1987): 98–110.

Gerčar, Janez. *Begunje: Priča narodovega trpljenja.* Ljubljana: Borec, 1969.

Gilbert, Martin. *Auschwitz and the Allies.* New York: Holt, Rinehart and Winston, 1981.

———. *The Second World War: A Complete History.* New York: Henry Holt and Company, 1989.

———. "The End of Auschwitz." In Gilbert, *Auschwitz and the Allies.*

———. "The Worst of All Camps." In Gilbert, *Auschwitz and the Allies.*

Grum, France, and Stane Pleško. *Svoboda v razvalinah: Grčarice–Turjak –Kočevje.* Cleveland, Ohio: Zgodovinski odsek Zveze slovenskih protikomunističnih borcev, 1961.

Gschwendtner, Jürg. *Deutsche Anti-Partisanenkriegführung: Gegenoffensive deutscher Verbände in Slowenien und Zentralkroatien September bis November 1943.* Allgemeine Schweizerische Militärzeitschrift, Frauenfeld. Frauenfeld: Huber & Co AG, Grafische Unternehmung und Verlag, 1986.

Harriman, Helga H. *Slovenia under Nazi Occupation, 1941–1945.* Studia Slovenica XI. New York–Washington: Studia Slovenica, 1977.

Herbert, Ulrich (Hg.). *Europa und der "Reichsheisatz": Ausländische Zivilarbeiter, Kriegsgefangene und KZ–Häftlinge in Deutschland 1938–1945.* Essen: Klartext Verlag, 1001.

Hnilicka, Karl. *Das Ende auf dem Balkan 1944/45: Die Militärische Räumung Jugoslaviens durch die Deutsche Wehrmacht.* Volume 13 of Studien und Dokumente zur Geschichte des Zweiten Weltkrieges. Göttingen Zurich Frankfurt: Musterschmidt, 1970.

Ivanič, Martin, ed. *Dachauski procesi (Raziskovalno poročilo z dokumenti).* Ljubljana: Komunist, 1990.

Jagschitz, Gerhard. *Der Putsch: Die Nationalsozialisten 1934 in Österreich.* Graz Wien Köln: Verlag Styria, 1976.

Jakac, Božidar, and Miran Jarc. *Odmevi rdeče zemlje.* Ljubljana: Jugoslovanska knjigarna, 1932.

Jedlicka, Ludwig. *Vom Alten zum Neuen Österreich: Fallstudien zur Österreicheschen Zeitgeschichte 1900–1975.* St. Pölten: Niederösterreichisches Pressehaus Druck-und VerlagsgesmbH, 1975.

———. "Der aussenpolitische Hintergrund der Ereignisse vom Frühsommer 1934 bis Oktober 1934." In *Das Jahr 1934: 25. Juli.* München: R. Oldenbourg Verlag, 1975.

Jedlicka, Ludwig, and Rudolf Neck, eds. *Das Jahr 1934: 25. Juli.* Protokoll des Symposiums in Wien am 8. Oktober 1974. Wissenschaftliche Kommission der Theodor-Körner-Stiftungsfonds und der Leopold-Kunschak-Preises zur Erforschung der österreichischen Geschichte der Jahre 1927 bis 1938, Veröffentlichungen. Munich: R. Oldenbourg Verlag, 1975.

Jezernik, Božidar. *Italijanska koncentracijska taborišča za Slovence med 2. svetovno vojno.* Ljubljana: Društvo za preučevanje zgodovine, literature in antropologije, 1997

Keegan, John, ed. *Geographia Atlas of the Second World War.* London: Times Books, 1989. Reprinted 1994, 1996. This Geographia edition first published in 1996.

Keyserlingk, Robert H. *Austria in World War II: An Anglo-American Dilemma.* Kingston and Montreal: McGill-Queen's University Press, 1988.

Kindermann, Gottfried-Karl. *Hitler's Defeat in Austria 1933–1934: Europe's First Containment of Nazi Expansionism.* Trans. Sonia Brough and David Taylor. Boulder, Colorado: Westview Press, 1984.

Kirk, Ford, Jr. *OSS and the Yugoslav Resistance, 1943–1945.* Texas A & M University Military History Series. College Station, Texas: Texas A & M University Press, 1992.

Kirk, Tim. "Limits of Germandom: Resistance to the Nazi Annexation of Slovenia." *The Slavonic and East European Review,* vol. 69, no. 4 (October 1991): 646–667.

Klopčič, Peter. "Bežigrajski študentje v Kočevskem Rogu, poletje 1942." Cleveland, Ohio: *Ameriška domovina* (April 18, 1996): 17–20.

Klusacek, Christine, and Kurt Stimmer, eds. *Dokumentation zur österreichischen Zeitgeschichte: 1928–1938.* Wien-München: Jugend und Volk, 1982.

Kocbek, Edvard. *Tovarišija: Dnevniški zapiski od 17. maja 1942 do 1. maja 1943.* Maribor: Založba Obzorja, 1967.

Kolar, Marjan, ed. *720 Let Ravne na Koroškem.* Mestna konferenca SZDL, vol. 1. Ravne na Koroškem: Koroška knjižnica, 1968.

Končar, Milojka. Notes smuggled from the Gestapo prison. July–September 1944. Photocopies in author's archive.

Korošec, Ivan. *Teharje: Krvave arene.* Ljubljana: Ilex–Impex, 1994.

Kos, Milko. *Zgodovina Slovencev: Od naselitve do petnajstega stoletja.* Ljubljana: Slovenska Matica, 1955.

Krivic, Vladimir. "Odlomki iz spominov na leto 1942," *Ljubljana v ilegali III: Mesto v žici.* Ljubljana, 1967.

Krivic, Vladimir, and others. *Ljubljana v ilegali II: Država v državi.* Mestna konferenca SDZL. Ljubljana: Državna založba Slovenije, 1961.

———. *Ljubljana v ilegali III: Mesto v žici.* Mestna konferenca SDZL. Ljubljana: Državna založba Slovenije, 1967.

———. *Ljubljana v ilegali IV: Do zloma okupatorjev.* Mestna konferenca SDZL. Ljubljana: Državna založba Slovenije, 1970.

Krivokapić, Radovan V. *Bibliografija vojnih izdanja 1945–1968.* Beograd: Vojnoizdavački zavod, 1969.

Kromer, Claudia. *Die Vereiningten Staaten von Amerika und die Frage Kärnten 1918–1920.* Aus Forschung und Kunst, Bd. 7. Klagenfurt: Geschichtsverein für Kärnten; Bonn: Habelt in Komm., 1970.

Lee, Loyd E. *A Global History of the Second World War.* Boston–London–Sydney–Wellington: Unwin Hyman, 1989.

Liberation of Auschwitz [videorecording]. Waltham, Mass.: National Center for Jewish Film. Brandeis University, 1985.

Lichem, Heinz von. *Der Tiroler Hochgebirgskrieg, 1915–1918 im Luftbild: die altösterreichische Luftwaffe.* Innsbruck: Steiger, 1985.

Lichtenstein, Heiner. *Warum Auschwitz nicht bombardiert wurde.* Köln: Bund Verlag, 1980.

Lindsay, Franklin. *Beacons in the Night: With OSS and Tito's Partisans in Wartime Yugoslavia.* Stanford, California: Stanford University Press, 1993.

Littlefield, Frank C. *Germany and Yugoslavia 1933–1941: The German Conquest of Yugoslavia.* East European Monographs, vol. No. CCXLIV. Boulder, Colorado: East European Monographs, 1988.

Lyons, Michael J. *World War II: A Short History*. Englewood Cliffs, New Jersey: Prentice Hall, 1989.

Magocsi, Paul Robert. *Historical Atlas of East Central Europe*. Seattle & London: University of Washington Press, 1993.

Malle, Avguštin, and Valentin Sima, eds. *Der 'Anschluss' und die Minderheiten in Österreich / Anšlus in manjšine Avstriji*. Slovenski znanstveni institut. Disertacije in razprave / Dissertationen und Abhandlungen. Klagenfurt/Celovec: Drava, 1989.

Matanle, Ivor. *World War II: 50th Anniversary Commemorative Edition*. New York: Military Press, 1989.

McEvedy, Colin. *The Penguin Atlas of Recent History: Europe since 1815*. London, New York: Penguin Books, 1982.

Medved, Jakob. *Mežiška dolina: Socialnogeografski razvoj zadnjih 100 let*. Ljubljana: Mladinska knjiga, 1967.

Medved, Jakob, ed. *Jugovzhodna Koroška*. Ljubljana: Geografsko društvo Slovenije, občine, Ravne na Koroškem, Slovenj Gradec, Dravograd, 1970.

Mikuž, Metod. *Pregled zgodovine narodno-osvobodilne borbe v Sloveniji*. Ljubljana, 1960.

———. *Zgodovina slovenskega osvobodilnega boja*. Ljubljana: Prešernova družba, 1970.

Milač, Jan. "Aus meinem Tagebuch." In *Der Krieg in der Wischberggruppe: Berichte einziger Mitkämpfer*, by Norbert Nau. Graz: Leykam Verlag, 1937: 26–33.

Milač, Metod M. "Spomini na študentovsko taborišče v Avstriji." *Nova zaveza*, letnik V, številka 4 (December 1995): 82–87.

———. "Iz mojih izkušenj v vojnih letih 1941–1945." Translated by Henrik Ciglič. *Nova revija: Mesečnik za kulturo*, XV (May 1996): 134–143.

———. "The War Years, 1941–1945: From My Experiences." *Slovene Studies: Journal of the Society for Slovene Studies* 16/2 (1994, published 1997): 31–47.

———. "Petje druži nove priseljence: ustanovitev in prva leta Pevskega zbora Korotan." (Choral Singing Unifies New Immigrants: Founding and First Years of Singing Society Korotan). In *Dve domovini/Two Homelands*. Ljubljana: Institut za slovensko izseljenstvo ZRC SAZU, 1997: 49–70.

Mitchell, Ian. *The Cost of a Reputation. Aldington versus Tolstoy: The Causes, Course and Consequences of the Notorious Libel Case*. Glasgow: Topical Books, 1997.

Moravec, Dušan. "Miran Jarc." In Krivic, *Ljubljana v ilegali, III.*

Müller, Rolf–Dieter. "Die Rekrutierung sowjetischer Zwangsarbeiter für die deutsche Kriegswirtschaft." In Herbert, *Europa und der 'Reichseisatz.'*

Nicolson, Nigel. *Long Life*. London: Weidenfeld & Nicolson, 1997.

Novak, Bogdan. *Trieste, 1941–1954: The Ethnic, Political, and Ideological Struggle*. Chicago, London: The University of Chicago Press, 1970.

Petrovic, Svetislav-Sveta. *Free Yugoslavia Calling*. Edited and translated by Joseph Ciszek Peters, Part IV. Yugoslavia. New York: The Greystone Press, 1941.

Piskernik, Angela. "Pričevanja 1944 Ravensbrück." In *FKL Žensko koncentracijsko taborišče Ravensbrück*. Ljubljana: Partizanska knjiga, 1971, 258–266.

Pleterski, Janko, Lojze Ude, and Tone Zorn, eds. *Koroški plebiscit: Razprave in članki*. Ljubljana: Slovenska Matica, 1970.

Plut-Pregelj, Leopoldina, and Carole Rogel. *Historical Dictionary of Slovenia*. European Historical Dictionaries, No. 13. Lanham, Md., and London: The Scarecrow Press, Inc., 1996.

Prušnik, Gašper Karel. *Gemsen auf der Rawine: der Kärntner Partisanenkampf*. Klagenfurt: Drava, 1979.

Rausch, Josef. *Der Partisanenkampf in Kärnten im Zweiten Weltkrieg*. Militärhistorische Schriftenreihe, vol. 39/40. Vienna: Heeresgeschichtliches Museum / Militärwissenschaftliches Institut, 1979.

Rechter, Peter (HG.). *Das Neue OstEuropa von A–Z*. München: Droemer Knaur, 1992.

Renker, Gustav. "Fünf Männer bauen einen Weg: Ein Alpenroman." *Delhagen & Klassings Monatshefte* 48. Jahr., no. 8 Heft (April 1934).

Rumpler, Helmut, and Arnold Suppan (HGs.). *Geschichte der Deutschen in Bereich des heutigen Slowenien 1848–1941 = Zgodovina Nemcev na območju današnje Slovenije 1848–1941*. Schriftenreihe des österreichischen Ost- und Südosteuropa–Institut, Band 13. Wien: Verlag für Geschichte und Politik, c1988.

Schausberger, Norbert (Hg.). *Zeitzeugen in Kärnten 1939–1945: Erinnerte Erfahrungen von Kärntnerinnen und Kärntnern während des Zweiten Weltkrieges*. Klagenfurt: Pädagogische Akademie des Bundes in Kärmten, 1991.

Schober, Eduard. *Das Lavanttal*. Wolfsberg: Druck- und Verlagshaus Ernst Ploetz, 1990.

Shelley, Lore, comp., trans., ed. *Auschwitz–The Nazi Civilization: Twenty-Three Women Prisoners' Accounts: Auschwitz Camp Administration and SS Enterprises and Workshops*. Lanham, New York, London: University Press of America, Inc., 1992.

Sirc, Ljubo. *Between Hitler and Tito: Nazi Occupation and Communist Oppression*. London: Andre Deutsch, 1989.

Smole'n, Kazimierz, ed. *From the History of KZ–Auschwitz*. Trans. Krystyna Michalik. New York: Howard Fertig, 1982.

Snuderl, Makso. *Osvobojene meje: Kronika Maribora in slovenske severne meje v letih 1918/19*. Maribor: Založba Obzorja, 1968.

Solzhenitsyn, Aleksandr I. *The Gulag Archipelago*. New York: Harper & Row, 1974.

Stafford, David. *Britain and European Resistance, 1940–1945: A Survey of the Special Operations Executive, with Documents*. Toronto and Buffalo: University of Toronto Press, 1980.

Stieber, Gabriela. *Refugee Need and Refugee Aid in Carinthia after 1945*. Klagenfurt: Verlag des Kärntner Landesarchivs, 1999.

Stojadinović, Milan M. *Ni rat ni pakt: Jugoslavija između dva rata*. Rijeka: Otokar Keršovani, 1963.

Strgar, Milica. *Litijski zbornik NOB*. Ljubljana: Delo, 1969.

Sulik, Alfred. "Volkstumpolitik und Arbeitseisatz: Zwangsarbeiten in der Grossindustrie Oberschlesiens." In Herbert (Hg.), *Europa und der "Reichseisatz."*

Sušnik, Franc. *In kaj so ljudje ko lesovi: Koroški zapisi*. Maribor: Založba Obzorja, 1968.

Swift, Michael, and Michael Sharpe. *Historical Maps of World War II Europe*. London: PRC Publishing Ltd., 2000.

Świebocka, Teresa, comp. and ed. *Auschwitz: A History in Photographs*. English edition prepared by Jonathan Webber and Connie Wilsack. Bloomington and Indianapolis: Indiana University Press, 1993.

Švajcer, Janez J., ed. *Boj za Maribor 1918–1919: Spominski zbornik ob sedemdesetletnici bojev za Maribor in severno mejo na slovenskem Štajerskem*. Maribor: Obzorja, 1988.

Terzić, Velimir. *Slom kraljevine Jugoslavije 1941: Uzroci i posledice poraza*. Ljubljana–Beograd: Partizanska knjiga, 1982.

Tolstoy, Nicolai. *The Minister and the Massacres*. London–Melbourne–Auckland–Johannesburg: Century Hutchinson Ltd, 1986.

———. "Vojni zločin—v mirnem času." *Pričevanja: Graški zbornik*. Knjižna zbirka: Celovški rokopisi, 2. France Vrbinc, ed. Uroš Roessmann, trans. Celovec–Ljubljana–Dunaj: Mohorjeva založba, 1996.

Turk, Ciril. *Ušli so smrti: Poročila treh rešencev iz množičnega groba v Kočevskem Rogu*. Celovec-Ljubljana-Dunaj: Mohorjeva založba, 1998.

Van Creveld, Martin L. *Hitler's Strategy 1940–1941: The Balkan Clue*. Cambridge: Cambridge University Press, 1973.

Vodušek Starič, Jera. *Prevzem oblasti: 1944–1946.* Ljubljana: Cankarjeva založba, 1992.

——. *"Dosje" Mačkovšek.* Ljubljana: Arhivsko društvo Slovenije, 1994.

Webster's New Geographical Dictionary. Springfield, MA: G. & C. Merriam Company, 1977, s.v. "Rab."

Weissensteiner, Friedrich. *Der Ungeliebte Staat: Österreich zwischen 1918 und 1938.* Vienna: Österreichischer Bundesverlag Gesellschaft m.b.H., 1990.

Young, Peter Brigadier, ed. *The World Almanac of World War II: The Complete and Comprehensive Documentary of World War II.* New York: Bison Books, 1981.

ZDSPB Tabor—Zgodovinski odsek. *Bela knjiga slovenskega protikomunističnega upora 1941–1945.* Printed in USA, n.d.

Zveza slovenskih protikomunističnih borcev. *Vetrinjska tragedija.* Cleveland, Ohio: Ameriška domovina, 1960.

——. *Svoboda v razvalinah: Grčarice–Turjak –Kočevje.* France Grum and Stane Pleško, eds. Cleveland, Ohio: Tiskala tiskarna sv. Mohorja v Celovcu, 1961.

Žebot, Ciril. *Neminljiva Slovenija.* Celovec: Mohorjeva, 1988.

Žugić, Miodrag, and Miodrag Milić. *Jugosloveni u koncentracionom logoru Aušvic 1941–1945.* Beograd: Institut za savremenu istoriju, 1989.

Index

⟨decorative flourish⟩

Studies in Modern European History

The monographs in this series focus upon aspects of the political, social, economic, cultural, and religious history of Europe from the Renaissance to the present. Emphasis is placed on the states of Western Europe, especially Great Britain, France, Italy, and Germany. While some of the volumes treat internal developments, others deal with movements such as liberalism, socialism, and industrialization, which transcend a particular country.

The series editor is:

Frank J. Coppa
Director, Doctor of Arts Program
in Modern World History
Department of History
St. John's University
Jamaica, New York 11439

To order other books in this series, please contact our Customer Service Department:

(800) 770-LANG (within the U.S.)
(212) 647-7706 (outside the U.S.)
(212) 647-7707 FAX

or browse online by series at:
WWW.PETERLANGUSA.COM